The Transformation of Rural England

'This book is about the development of England's rural landscape in the eighteenth and nineteenth centuries: about enclosure and reclamation, land use and settlement, hedges and walls, farm buildings, the archaeology of farming, and much else. But it is also an examination, from the perspective of landscape history, of the complex process of agrarian change usually referred to as the 'Agricultural Revolution'. Many eminent scholars have written on this subject: economic historians, economists, geographers. Landscape history can add another exciting dimension, and one perhaps more rooted in the environment, and in the realities of farming life, than some of the rarified models currently propagated; models evidently produced by people more familiar with computers than with the soil. Landscape history has come of age. It is time to use its particular insights and approaches to contribute to wider debates in social and economic history.' *From the Introduction by Tom Williamson*

Tom Williamson is Lecturer in Landscape History at the University of East Anglia.

D1351419

205 514

Paperback cover image: Parliamentary enclosure surveyors at work in Henlow, Bedfordshire (reproduced with the permission of Bedfordshire and Luton Archives and Record Service)

The Transformation of Rural England

Farming and the Landscape 1700–1870

TOM WILLIAMSON

NORWICH CITY COLLEGE LIBRARY

205514

Stock No

Class 942.07 WIL

Cat. Proc.

UNIVERSITY
of
EXETER
PRESS

First published in 2002 by
University of Exeter Press
Reed Hall, Streatham Drive
Exeter EX4 4QR
UK
www.ex.ac.uk/uep/

Reprinted 2003

© Tom Williamson 2002

The right of Tom Williamson to be identified as author
of this work has been asserted by him in accordance with
the Copyright, Designs & Patents Act 1988.

British Library Cataloguing in Publication Data
A catalogue record of this book is available
from the British Library.

Paperback ISBN 0 85989 634 X
Hardback ISBN 0 85989 627 7

Typeset in 10.75 on 12.5 pt Palatino Light by Exe Valley Dataset Ltd, Exeter

Printed and bound in Great Britain by
J.W. Arrowsmith Ltd, Bristol

Contents

Figures

Notes on Figures

Figure 10 is based on the maps of Buckinghamshire, Bedfordshire, Cambridgeshire and Warwickshire produced by Harrison *et al.* 1965; and on the map of Northamptonshire published by the Royal Commission on Historical Monuments, England, in 1984.

Figure 20 is based on three sources: a map of the parish of Ardeley, 1744 (HRO D/Z 110 P1); the Ardeley Tithe Award Map (HRO DSA 4/5/2); and the OS 6 inch First Edition, 1880.

Figure 22 is based on an undated early eighteenth-century survey by Jonas More: 'A Map of the Great Level of the Fens . . . as it is now Drained' (Wisbech Museum).

Figures 26 and 27 are based on information from Tate 1978. The upland soils are from Avery *et al.* 1974: the classes mapped are 66 (stagnopodzols), 67 (rankers/ stagnohumic gleys), 70 (peat soils) and 71 (raw peat soils).

Figure 33 is based on the *c.*1836 Tithe Files, published in CD-Rom form by Kain 1995. Natural soil regions were defined using Avery *et al.* 1974, and the average area under tilth calculated for each. In the majority of cases values were relatively homogenous within soil types but in the vicinity of some urban areas, in particular, some variation was apparent. In such cases, regions were subdivided on a subjective basis and the data mapped accordingly.

Acknowledgements

Many people have helped with this book, providing advice, encouragement, information or inspiration. My greatest debt is to Susanna Wade Martins, who taught me so much about the agricultural revolution; particular thanks must also go to Liz Bellamy, David Brown, Liam Brunt, Andrew Done, Keith Snell, Anne Rowe, Arthur Teece and Hadrian Cook for advice and information. As always, colleagues, students and former students at the Centre of East Anglian Studies provided criticism and help, especially Richard Wilson, Jenni Tanimoto, Christopher Harper-Bill, Jonathan Theobald, Keith Bacon, Jo Parmenter, Robert Liddiard, Kate Skipper and Sarah Birtles. Above all, I would like to thank Michael Turner, who kindly read an earlier draft of this book, and made a number of very useful comments. He and his co-workers, Bethanie Afton and John Beckett, also allowed me to see (in advance of publication) some of their important new data on crop yields. The illustrations were drawn by Philip Judge. My thanks to the staff of the Buckinghamshire, Essex, Hertfordshire, Lincolnshire, Norfolk and Suffolk Record Offices, and of Wisbech Museum, for all their kindness and assistance; to the Rural History Centre, Reading University, for permission to reproduce Figure 12; to Richard Muir, for Figures 19 and 31; to the Spalding Gentlemen's Society, for Figure 23; to *Farmers Weekly*, for Figure 30; and to the Cambridge University Committee for Aerial Photography, for permission to reproduce Figures 9 and 21. Finally, my thanks as ever to my family for all their tolerance and understanding.

Abbreviations

BPP   British Parliamentary Papers
BRO   Buckinghamshire Record Office
ERO   Essex Record Office
ESRO   East Suffolk Record Office
HRO   Hertfordshire Record Office
LRO   Lincolnshire Record Office
NRO   Norfolk Record Office
PRO   Public Records Office, Chiswick
WSRO   West Suffolk Record Office

Acres/hectares

For reasons of historical context and to avoid breaking up the text I have for the most part retained the use of the term acre without converting to hectares.

1 acre = 0.4 of a hectare

CHAPTER 1

Revolutions in Agriculture

Introduction

This book is about the development of England's rural landscape in the eighteenth and nineteenth centuries: about enclosure and reclamation, land use and settlement, hedges and walls, farm buildings, the archaeology of farming, and much else. But it is also an examination, from the perspective of landscape history, of the complex process of agrarian change usually referred to as the 'Agricultural Revolution'. Many eminent scholars have written on this subject: economic historians, economists, geographers. Landscape history can add another exciting dimension, and one perhaps more rooted in the environment, and in the realities of farming life, than some of the rarefied models currently propagated—models evidently produced by people more familiar with computers than with the soil. Landscape history has come of age. It is time to use its particular insights and approaches to contribute to wider debates in social and economic history.

The book is not, therefore, intended as a comprehensive account of the development of the English landscape in the period from the late seventeenth to the late nineteenth century. It has a more limited aim than this, although an immensely important one. It argues that the momentous agrarian changes of the eighteenth and nineteenth centuries can only be understood in terms of fundamental patterns of landscape and land use change. These changes not only allowed the growing population of industrialising Britain to be fed. They also created much of the essential fabric of the countryside we enjoy today.

Historians have long argued about the nature, timing and even the existence of an 'agricultural revolution'. The traditional view, expressed by Lord Ernle in his survey of 1912, was that the 'revolution' was a phenomenon of the period c.1750–1850 (Ernle 1912). It involved the large-scale enclosure of open fields and common land, the use of new forms of machinery such as the seed drill, the improvement of livestock breeds and, fundamentally, the adoption of new crops— especially turnips and clover. Together, these improvements allowed the growing cities of industrial England to be fed, both through increasing the yields from existing farmland and by expanding the area under cultivation. Ernle's views were not entirely new: later eighteenth- and early nineteenth-century writers, such as Arthur Young, had been confident that they were living through a time of rapid change, and in many ways Ernle's 'revolution' was defined in their terms.

Ernle's views were refined by a number of twentieth-century historians, most notably J.D. Chambers and George Mingay (1966). The assumption underlying this 'traditional' position was that, before the changes of the eighteenth century, agriculture in England had been carried out on essentially medieval lines. Extensive tracts of country were given over to poor, unproductive waste ground and permanent pasture of various kinds. These were kept quite distinct from the equally permanent arable, which often took the form of 'open fields' in which the holdings of individual farmers lay in numerous tiny unhedged strips, intermingled with those of their neighbours. There were usually two or three great fields in a township, one of which lay 'fallow' each year: that is, left unsown and grazed by the common flocks. Fallowing helped prevent the build-up of diseases and allowed the land to be cleansed of weeds, for at the end of the season the land was ploughed, effectively burying all unwanted plants. It also allowed the land to 'rest': that is, helped restore fertility, which was depleted by repeated cropping. Nitrogen and other vital elements were restored by the decay of the ploughed-in weed growth and, more importantly, by the manure dropped by the animals herded or folded in the field, foraging among the weeds. Yields were low largely because the numbers of animals kept, and thus the quantities of manure produced, were limited by the 'fodder gap'. No grass grew in the winter, and so stocking levels depended on the amounts of hay which could be harvested in the summer from the restricted areas of low-lying meadow land.

The agricultural revolution changed all this. The tracts of common grazing were now ploughed up, thus dissolving the old distinction between permanent grass and permanent arable. In addition, the widespread adoption of turnips and clover—combined with cereals in regular rotations of which the 'Norfolk four-course' was the most famous—brought great improvements to existing arable land. Turnips were a fodder crop, fed off in the fields by sheep or taken to cattle stalled in yards. Clover also provided food for livestock—it was both grazed directly and cut for hay—but in addition it fixed nitrogen in the soil directly from the

atmosphere. Bare fallows were eliminated and yet more livestock could be kept, more manure produced, and thus higher yields achieved (Beckett 1990, 11–18). This 'revolution' was pioneered, according to many, by a small group of enlightened aristocrats, and their principal tenants—large capitalist farmers. Contemporaries placed particular emphasis on the achievements of landowners in Norfolk, and to a lesser extent Suffolk and Lincolnshire: on men like 'Turnip' Townshend, owner of the Raynham estate in west Norfolk, and Thomas William Coke, 'Coke of Norfolk' (Riches 1937). Such men undertook large-scale enclosure of open fields and heaths, and used long leases with detailed husbandry clauses in order to enforce 'best practice' on their tenants.

This traditional view of the eighteenth-century 'revolution' was forcibly challenged in the 1960s by the historian Eric Kerridge (Kerridge 1967 and 1969). He suggested that the sixteenth and seventeenth centuries were, in fact, the period in which there was a decisive break with medieval husbandry practices. Some of the features of the traditional model, such as the adoption of machinery like the seed drill, were simply irrelevant or mythical. Others, he argued, such as the cultivation of clover and turnips, had become widespread well before 1750, in some cases before 1700. Much of England's landscape had long been enclosed by 1500, and much was enclosed during the following two centuries. More importantly, Kerridge drew attention to a number of important innovations which historians had previously ignored. One was convertible or 'up-and-down' husbandry—the practice of alternating long pasture leys and periods of cropping on the same piece of land—something which served both to improve the quality of the pasture and to improve arable yields (Kerridge 1967, 181–220). Another was the 'floating', or artificial irrigation, of water meadows. Watering during the winter months made the grass grow earlier, and thus shortened the period during which livestock had to be kept on fodder; watering in the summer served to increase sub-stantially the size of the hay harvest, and thus the quantities of fodder available to the farmer (Kerridge 1967, 251–67). Both served to raise significantly the numbers of animals which could be kept, and thus to increase the quantities of manure reaching the soil. These and other practices revolutionised English agriculture, and in Kerridge's view the main force of agrarian change was spent before 1670 (Kerridge 1967, 15–40, 326–48). Kerridge's ideas have been challenged on many occasions, and on a number of different grounds, but the concept of the 'early' agricultural revolution has recently received considerable support from the economist Robert Allen. In his view, the seventeenth century was the key period of improvement—what he called the 'yeoman's revolution', featuring in particular the improvement of cereal yields through the careful selection of seed. The eighteenth century, in contrast, was a period of institutional change, involving the amal-gamation of farms and enclosure, which redistributed agricultural wealth upwards to the landlord but which did little to improve agricultural output (Allen 1991 and 1992). Another economist, Gregory Clark, has also strongly argued that 'there was no agri-cultural revolution during the Industrial Revolution', and that the major improve-ments in productivity occurred in the period before c.1700 (Clark 1988, 249).

During the 1980s, however, arguments about the nature and timing of agrarian change were made more complex by the research of Bruce Campbell and others which revealed that, for some areas of England at least, the traditional image of medieval farming as backward and conservative—and thus desperately in need of some kind of post-medieval 'revolution'—was flawed. Campbell demonstrated that in parts of thirteenth-century Norfolk fodder crops, principally peas and beans, were widely substituted for year-long fallows; fertilisers were assiduously applied; and high labour inputs allowed yields to be achieved which were well up to those of the post-medieval centuries (Campbell 1983). Similar evidence for innovation was soon forthcoming from other areas of medieval England, such as northern Kent (Mate 1985). Yet by this time claims were being made for a 'revolution' at the other end of the chronological scale. F.M.L. Thompson identified a first agri-cultural revolution in the eighteenth century, involving enclosure and improved husbandry techniques; but also a second, characterised by the buying-in of inputs such as animal feeds and artificial fertilisers, associated with the capital-intensive 'high farming' of the mid-nineteenth century (F.M.L. Thompson 1968). According to this view, it was in the period after 1830 that the most significant improvements in agricultural productivity were achieved. Mingay has since gone further, arguing that the hundred years up to 1850 represented merely 'a base, or rather a preparation . . . for the greater changes yet to come' (Mingay 1989a, 971).

In the face of such conflicting arguments some historians would now question whether the term 'agricultural revolution' has any real meaning, agreeing with Joan Thirsk that English agricultural development is best understood as a 'continuum, to be divided between periods of more or less rapid change' (Thirsk 1987, 57–8). There may be much merit in such a view. But if so, then there can be little doubt that the eighteenth and early nineteenth centuries were one of the periods of rapid change. As Beckett has argued, 'The primary task of the farming community was to feed the population, and if this is taken as the essential criterion for defining an agricultural revolution, the concept is clearly justified' on this period (Beckett 1990, 9). It is true that changes in dietary requirements may have been a factor in feeding the population, for industrial workers arguably require fewer calories than those undertaking heavy agricultural manual work, and this was a period in which a higher and higher proportion of the population worked in factories rather than fields (Clark 1988). For some sections of the population, moreover, nutritional standards may simply have declined in this period. Nevertheless, the scale of the achievement, looked at in the long term, was considerable.

As landscape archaeologists are now well aware, prior to the eighteenth century the demographic graph of England and Wales resembles a series of great waves. In late Romano-British times—in the fourth century—the population may have reached 4 million, and in the late thirteenth century, around 5 million, but these peaks were followed by drastic demographic declines brought about in the latter case certainly, and in the former probably, by epidemic disease. Evidently, with the available technology, population growth beyond these kinds of levels could not be sustained. Another great wave of growth commenced in the sixteenth century and this likewise ground to a halt in the later seventeenth century, this time levelling off at around $5-5^1/_2$ million. In this case population levels then declined more gradually to the end of the century, and afterwards remained comparatively stable in the early years of the eighteenth century, before rising fairly slowly to around 6 million by c.1750. But thereafter the population grew almost exponentially, reaching around 9 million by 1800 and nearly 18 million by 1851 (Mitchell and Deane 1962, 5–6). Of course, the scale of the country's agricultural achievement should not be exaggerated. In the years around 1800, when French blockades coincided with a series of poor harvests, there were acute shortages of grain and prices rose to dangerous levels. Nevertheless, output had clearly been increased to an astonishing extent: England had broken out of the Malthusian trap.

Even in 1851 imports amounted to only 16 per cent of foodstuffs consumed in England and Wales. To feed the expanding population, therefore, the volume of wheat produced may have more than doubled, and the quantity of barley may have increased by over two-thirds. Increases in the production of other foodstuffs were probably of a similar order (Holderness 1989, 145; Beckett 1990, 9). What is particularly striking is that the expansion of production was achieved at the same time as a marked improvement in what economic historians call 'labour productivity': the amount of people required to produce a given amount of food (Overton 1996a, 121–8). In 1760 the output of each agricultural worker could feed around one other person; by 1841 it could feed another 2.7. This is of vital importance, because England was also experiencing an industrial revolution at this time, with more and more workers employed full-time in mines, mills and factories. Indeed, if the home production of grain had not kept pace with population growth, increasing imports might have stifled this other revolution, by reducing the amount of investment available for industry. It is hard to quarrel with Mark Overton's trenchant statement: 'The evidence overwhelmingly favours the century after 1750 as the period of most rapid and fundamental change in output and productivity' (Overton 1996b, 20).

Raising Yields

How was all this achieved? As already indicated, historians generally agree that there were, and indeed are, two main ways of increasing the production of food. Firstly, agricultural methods can be improved so that each acre of land produces more grain, meat or whatever. Secondly, the actual area of productive land can be increased, through the reclamation of marginal land. Attempts have been made to quantify both these processes in the period under discussion.

The greatest ingenuity has been shown in calculating changes in yields per acre. For the late eighteenth and nineteenth centuries yields of the principal grain crops are readily available from two main sources: government surveys and reports, and the comments of agricultural writers like Arthur Young. Such broad generalisations are not always very reliable, however. Moreover, for the period before the 1760s such evidence does not really exist at all, and while there are documents (such as farming diaries or estate accounts) which provide us directly with this kind of information, they are widely scattered, comparatively few in number, and have until recently not been collated on a national or regional scale. The historian Mark Overton, however, realised in the 1970s that a large number of documents exist which can provide information on crop yields *indirectly*. From the early sixteenth century documents called *probate inventories* were produced when people of anything above modest means died. These were valuations of the 'goods, chattels etc.' of the individuals in question, usually made by neighbours. Those made for farmers often include estimates of the value of crops growing in the fields: 'item four acres of wheat in a close called stubbings . . . £4'. If we know the current price of wheat—say, in this case, 5 shillings

a comb—then we can calculate that this particular appraiser estimated that the field in question would produce 4 combs per acre (Overton 1979). Overton's initial method of calculating yields was subsequently criticised by Paul Glennie, who suggested that it did not make allowance for the costs of harvesting and carting the crop, nor for the tithe which the vicar or rector would be expected to take (Glennie 1988). These refinements accepted, the method has been used by a number of historians to chart changes in yields during the sixteenth, seventeenth and eighteenth centuries (Allen 1988; Overton 1990 and 1991; Glennie 1988 and 1991).

Such studies have suggested different patterns in different areas, but have in general given some support to the idea of a sixteenth/seventeenth-century 'revolution', while at the same time demonstrating the scale of the eighteenth-century achievement. In Norfolk, according to Overton's calculations, cereal yields rose steadily through the seventeenth century, and by the period 1680–1709 averaged 15.9 bushels per acre for wheat and 16.1 for barley. Over the period 1710–39, in contrast, the figures were 19.2 and 20.8—a significant increase. Overton compared these figures with those supplied by the kinds of late eighteenth- and nineteenth-century sources already mentioned, and suggested that increases continued fairly steadily thereafter. By the 1760s, according to information presented in Arthur Young's *Farmers Tour* (1771), wheat yields in the county had reached 26.5 bushels and barley 32.5 bushels per acre, although by 1801, according to the House of Lords *Report on the Dearth of Provisions*, they had dropped back slightly to 22.4 and 32 respectively, and shortly afterwards—in 1804—Young estimated that the average yields per acre for the county as a whole were 23 bushels per acre for wheat and 34 for barley (Overton 1991,

298–305). In Lincolnshire the pattern was slightly different, with more achieved in the period before c.1700. Yields in c.1550 of 9.5 bushels for wheat and 8 for barley rose to 15.8 and 10.7 respectively by the end of the seventeenth century. By 1750, wheat yields were averaging 20 bushels per acre, barley 13.5; by the end of the century, the figures were 21 and 15.8 respectively. Further increases brought the figures to 23 and 20 bushels an acre by the 1830s (Overton 1991, 303). In Hertfordshire, Paul Glennie's work suggests that wheat yields rose rather faster in the late sixteenth and early seventeenth centuries than in the period 1650–1700: from an average of around 9 bushels an acre in c.1550 to 12.2 in c.1660 to 16 in c.1650, but thereafter only climbing to 17 in c.1700. Nevertheless, here—as in Norfolk—the scale of subsequent increase was substantial, with yields of 24 bushels an acre being recorded by the start of the nineteenth century, and 28 by the middle of the century (Glennie 1991; Overton 1996a, 77). In all three counties, therefore, significant increases in yields per acre were made in the period before the late seventeenth century, but all saw further improvements in the period under consideration here.

The scale of these improvements—in the course of the eighteenth and nineteenth centuries—has recently been charted on a national basis by Michael Turner, John Beckett and Bethanie Afton. Through a programme of detailed research in record offices they were able to assemble a large number of *direct* references to crop yields contained in farming diaries, account books and the like, covering the period 1720–1920 (Turner *et al.* 2001). Such records are widely scattered, and for any decade relatively few in number, but the story they tell is clear enough. Between 1720 and the 1840s wheat yields increased by some 50 per cent, from

around 20 to 30 bushels an acre; the improvements for barley were even more striking, from 25 to nearly 50 bushels an acre (Turner *et al.* 2001, 129, 158).

How were yields increased? There has been almost universal agreement that, at least in the period before c.1840, the key factor was the adoption of the new crops and rotations (Campbell and Overton 1993; Overton 1996a, 131). In the words of the economic historian Patrick O'Brien, 'at the core of a protracted process was a set of fodder crops which offered a solution to the age-old problem of how to raise the capacity of farmland to carry more animals'—and thus increase the supply of manure (O'Brien 1985, 779). In the period before 1800 there were few other forms of fertiliser available to farmers. Night soil from towns, dredgings from streams and rivers, and even seaweed might be applied to the fields (Brunt 2000), but animal dung was, without question, the key source of fertility. This central feature of Ernle's 'revolution' has thus stood the test of time: indeed, a number of more recent studies have explored the efficacy of the new crops in replenishing, directly or indirectly, the nitrogen lost through repeated cropping (Chorley 1981; Sheil 1991). The uptake of the new crops may have been gradual. It has been suggested that even in Norfolk, a county long acknowledged to be at the forefront of the agricultural revolution, only c.3 per cent of farm acreage was devoted to clover, and 8 per cent to turnips, in the middle of the eighteenth century. By the 1830s, however, the documents known as the Tithe Files—drawn up in the 1830s on a parish-by-parish basis, in advance of the commutation of tithes—suggest that their use was very widespread, often in the form of the 'Norfolk four-course'. In Norfolk itself 'wheat, turnips, barley and clover each accounted for about a quarter of the arable acreage in the 1830s. In other counties the proportions were lower, but still suggest the prevalence of the rotation' (Overton 1996a, 119). Of course, modern agricultural historians have acknowledged the contribution made by other changes in farming, such as marling—the practice of spreading a calcareous subsoil on the surface of the fields in order to neutralise soil acidity (Allen 1994). These, however, almost always take second place to the new crops and rotations.

Enclosure and Reclamation

Almost all historians agree that as well as changes in the practice of farming, fundamental institutional changes played a crucial role in raising production: most importantly, the interconnected processes of enclosure and increases in farm size. Enclosure, as most landscape historians will be well aware, is an immensely long and complex process. Indeed, in spite of its centrality to many discussions of the agricultural revolution, most of England had already been enclosed by the start of the eighteenth century. Much land, even in the Middle Ages, had been held 'in severalty'—that is, in walled or hedged fields under the control of a single individual. But at this stage the majority had, indeed, comprised arable 'open fields' and areas of unfenced common grazing, the latter usually occupying the most agriculturally marginal land. Enclosure is the process by which, from late medieval times, such land was converted into private property. It was achieved in two principal ways. *Piecemeal enclosure* involved a series of private agreements which led to the amalgamation, through purchase and exchange, of groups of contiguous open-field strips, and their subsequent fencing or hedging (Yelling 1977, 11–29). *General enclosure* in contrast involved the community of proprietors acting together to replan the

landscape at a stroke, usually (although not invariably) enclosing the totality of the remaining open land in a township. In many (perhaps most) townships general enclosure completed a process which had already proceeded some way through piecemeal enclosure. Many open-field systems were too extensive and complex to be easily removed in their totality through this latter form of enclosure, which also, by its very nature, made relatively little impact on common grazing land, for the simple reason that this comprised areas of shared use-rights rather than intermixed properties (Yelling 1977, 86; Williamson 2000, 59).

Piecemeal enclosure generally leaves sparse traces in the documentary record. But it often leaves clear signs in the landscape, in two ways. Firstly, open-field plough strips seldom had dead straight boundaries: they were usually slightly sinuous in plan, characteristically taking the form of a shallow 'reversed S', caused by the way in which the ploughman moved to the left with his team as he approached the headland at the end of the strip, in order to avoid too tight a turning circle (Eyre 1955). Because the new walls and hedges were established along the edges of bundles of strips, they served to preserve, in simplified form, the slightly wavy lines of the earlier landscape (Figure 1). Secondly, because open-field strips running end to end seldom came to be enclosed in line by this method, field patterns produced by piecemeal enclosure often exhibit a number of small 'kinks', tiny dog-legs, where the boundary of one field will run, not to the corner of the next field, but to a point some way along the boundary line, a strip or two strips' distance away. Unfortunately, piecemeal enclosure is not always so obviously displayed in the field pattern. This is because the process was often associated with engrossment, as large estates steadily

Figure 1   Field walls created by piecemeal enclosure near Wardlow, Derbyshire

and systematically bought out their neighbours, often leading to their complete ownership of a parish. In such circumstances, the irregular field pattern produced by piecemeal enclosure might be rationalised at a later date, with old boundaries straightened or removed and new ones laid out, thus erasing, to some extent at least, the earlier pattern.

General enclosure took a number of forms (Yelling 1977, 5–10). 'Enclosure by unity of possession' occurred when a single individual acquired all the land in a township: the common rights were terminated and the landscape could be hedged, walled or otherwise rearranged at will. The earliest general enclosures, those associated with the depopulation of Midland villages in the late fourteenth and fifteenth centuries, generally fall into this category. In the sixteenth and seventeenth centuries these were largely superseded by enclosures carried out 'by agreement'. The majority of proprietors in a community agreed to enclose and, having carried out the necessary surveys, re-allotted open-field strips in consolidated holdings, and divided up areas of common grazing in proportion to the rights which proprietors had exercised over them. Sometimes stability was given to the new dispensation by an ingenious legal device: a fictitious legal dispute was brought in the court of Chancery, contesting the enclosure (Yelling 1977, 8). Once the court had ruled against the plaintiff the enclosure was secure.

Figure 2 'Planned countryside': the landscape of parliamentary enclosure near Duxford, Cambridgeshire

In the course of the eighteenth century these forms of enclosure were largely, although not entirely, superseded by parliamentary enclosure (Turner 1980 and 1984a; Mingay 1997). Landowners petitioned for a parliamentary act, which was followed by survey and award, a process which was considerably simplified by the passing of the General Enclosure Act in 1836. The key feature of parliamentary enclosure was that it could be carried through even if the majority of landowners opposed it: what was now required was not a majority of landowners, but the agreement of those who held most of the land in a township—generally three-quarters by value (Mingay 1997, 60). In the words of the Hammonds, 'the suffrage was weighed, not counted' (1911, 104).

The various forms of general enclosure usually produced field patterns much less closely related to earlier arrangements than piecemeal enclosure: networks of linear boundaries and rectilinear fields, most strikingly so in the case of parliamentary enclosure. Such field patterns dominate many upland districts where extensive tracts of open moorland were enclosed in the seventeenth, eighteenth and nineteenth centuries. They are most striking and continuous, however, in a broad swathe of country running through the middle of England, from Dorset in the south to Yorkshire in the north. This was the area of medieval England in which open fields had been most developed and most pervasive: where vast tracts of land had been farmed in

Figure 3   *'Ancient countryside': sunken lane near Duddenhoe End, Elmdon, north Essex*

'regular' open-field systems, often approximating to the textbook norm. Farmers normally resided in nucleated villages and their land was scattered, fairly evenly, through two or three great unhedged fields, one of which lay fallow each year. Many aspects of agrarian life were rigidly controlled by community and custom in these regions and this, together with the excessive intermixture of properties, ensured that open fields here were particularly resistant to enclosure and thus survived *en masse* into the post-medieval period. Hence the dominance in this region of the particularly rectilinear landscapes characteristic of parliamentary enclosure (Figure 2). This, to use Rackham's term, is the region of 'planned countryside': 'The *champagne* . . . the land of brick box-like farms in exposed positions, of thin hawthorn hedges, of ivy-laden clumps of trees in the corners of fields, of relatively few woods, and above all of straight lines' (1976, 17).

In the south and east of England, and across much of the west, very different landscapes can be found, for here enclosure was largely completed before 1700. These are Rackham's 'ancient countrysides': 'The land of hamlets, of medieval farms in hollows of the hills, of lonely moats in the clay-lands, of immense mileages of quiet minor roads, hollow-ways, and intricate footpaths; of irregularly shaped groves and thick hedges colourful with maple, dogwood, and spindle' (1976, 17) (Figure 3).

Beyond the western belt of 'ancient countryside' lay Rackham's third broad landscape region: the highland zone, characterised by 'moors, dales, and a mountain way of life' (1986, 4).

The map of these regions produced by Rackham (Figure 4) represents, as he himself emphasised, a broad generalisation; and one could argue about precise boundaries and

Highland Zone
Predominantly Ancient Countryside
Predominantly Planned Countryside

Figure 4   Oliver Rackham's simplified landscape regions

particular classifications, not least because certain districts display characteristic features of more than one landscape type. Nevertheless, Rackham's map undoubtedly has a sound basis, and in particular it is clear that the south and east of England (including much of East Anglia), the west Midlands and much of the West Country were all substantially enclosed before the period of the 'agricultural revolution'.

The distinctive character of these ancient countryside areas is usually still very apparent, in spite of modern changes to the landscape, not only in the more scattered pattern of settlement but in the shape of fields and the character of hedges. As Rackham suggests, these are usually much more mixed and species-rich than those more recently established in planned country-side areas. It is often assumed that this is simply due to the fact that they have had more time to be colonised by a range of additional species. But it was also because they were often originally planted with hazel, ash and other plants, in addition to thorn. This was because early enclosers looked to their hedges as a source of fruit and fuel, as well as regarding them simply as a barrier to livestock, and planted accordingly (Johnson 1978). Thomas Tusser, writing in 1573, thus advocated including elm, ash, crab, hazel, sallow and holly in hedges, and, in praising the advantages of 'severall' or ancient countryside over champion, emphasised the fact that there was an abundance of fuel and fruit to be found in the hedges (Tusser 1812, 102). John Norden's *Surveyor's Dialogue* of 1607/1610 commented on the abundance of fruit trees in the hedges of Devon, Gloucestershire, Kent, Shropshire, Somerset and Worcestershire and lamented the fact that they were gradually disappearing from the hedges of Middlesex and south Hertfordshire, as the modern generation failed to replace those which had grown old and died (Norden 1607, 53). Even at the start of the nineteenth century Arthur Young was able to describe how the farmers in Hertfordshire 'fill the old hedges everywhere with oak, ash, sallow and with all sorts of plants more generally calculated for fuel than fences' (Young 1813a, 49).

It is often assumed that 'ancient country-side' had never had much in the way of open fields but in fact these had once been present in many such areas, and often persisted into the post-medieval period (Roden 1973; Roberts 1973; Baker 1973; Skipper 1989; Williamson 2000). They were not, however, usually like the great open fields of the 'champion' Midlands. They were 'irregular' field systems, in the sense that the holdings of individuals were clustered in the area close to the farm rather than (as in the Midlands) being scattered evenly across two or three great fields. Often there were numerous named fields (Gaddesden in Hertfordshire had twenty) and communal controls were generally less rigorous and less pervasive than in the Midlands. The distinction between the Midlands and the 'ancient countryside' areas was thus not simply, or even mainly, a contrast between landscapes anciently enclosed and landscapes of open fields—although there were some areas, such as central Essex, in which the extent of common arable seems always to have been limited. It was rather one between regions where the open-field systems were regular and regions where they were irregular in character. The latter systems tended to disappear quietly, and at an early date, and it is evident from landscape evidence that this was normally through piecemeal rather than general enclosure. Because communal agriculture was less deeply entrenched in these districts, and because properties were less thoroughly intermixed (most areas of arable contained the strips of relatively few proprietors), irregular open fields were much more susceptible than regular systems to this form of enclosure. But the areas of common grazing in such districts, which could be extensive, usually survived up until the time of parliamentary enclosure in the late eighteenth or early nineteenth century.

The enclosure history of many 'upland' areas of the north and west of England was broadly similar. Here, too, the medieval landscape had comprised varying mixtures of enclosed land and open fields, often of 'irregular' form. But here there were particularly extensive tracts of common grazing on the poorer, higher land. The open fields were mainly enclosed gradually, and piecemeal, leaving the common grazing to be removed in the eighteenth or nineteenth centuries by some form of general—normally parliamentary—enclosure.

The precise chronology of English enclosure remains contentious. Uncertainties about the relative extent of open and enclosed land in the Middle Ages, and the poorly documented nature of piecemeal (and some early forms of general) enclosure, conspire to make this a particularly intractable problem. Even the history of enclosure in the period under consideration here remains contentious. The painstaking research of Michael Turner and W.O. Tate suggests that around 20 per cent of England, comprising both open fields and commons, was enclosed by parliamentary act in the period after 1750, around 21 per cent of the total of enclosed land (i.e. excluding land that remained as common at the start of the twentieth century) (Wordie 1983, 486), and that this occurred in two distinct waves of activity, peaking in the 1770s and again during the Napoleonic War years (Turner 1980). These two peaks, as we shall see, tended to affect different areas of England and different kinds of land. However, John Chapman has argued that Turner's figures, based on the acreage summaries contained in the various enclosure awards, underestimate the true area affected. A detailed analysis of a 10 per cent sample of awards, looking at the area actually allotted, suggested that another 500,000 acres should be added to Turner's total, suggesting that as much as 21 per cent of England was enclosed by act. Although Chapman's arguments have been questioned on statistical grounds, they remain convincing (Chapman 1987; Walton 1990 and 1991). What remains more contentious is the extent to which other forms of enclosure—piecemeal enclosure and (in particular) enclosure effected by the simple expedient of buying up an entire

township—continued into the late eighteenth century and beyond. It used to be assumed that after c.1750 non-Parliamentary enclosure was of negligible importance. Indeed, Wordie in 1983 suggested that such enclosures accounted for no more than 1 per cent of the land area of England (Wordie 1983, 488). But more recently Chapman and Seeliger have shown that in Hampshire non-Parliamentary enclosure continued on some scale into the eighteenth century (Chapman and Seeliger 1995). In a detailed study they discovered 64 private enclosure agreements, including 32 from the eighteenth century and 10 from the nineteenth, and suggested that 45 per cent of eighteenth-century enclosure in the county had been made without recourse to parliament. They suggested, moreover, that such enclosures by formal agreement represented 'the tip of a far greater hidden iceberg of eighteenth and nineteenth-century enclosure' (Chapman and Seeliger 1995, 44). As we shall see, the results of this study cannot easily be extrapolated to the whole of England. In many Midland counties, in particular, non-parliamentary enclosures were of negligible importance. Nevertheless, the Hampshire experience can certainly be paralleled elsewhere, and if we assume that, nationally, all such activity accounted for no more than 20 per cent of the area affected by parliamentary enclosure—surely an underestimate—over 25 per cent of England must have been enclosed in the period after c.1750. Only detailed local and regional research will be able to show how much enclosure took place from c.1700 to c.1750, but—to judge from counties like Northamptonshire, where such studies have been made—it is hardly likely to have been less than a fifth of this total. It would thus seem reasonable to assume that, in the period under consideration here, as much as

30 per cent of the land area of England may have been enclosed, a very considerable proportion. In other words, while some early students of the agricultural revolution certainly overemphasised the extent to which open fields and common land survived at the start of the eighteenth century, recent research has tended to reverse this trend, and thus to reinstate the significance of the enclosure as a factor in agricultural change.

The Significance of Enclosure

Historians have long argued that enclosure was important for a number of reasons. Firstly, the adoption of the new rotations was difficult in an open-field context. Turnips, because they were planted in place of the fallow, would be fed off by the common flocks at an early stage of growth unless the strip on which they grew was temporarily fenced—something which could only take place with the permission of fellow cultivators. It is true that a number of scholars—such as Michael Havinden—have argued that even the 'regular' open fields of the Midlands allowed a degree of flexibility, and that open-field farmers were able to reorganise their cropping patterns in order to use the new rotations (Havinden 1961). But this argument should not be taken too far. Innovators often remained in a precarious position, dependent on the whims of neighbours. Moreover, there is little doubt that in many Midland parishes the old three-course rotation, of two crops and a fallow, still held sway even at the start of the nineteenth century. The vicars and rectors who responded to the enquiry mounted by the government in 1801 into the likely state of the coming harvest (a source generally known as the Crop Returns) recorded turnips and clover in many open-field parishes. But some, like the vicar of Congerstone in Leicestershire, described

how their parish was 'an open field lordship, one-third of which is every year fallow' (Turner 1982a, II, 54). In Marston Trussell in Northamptonshire, similarly, the parish was said to be 'divided into three fields, *viz*, one sown with wheat and barley, another with beans or beans and peas mixed . . . and the third field fallow annually in rotation . . . Turnips perhaps half an acre' (Turner 1982a, II, 147).

But the connections between enclosure and improvement, according to many, went further than this. Drainage, marling, and the general management of the land were all more difficult in scattered, open parcels, and there were perennial problems with theft and trespass. Some modern historians might argue against all this, but the relative value of open and enclosed land—the former commanding rents more than twice that of the latter, according to the more enthusiastic improvers—suggests otherwise (Chambers and Mingay 1966, 85). In part this reflected the greater efficiency with which compact parcels of land could be worked, and consequent savings on labour costs, and in part it reflected increases in production. But above all, enclosure allowed farmers to follow particular kinds of husbandry which were impossible in an open-field context. In particular, specialisation in livestock husbandry was simply not feasible, on any significant scale, where land lay in small, widely scattered, unhedged strips, intermixed with land under crops. In the words of the historian Mark Overton:

> Enclosure facilitated innovation and change in land use because the constraints imposed by common property rights, the scattering of land, and collective decision making could be overcome. Contemporaries were virtually unanimous that enclosed fields offered more opportunities

for money-making than did commonfields (Overton 1996a, 165).

There are thus good *a priori* grounds for believing that enclosure of open-field arable will have led to increases in agricultural production. But, as John Chapman has demonstrated, the majority of parliamentary enclosures in the period actually affected not arable fields but common grazing land (Chapman 1987). Around 1.8 million acres (728,450 hectares) of common heaths, downs, fens and moors were enclosed in the period up to 1836 by acts which dealt exclusively with common land (Turner 1980, 178); a further half million acres were enclosed after 1836. In addition, enclosure acts dealing primarily with open fields almost invariably included some common pasture, and those in light land districts often included very extensive areas. Indeed, Chapman has suggested—on the basis on a detailed analysis of a sample of such acts— that around 60 per cent of all land enclosed by act in England was, in fact, grazing land: a total of, perhaps, some 4.4 million acres (1.8 million hectares). This large-scale conversion of common grazing to land held in severalty was often accompanied by land improve- ment and reclamation, and this was, according to many, a major factor in the expansion of food production in this period.

Of necessity, large-scale schemes of enclosure and reclamation were spearheaded by large landowners. This was partly because they required large amounts of capital. But it was also because the largest tracts of common 'waste' tended—with one or two significant exceptions—to be found on the more agriculturally marginal land, and it was here that large estates were most in evidence. There were a number of reasons for this. In the early Middle Ages fertile land made for dense populations of wealthy peasants, able

to resist the domination of single lords, while poor lands made for the reverse. Moreover, in the late Middle Ages, as population fell in the wake of the Black Death, marginal land was vacated *en masse* by farmers now able to take up more profitable holdings elsewhere, allowing manorial lords to acquire complete proprietorial rights over many townships. In the post-medieval centuries, moreover, fertile land was expensive land, and therefore difficult to acquire in large, continuous blocks. Poor land in contrast was cheaper, and could be so acquired. For all these and other reasons large landowners dominated most of the more marginal areas of England, and were thus centrally implicated in land reclamation in the course of the eighteenth and nineteenth centuries.

Owners and Farmers

Of course, large estates extending over 5,000 acres or more were not restricted to such areas. They could be found in most parts of England, although in more fertile districts they existed alongside a plethora of smaller properties, those of the local gentry and small freeholders (Habbakuk 1953; Beckett 1977, 1984 and 1986). The amount of land owned by the gentry and aristocracy seems to have increased steadily throughout the post-medieval period, as they gradually absorbed the property of those holding by the less secure forms of traditional 'copy- hold'. But large estates expanded most rapidly from the late seventeenth century, when the development of the legal devices known as entails and strict settlements made their fragmentation less likely, and the development of mortgages allowed them to grow further through the purchase of small freehold farms in a time of agricultural recession (Allen 1992, 14–15, 86).

During the period studied here only a minority of farmers were owner-occupiers. Most held on tenancies of varying duration. The farmer provided the working capital—tools, seed, livestock—and maintained the hedges, fences and the like; the landlord usually erected and repaired the farm buildings, and paid for or subsidised major improvements whose effects were of long duration. In some districts, by the start of the eighteenth century the terms of the agreement between the two parties was enshrined in a written lease which might stipulate the particular mode of husbandry which was to be employed on the farm (Habbakuk 1953; Clay 1985, 229). Even in those districts (usually those with the most fertile soils) where small proprietors still existed in some numbers, owner-occupiers were often in a minority. Many small properties were owned by petty traders, or by aspiring professionals. They provided a form of secure investment, and were leased out in order to provide a regular income.

Throughout the post-medieval period landowners and their agents encouraged the growth of average farm size by gradually amalgamating holdings. They preferred men with capital, able to stock a farm well and maintain it in reasonable heart. They disliked dealing with large numbers of small farms, not least because this increased the quantity of buildings and houses which required maintenance. But the growth of larger farms was also encouraged by wider economic factors—the inability of small holdings to compete in an increasingly market-orientated economy (Mingay 1961–2, 484).

Historians have long debated the chronology of changes in farm size (Beckett 1983; Ginter 1991; Grigg 1987). Particular circumstances seem to have encouraged the decline, nationally or locally, of small cultivators: the recessions of the early eighteenth century or

the 1820s, or (in particular) parliamentary enclosure, when many small owner-occupiers were forced to sell up, in order to cover the legal costs of the process. Thus Sheppard has discussed the marked decline in small farmers in the post-Napoleonic War depression in Sussex, Martin the pattern of 'dislocation and change' during the years of enclosure in Warwickshire, Turner the effects of enclosure in Buckinghamshire (Sheppard 1992; Martin 1979; Turner 1975). But the issue is an immensely complicated one, not helped by the perennial confusion between small owners and small farmers, nor by the fact that the definition of 'small farm' changed constantly over the centuries, as average farm size increased. Moreover, in any period the average size of farms, and the mixture of large and small farms, varied greatly from district to district and region to region. To some extent such variation was related to forms of husbandry—arable farming tended to encourage larger farm units than, say, dairying. But in large measure it was, like the size of estates, a function of soil fertility. By and large, poor land made for large farms: where yields were low farms had to be large, in order to provide the farmer with a decent living and enough money to pay the rent. By the nineteenth century contrasts could be very marked, even over short distances. In the county of Norfolk, for example, as late as 1851 many small family farms remained viable on the fertile soils of the Flegg loams or the Fens. In these districts over 40 per cent of the holdings recorded in the census of that year were of under 50 acres, and the average size was 104 and 110 acres respectively. On the poor light soils of north-west Norfolk or Breckland, in contrast, small farms of 50 acres or less were virtually unknown: the average farm size was around 420 and 450 acres respectively (Wade Martins and Williamson 1999a, 76–9).

Alan Howkins has rightly drawn attention to the fact that in some ways the 'disappearance' of the small farmer in the course of the eighteenth and nineteenth centuries has been overstated by historians. As late as 1880, 71 per cent of farm holdings in England covered less than 50 acres (Howkins 1994, 53). But for some purposes this is a misleading figure, for we need to distinguish between, on the one hand, the number of farms of different sizes, and on the other, the proportion of land farmed by units of varying size. The important point here is that even in areas like Flegg and the Fens many large farms, of 150, 200 or even 300 acres, still existed in 1851 alongside the small units of 50 acres and less. Although such farms might *numerically* be in the minority, in many parishes they nevertheless farmed the majority of the land. In Flegg, 53 per cent of the land was farmed in units of more than 150 acres; in the Fens as much as 66 per cent. Even the proportion of land cultivated in units of 300 acres or more was surprisingly high by 1851, approaching a quarter in both districts.

The overall impression produced by a large number of local and regional studies is that much consolidation of holdings had occurred by the start of the period studied here, but that farm size continued to grow. The precise chronology of this process clearly varied greatly, from region to region, but everywhere farms continued to grow larger in area and smaller in number. In Allen's words, 'By the early 19th century, most of England's farmland had passed from family farms to large scale capitalist tenants' (Allen 1992, 265).

Readers may be wondering why so much space has been devoted to this particular issue. The reason is simple. Most contemporary commentators believed, and many modern historians believe, that large farms were more productive than small. Their owners used labour more efficiently and produced more food per acre. Large farmers had more capital to invest in improvements and were more likely to adopt new methods and techniques. In short, the transition from small to large farms ensured that more food was produced, more efficiently.

Problems and Queries

This, then, is the agricultural revolution which features in most textbooks. True, any attempt to summarise briefly the current state of play in a complex historical debate runs the risk of oversimplifying, and of lumping together dissonant views and suppressing differences of emphasis. Nevertheless, while it is true that not all scholars would subscribe to all the arguments outlined above, many would probably subscribe to most of them. The rapidly rising population of industrialising England was fed both by increasing the area under cultivation—through the reclamation of 'waste'—and by raising yields on cultivated land. The latter was principally achieved by the use of new crops and rotations, which ensured that stocking levels increased and with them, the amount of manure applied to the land. Other improvements and efficiencies—including improvements to livestock—were made possible by enclosure, and by the gradual increase in the size of farms. New techniques were often pioneered by large tenant farms and large landowners, and the latter were particularly involved in the large-scale reclamation of 'waste'.

The essential argument of this book is a simple one: that a number of other factors, generally neglected by historians, were also of importance in increasing production; and that the reclamation of marginal land and the improvement of yields per acre would never in themselves have been enough to feed England's rapidly expanding population in the period after *c*.1750. In the chapters that follow some of the difficulties with the 'conventional' revolution, if I may call it that, will be explored. But it might be useful at this stage to highlight one or two general problems.

Firstly, as we have seen, a very great deal of ingenuity has been expended in calculating changes in the yields per acre of the principal grain crops. But the figures thus produced, while certainly not meaningless, can be misleading. It is often assumed or implied that yields are a good guide to the amount of grain being produced on a given farm, in a given township, or in a given county. But this was also a function of the frequency with which the land was cropped. In many parts of England seventeenth-century farmers practised a three-course rotation with a fallow every third year. Under such a system, one-third of the farm was commonly under wheat each year. By the 1830s, many such districts had adopted a four-course rotation, featuring turnips and clover. In any year, half the land was now under 'restorative' fodder crops which, directly or indirectly, returned nitrogen and other nutrients to the soil. Across England as a whole, according to some authorities, this ensured that wheat yields increased by some 38 per cent (Overton 1996a, 77). But because less land was now sown with wheat—a quarter, rather than a third—the actual increases in *production* would have been less impressive, at around 4.5 per cent. Of course, this does not mean that the farm as a whole was less productive—as we shall see, the adoption of the new rotations allowed more fodder crops to be grown, and thus increased the quantity of meat produced. Moreover, many farms followed very different forms of husbandry both at the start and at the end of

this stated period. Nevertheless, the trend in cropping was almost everywhere the same: the substitution of fodder crops, in two or more courses, for a bare fallow every third year reduced the frequency of cereal cropping, and thereby lowered the amount of grain, and especially wheat, being cultivated. The production of cereals certainly increased but seldom by as much as the 'raw' yield figures presented by historians like Overton or Glennie might suggest, and these can therefore provide, in isolation, a rather misleading picture of agricultural performance. This is an obvious point, and an uncontentious one perhaps, but it is often neglected and certainly worth emphasising at the start of an enquiry like this.

We should also note, in passing, that crop yields were not only affected by what men did to the soil or to their crops. They were also influenced by weather and climate. Areas in the far north of England, for example, could never produce crop yields as high as those in the south, whatever improvements were carried out there, because of the amounts of rain these areas received, and the shortness of the growing season. And in all districts improvements in average yields brought about by changes in farming practices might be enhanced—or diminished—by short-term climatic trends. Thus any gains made though agricultural improvement might be temporarily offset by a period of poor harvests, resulting from a run of late springs or wet summers. We should not assume, as many agricultural historians are wont to do, that trends in crop yields were, in the short or medium term, entirely a consequence of human actions.

There are rather different problems with the simple idea that England's rising population was fed by expanding the area of farmland though enclosure and reclamation. Historians have often followed eighteenth-century commentators in assuming that large areas of under-utilised land, awaiting improvement, existed in c.1700, but this oversimplifies a complex situation. What contemporaries categorised as 'waste' took many forms but most fell into four main categories: upland moor, lowland heath, chalk downland and fen. Historians have generally been dismissive about the economic importance of these areas prior to enclosure and reclamation, but some of them, especially the heaths and downs, were intensively used, and central to the sophisticated farming systems which had developed in these areas over the long centuries before the period of 'improvements'. The very fact that such areas remained as open pasture or heath, and did not become colonised by scrub and trees, is testimony enough to the intensity of their exploitation. Moreover, many such areas had survived unploughed because they were marginal for arable cultivation. This was particularly true of the high, windswept moors of northern England, which comprised by far the largest single type of 'waste' still extant at the start of the eighteenth century. Many such areas, even if enclosed, could neither be reclaimed nor improved, or only ever turned in relatively low yields. The only extensive area of good-quality, naturally fertile 'waste' reclaimed and successfully put to the plough in this period was—as we shall see—the East Anglian Fens, and reclamation here did indeed make a very major contribution to England's grain requirements. But the assumption that, *in general*, enclosure of 'waste land' transformed large areas of unproductive land to fertile farmland is at best questionable.

The enclosure and reclamation of 'wastes' were often the work of large landowners, and their major tenants, and these people have often been viewed as the key actors in the drama of the 'revolution' (e.g. Riches 1937). True, they have loomed less large in more recent accounts (e.g. Overton 1996a), but their importance remains entrenched in popular perceptions of the period as well as in the work of particular historians (e.g. Rosenheim 1989). It might therefore be worth noting the difficulties with such a view. Large landowners were not simply interested in producing more grain or meat. They were interested in making money, and this often involved forms of estate management which did not maximise food production at all, but served instead to preserve the long-term value of their land—the two aims might, on occasions, come into direct conflict. They had wider interests, too, which could oppose those of agricultural improvement: they wanted good hunting and shooting, extensive parks and gardens. They often knew little about the practicalities of agriculture, adopting fashionable improvements quite unsuitable to the local environment, or indulging in land improvement schemes which had little, if any, real hope of success (Wade Martins and Williamson 1999a, 191–4). Programmes of reclamation were motivated as much by social and aesthetic as by economic considerations: contemporaries used the term 'improvement' indiscriminately for the reclamation of 'waste', for schemes of afforestation, and for the laying out of parks and elaborate pleasure grounds.

Nor should we meekly follow the prejudices of Young and most of his contemporaries in assuming that large farms were more productive than small, or large farmers necessarily more efficient, or more innovative, than their less wealthy neighbours. The consensus arising from a number of recent studies appears to be that crop yields, at least in the period studied here, were largely independent of farm size (Overton 1996a, 205). On average, large farms actually produced *lower* yields than small ones because small farms were generally found in areas of more fertile soil and large ones in less favoured areas. But within particular districts there is little hard evidence that large farms produced significantly more per acre. Randall Burroughes of Wymondham in central Norfolk was an assiduous improver, mentioned by Arthur Young in his *General View of the Agriculture of Norfolk* (1804a), a man keen to adopt every fashionable innovation that came his way. He farmed over 300 acres and during the 1790s produced average yields of barley of around 31 bushels, and average yields of wheat of around 22 bushels an acre (Wade Martins and Williamson 1995, 12–18). A few years before, some 12 kilometres down the road at Mattishall, on identical soils, the vicar recorded in some detail the farms and their yields in his tithe book. There were 38 farms, some little more than smallholdings, with an average area of 37 acres. Only one farm covered more than 150 acres, most of the land being cultivated by farms less than half the size of Burroughes' (Gonville and Caius archives; Lloyd-Pritchard 1953). While the barley yields in the parish were slightly lower than those produced by Burroughes (at 29 bushels per acre), the wheat yields were identical. To some extent this is unsurprising, given that Mattishall farmers—even those with a tiny acreage—were as keen to grow turnips, clover and the rest as Burroughes. Large farms may have been more productive than small, but there is little evidence to suggest that the difference was very great.

Perhaps the greatest problem with many traditional accounts of the agricultural revolution, however, is that they place too much emphasis on a limited range of innovations, and neglect other practices which were of equal or greater importance. Not all soils, not all environments, could be

improved by the familiar textbook techniques. In some districts these could not be adopted at all; in others they might be positively harmful. Marling and the four-course rotation were, essentially, suitable improvements for light, 'hungry' land, in which nutrients and lime were constantly being leached from the porous soil. But other kinds of soil demanded different treatment in order to increase yields. In heavy clay districts, for example, lack of nutrients was not usually a major problem. Such soils often retain well the principal chemicals necessary for plant growth, and over much of England are alkaline or neutral below the top few centimetres. Here seasonal waterlogging was the main feature limiting crop yields, a problem which turnips or marl could do nothing to rectify. Indeed, on heavy land it could be hard or impossible to introduce the new rotations. In stiffer soil it was difficult to obtain the fine seed-bed required for turnips, while waterlogging encouraged the crop's principal pest, club root or finger-and-toe disease (*Plasmodiophora brassicae*). In addition, on stiff soils during the winter months it was often impossible to feed the crop off in the field—because stock 'poached' the damp land—yet also difficult to draw it for removal to farmyards (D.H. Robinson 1949, 332). Although, as we shall see, drainage improved dramatically in the eighteenth and nineteenth centuries in many clayland districts, there remained many places where turnips simply would not grow. We might expect, given the emphasis placed on this worthy crop in many conventional accounts, that such places would have been characterised by particularly low yields, but there is remarkably little evidence for this. In Essex, for example, the 1836 Tithe Files record that 89 out of the 246 parishes for which the information is listed—28 per cent—grew no turnips at all. Yet their average recorded wheat yield, at 24.2 bushels an acre, was virtually identical to the county average, of 24.6 bushels. Indeed, of the 21 parishes in England as a whole recording the highest wheat yields per acre in the Tithe Files (35 bushels or more per acre) as many as a third grew no turnips.

Landscape History and the 'Revolution'

This brings us to the purpose and character of this book. As I noted in the introduction, it is an investigation into agricultural change from one specific perspective: that of landscape history or, as it is sometimes termed, landscape archaeology. This is not as well-established as many perspectives upon the past and, moreover, most of its practitioners have concerned themselves primarily with the prehistoric, Roman or medieval periods, so it may be necessary to explain briefly what it actually involves (Williamson 1998a, 18; Lewis *et al.* 1997, 22–4). In some ways landscape historians do what historical geographers used to do, before many of them lost interest in maps and embraced post-modernism. They focus upon the landscape—on physical structures and spatial relationships, past and present—and try to explain these in terms of social organisation and economic activity. At the same time, they use such landscape patterns to throw new, independent light on social and economic history. In addition, their work often displays an acute awareness of the subtle interplay between the natural and the cultural, the environmental and the social: humans are not, perhaps, placed quite so close to the centre of the stage as in most varieties of history. Moreover, from archaeology the discipline derives the firm belief that not all human activity, or its manifestations in physical form in the landscape, can be understood simply in economic terms. Issues of ideology and social status can at times override simple considerations of financial gain, and the spatial organisation of the landscape might itself play an *active* rather than merely reflective role in the articulation of social relationships. Above all, landscape historians employ a particularly wide range of evidence—documentary, cartographic, archaeological, environmental—and normally study wide areas over extended periods of time. In other words, they tend to be generalists, 'jacks-of-all-trades', rather than period specialists. This does not mean that they avoid the study of particular issues or periods: far from it. But such studies are always informed by three considerations given less prominence in, for example, conventional economic history.

The first is the importance of the natural environment in moulding social, economic and agrarian arrangements. This role might be obvious and direct, as when particular soil conditions encouraged or precluded the growth of particular crops. Or it might be subtle and indirect, as for example when environmental conditions structured aspects of agrarian arrangements, which in turn had effects upon social organisation or institutional structures. The second is the recognition that inherited patterns, 'antecedent structures', are often as important in the development of social and economic forms as contemporary circumstances, and that spatial patterns and relationships (and associated institutional forms) can persist, as an active and structuring force, long after the circumstances that engendered them have changed beyond recognition. The classic open-field system of the Midlands, originating in the early Middle Ages yet persisting, in some cases, into the nineteenth century, is one particularly striking example. Lastly, variations in soils, climate and topography, and the enduring patterns of fields and settlements which these helped engender, were strongly regional in nature. Local societies and their landscapes tended, to a significant extent, to develop along their own trajectories, crucially effected of course by national and international trends, but moving nevertheless with a measure of autonomy. These societies and landscapes, like the environmental patterns to which they were related, were always poorly correlated with administrative structures: they were seldom if ever neatly constrained by county boundaries. The soils, farming systems and landscapes of the south Buckinghamshire Chilterns flow seamlessly across the county boundary into west Hertfordshire, but have little in common with those found in the clay vales in the north of Buckinghamshire.

Regions

The meaning and implication of these approaches will become apparent in the course of this book, but one particular aspect needs to be emphasised here. The English landscape at the start of the agricultural revolution period displayed a quite bewildering degree of variation, not only in terms of the natural environment (relief, climate, soils) but also in terms of the human landscape, and the institutional structures embedded within it (settlement patterns, the extent of open and enclosed land, the layout and character of field systems).

I have already drawn attention to the three main landscape zones of medieval England—the highland zone; the 'champion' regions, dominated by nucleated villages and extensive, and usually tightly-regulated, open fields; and the areas to either side of this broad belt, characterised by more dispersed settlement and by landscapes of enclosed fields and 'irregular' field systems. A further

distinction in the medieval landscape, vital for any understanding of eighteenth-century developments, can now be made. The champion belt can itself be divided into two broad kinds of landscape. Within the central core of the Midlands—a region of heavy clay soils—most parishes had open fields which, by the thirteenth century, often ran to the very margins of the township (Hall 1995, 2). There was very little in the way of 'waste' or common grazing land. In contrast, on the lighter lands around the margins of this central core—on the chalklands of Wessex, in parts of the Chilterns, in western East Anglia, on the South Downs, on the Wolds of Yorkshire and Lincolnshire, and (though to a lesser extent) in the Cotswolds—rather different forms of champion landscape could be found. Here open fields co-existed with extensive tracts of open grazing—downs, sheepwalks, and heaths. These were, to use the term current by the sixteenth century, 'sheep-corn' countries. Large flocks were grazed by day on the downs and heaths, and folded by night on the open fields, thus ensuring a continuous flow of nutrients which kept these thin, easily leached soils in heart (Kerridge 1967, 42–6).

Both of these broad types of 'champion' landscape were primarily arable countries, but in this respect they were not necessary special or unique. Although in some of the areas to the south and east, and to the north and west, of the champion belt, pasture farming played a more prominent role, most farmers in the Middle Ages were mixed cultivators, and all grew some arable crops. This was even true of those dwelling in the far north and west, in the 'highland zone'. In the valleys and vales cutting through the high moorland plateaux, arable land was a far more prominent feature of the landscape than it was to become by the eighteenth century, or is today.

The early medieval agrarian economy may have exhibited more regional specialisation than was once thought (Campbell 2000) but it was only in the wake of the Black Death that recognisable farming regions really began to develop. Their configuration—which has been studied in considerable detail by scholars like Joan Thirsk and Eric Kerridge (Kerridge 1967; Thirsk 1987)—underwent a number of changes but the main character-istics remained in place at the end of the seventeenth century (Figure 5). The old village-dominated champion lands—the light soils of the sheep-corn districts, and the Midland clay vales—remained arable districts, although cereals were also important in some areas of irregular field systems and dispersed settlement, such as the Chiltern dipslope (the areas shown as 'Wolds and downlands', 'Heathland', and 'Arable vale lands' on Figure 5). Elsewhere pasture became more extensive, and the area in tilth declined: in the lands to the west of the Midland belt (in what Thirsk has called the 'pastoral vale lands'); in the islands of 'forest' land scattered across the Midlands Plain; and in particular on heavy soils in the south and east of England, especially in the Weald and on the boulder clay plateau of East Anglia. The various areas of fenland and marsh depicted on Thirsk's map were also primarily pasture-farming areas, although some were wilder landscapes, in which the cutting of peat, marsh hay and thatching materials were of more importance than grazing. Some of these lowland districts were primarily devoted to dairying, some to fattening, and although they certainly bred some of their own cattle and sheep, a substantial proportion were raised elsewhere, often in the remote uplands, in what Thirsk has termed the 'fell and moorland' regions.

The distribution of early modern farming regions was, to a significant extent, deter-mined by soils and climatic conditions: the heavier clay soils of the lowlands made for lush pastures; the sheltered valleys of the north and west grew better grass than grain. But this was not always the case. Dairying, stock-rearing and grazing were not every-where an option open to farmers, even where environmental circumstances were favourable. Specialised livestock production generally required enclosure, and the most important pasture-farming districts were to be found in areas in which enclosed fields already dominated the landscape or in which open-field systems of 'irregular' form had

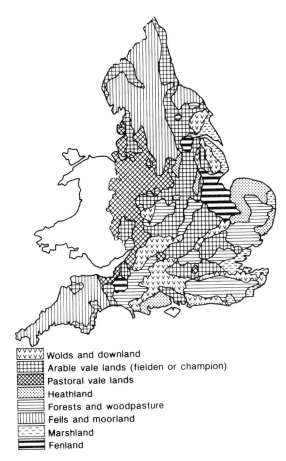

Wolds and downland
Arable vale lands (fielden or champion)
Pastoral vale lands
Heathland
Forests and woodpasture
Fells and moorland
Marshland
Fenland

Figure 5   Joan Thirsk's simplified schedule of early modern farming regions

existed, which could be enclosed piecemeal with relative ease. In the champion Midlands, in contrast, although the soils were often well suited to livestock farming, open fields of regular form were the norm, and enclosure and conversion to pasture was a more limited and more traumatic process, associated with the shrinkage or depopulation of settlements. The Midlands remained a largely arable region in the early modern period, a classic example of the way in which antecedent structures can have a determining influence on subsequent economic development. The pattern of farming in early modern England did not, therefore, directly mirror soil types. The clay plateau of East Anglia and the clay vales of the Midlands, despite both having heavy clay soils, developed contrasting systems of husbandry (Figures 5 and 6).

England at the end of the seventeenth century was thus a complex mosaic of farming regions, and even Figure 5 presents a highly simplified picture—each region could, if we so desired, be subdivided into smaller and smaller subregions. But as a number of historians have also emphasised, these regions were not simply *agricultural* entities. Factors operating both in the medieval past and in more recent times had ensured that particular kinds of social and tenurial structure were—rather broadly—associated with different kinds of farming economy. Pasture-farming districts thus tended to have less hierarchical social structures than arable areas: much of their land was owned by small owner-occupiers and members of the lesser gentry, and farmed by relatively small family farms (Thirsk 1970). Many had been poorly manorialised in the Middle Ages: sometimes because they were extensively cleared and settled at a relatively late date, in later Saxon or even post-Conquest times; sometimes because they remained thinly

populated, so that many dwelt far from their lord; sometimes for other reasons. Lack of manorial control, coupled with the fact that dairy farming and grazing often left time for other pursuits, ensured that in many of these districts industrial by-employments— weaving, iron-production, coal-mining—were well developed by the seventeenth century.

The arable lands were more hierarchical in character. Most had been highly manorialised in medieval times, and a continuing emphasis on arable production, in the increasingly market-orientated climate of the sixteenth and seventeenth centuries, ensured that small owner-occupiers continued to decline in importance. Small arable farmers tended to be more vulnerable to the vagaries of the harvest than large ones. Because they consumed a higher proportion of their own produce, a poor harvest might mean that they were forced into debt. Conversely, when the harvest was good and prices fell, they could make less of a profit from their relatively meagre surplus than larger producers, who had larger reserves to dispose of, and who had more opportunity to speculate on the longer-term development of the market. And as we have seen, the decline of small owner-occupiers was most marked in areas of the poorest land—the sandy heaths and thin chalk soils. It was here that the largest estates were most developed by the close of the seventeenth century, where land was relatively cheap. Their grip on the landscape was to grow ever tighter in the course of the period examined here.

We need to be a little cautious about accepting some of these arguments. In particular, the correlation between farming systems and early industrial development has a number of important exceptions (Overton 1996a, 57). Their more extreme versions are especially suspect. It has, for example, been argued that pasture areas

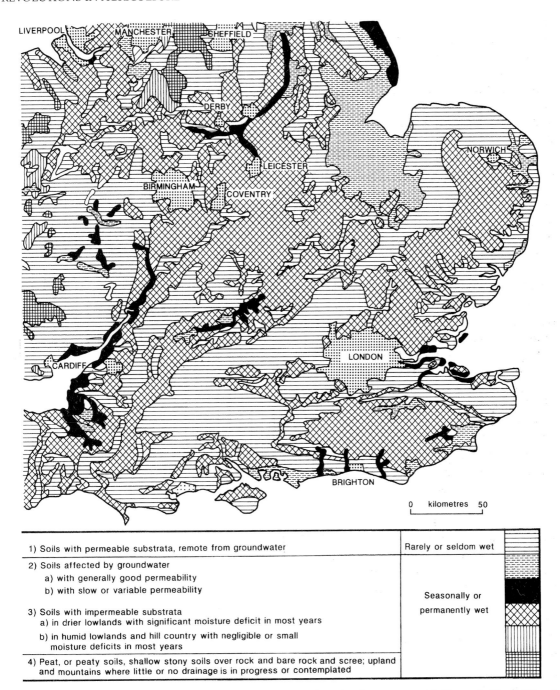

1) Soils with permeable substrata, remote from groundwater	Rarely or seldom wet

2) Soils affected by groundwater
    a) with generally good permeability
    b) with slow or variable permeability
	Seasonally or
	permanently wet

3) Soils with impermeable substrata
    a) in drier lowlands with significant moisture deficit in most years
    b) in humid lowlands and hill country with negligible or small
       moisture deficits in most years	

4) Peat, or peaty soils, shallow stony soils over rock and bare rock and scree; upland and mountains where little or no drainage is in progress or contemplated	

*Figure 6   Soils and drainage in southern and Midland England: compare with Figure 5. The Midlands
and the heavy clays of East Anglia and the south-east developed along very different lines
in the early modern period, in spite of similarities in soil drainage potential*

tended to be ideologically dissident. Puritan and non-conformist, they generally supported the parliamentary cause during the Civil War. Arable areas, in contrast, were conformist in religious outlook and Royalist in sympathies: they were more deferential societies (Underdown 1985). Such contrasts are probably too sweeping and simplistic, and they will play little part in the argument that unfolds in the chapters that follow. For our purposes, it is more important to emphasise that as well as being economic entities, farming regions also had an *ecological* aspect. Particular patterns of farming were closely associated with particular habitats and environments. Most heaths, for example, were associated with sheep-corn husbandry. Deforested in the Bronze Age, their acid soils favoured the development of a characteristic undershrub vegetation, dominated by heather or ling (*Calluna vulgaris*), bell heather (*Erica cinera*), gorse (*Ulex europaeus*) and broom (*Sarothamnus scoparius*). This is turn encouraged the development of the characteristic soil of the heathlands, the *podzol*, in which grey upper levels, leached of humus and iron, overlie hard layers of humus pan and iron pan, where these have been redeposited. Characteristic grasses thrive in such an environment, including sheep's fescue (*Festuca ovina*), wavy hair grass (*Deschampsia flexnosa*), and common bent (*Agrostis tenuis*), while some areas become dominated by bracken. The coarse character of the heathland vegetation helped to determine the nature of the heathland sheep breeds, and in particular the character of their fleeces. Yet the heaths did not constitute a stable 'climax' vegetation. They were not only created, but also sustained, by human activity. Had the intensity of grazing been reduced—as happened in many areas in the course of the twentieth century—the character of the vegetation would have

rapidly changed. Gorse and bracken would soon invade the land; next, birch and oak would gain a hold; finally, woodland would regenerate. Fen, downland and moorland were likewise distinctive, semi-natural habitats, first created in the distant past but maintained by, and in turn influencing the character of, regional farming systems.

Not all early-modern farming systems were intimately associated with ancient environments like these. Some, like the pasture districts of the south and east, had gained much of their ecological character in the post-medieval centuries, as the acreage of pasture increased at the expense of tillage, and as hedges and trees proliferated. And some 'traditional' farming systems were associated with relatively impoverished environments. In particular, the open-field parishes in the Midlands were not only largely treeless and hedgeless. They often had only limited reserves of pasture. Their landscape was dominated by ploughland, their ecology by arable weeds.

Society and landscape, farming and ecology, were thus intimately connected, forming a pattern of distinctive regions. The agricultural changes of the eighteenth and nineteenth centuries did not act on a blank and undifferentiated slate, and no single body of 'improvements' could raise productivity in all these varied circumstances. In the final analysis much of this variation was related to the natural environment—to the character of the climate, topography and soils. And the agricultural revolution was, above all, an ecological revolution, which in many districts changed the very nature of the soil, and destroyed forever environments and habitats which had been stable for centuries or millennia.

The great changes of the eighteenth and nineteenth centuries can thus only be understood within a regional context. But, in a book such as this, it is impossible to do real justice to the extent of local and regional variation in farming and landscape. Simplification is inevitable. The following chapters will deal, in turn, with the changes taking place in four broad types of landscape: the central, clayland core of the champion Midlands; the light heaths and chalklands of the south and east; the clays and fens of the Home Counties and East Anglia; and the districts lying to the north and west of the Midland Plain. Each of these broad districts developed along very different lines in the course of the eighteenth and early nineteenth centuries. There was not one agricultural revolution in England, but many.

CHAPTER 2

Grassing Down the Shires

The Midland Plain

We will begin our enquiry with the classic 'champion' landscapes which occupied the central core of the Midlands: the region affected, more than any other, by eighteenth- and nineteenth-century enclosure. It was here that old modes of open-field farming continued on some scale into the eighteenth century; it is here that we might expect to see the most dramatic effects of the new husbandry.

The area under discussion covers some 2,223,900 acres (900,000 hectares), embracing the counties of Northamptonshire and Leicestershire; the old county of Rutland; the southern and eastern half of Warwickshire; Buckinghamshire north of the Chilterns; and western Bedfordshire; but with atten- uated extensions, running through south Nottinghamshire into western Lincolnshire, and south-westwards, through north Berkshire and central Oxfordshire, to Swindon and beyond (Figure 7). Most of this extensive area is characterised by poorly draining clay soils, formed in part in chalky boulder clay, in part in Jurassic and Cretaceous clays (Ragg *et al*. 1984). Pockets of more freely draining soils certainly do occur, mainly in the valleys of the principal rivers such as the Nene and the Ouse, where lighter formations—Jurassic limestone and gravels—are exposed. Scattered areas of freely draining soils can likewise be found on higher ground, especially where the Jurassic Ironstone outcrops. Nevertheless, these exceptions should not detract from the crucial observation that most of the farmers in this region had to contend with soils which, if moderately fertile, were seasonally waterlogged and tenacious, hard and expen- sive to cultivate (Sturgess 1966, 105). This region forms the core of Rackham's 'planned countryside'; and it was here, in what Roberts has termed the 'Central Province' (Roberts and Wrathmell 1998, 100–10), that open-field agriculture reached its most complex form, and was most deeply entrenched.

The Open-Field Landscape

Precisely why this region of England came to be dominated by tightly nucleated villages and highly regular open fields is a matter over which historians and archaeologists continue to argue. Indeed, even the date at which open fields developed remains a matter of contention. What is generally agreed is that some time during the middle or later Saxon periods—that is, between the eighth and the eleventh centuries—there was a revolution in the Midland landscape. A settlement pattern consisting of hamlets and isolated farms was replaced by one of nucleated villages and—possibly at the same time, possibly later—the surrounding farm- land was reorganised in the form of large, unhedged open fields (Brown and Foard 1998; Fox 1981; Hall 1982). By the time that documents become sufficiently numerous and detailed to provide a picture of the typical Midland village, in the thirteenth century, each farmer had a holding which was scattered throughout the township in a large number of small, unhedged strips, called *lands*, each normally between a quarter and a half an acre in extent. Strips were grouped into bundles called *furlongs*, which formed the basic unit for cropping; and the furlongs in turn were grouped into large blocks called *fields* (Hall 1982 and 1995).

There were usually three fields, occasionally two, in each township, one of which lay

Figure 7   The location of some of the regions discussed in the text

fallow or uncropped each year. In a three-field system, the other fields lay under a spring-sown crop and an autumn-sown crop, such as beans and wheat respectively, crops well suited to the heavy soils. The fallow provided crucial grazing for the village livestock which were herded or folded there, and their dung returned to the soil the nitrogen and other nutrients which were depleted by cropping. This was not the only way in which nitrogen could be replenished, for beans served, to some extent, to fix it in the soil directly from the atmosphere. The weeds growing in the fallow, moreover, were ploughed in at the end of the season to provide 'green manure', a practice which also provided some measure of control over the rank weed growth to which these heavy, damp soils were particularly prone. Farming activities were carried out, for the most part, on an individual basis, but the organisation of the farming year was subject to strong communal controls, usually laid down by the court of the principal manor.

These were, by the thirteenth century, landscapes of almost unrelieved arable. Most villages had at least 80 per cent, some more than 90 per cent, of their land under the plough (Hall 1995, 2). The ploughlands of one village often ran all the way to the parish boundary, meeting the arable of the next community, with no intervening woodland or 'waste'. 'Only river meadows liable to flooding, wet areas along the sides of brooks where springs emerged, and areas with steep and rough ground, were left unploughed' (Hall 1995, 2). Indeed, many historians believe that it was this paucity of pasture, and the need to utilise more systematically and intensively the grazing offered by the fallows and the harvest aftermath, that was one of the main reasons behind the adoption of the 'Midland system' in the first place (Thirsk 1964; Fox 1981). The Midland

landscape would thus have appeared as a vast prairie (or, in the winter months, as a great sea of mud) with few hedges and trees, except in the immediate vicinity of the village. But the fields were not quite as featureless as the immense arable fields now to be found in many areas of England. It was usual for each strip to be ploughed in ridges, and the subsequent conversion of many of these areas to pasture has created what was, until relatively recently, the commonest type of earthwork in England—ridge and furrow (Figure 8).

The practice of ploughing in ridges was not entirely confined to the open fields of the Midlands, but was certainly strongly concentrated here (Beresford 1948). Even today large areas of ridge and furrow survive in the region, generally on the heaviest soils, especially along the border of Warwickshire and Northamptonshire, in southern Leicestershire and in north Buckinghamshire. The process of ridging is described by a number of early agricultural writers. The plough cut a single furrow and the mould board turned the soil towards the right as the ploughteam moved down the strip. Each 'land' was usually ploughed in a clockwise direction, starting in the middle and going round and round until the edge was reached. This served to move soil towards the centre of the strip, and over the years this led to the formation of a permanent ridge (Hall 1999, 55). Strips were not, however, ploughed in the same direction every year for this would have created very high ridges with very deep and wide furrows, cutting into the infertile subsoil. An anti-clockwise motion was thus adopted in the fallow season in order to move some of the soil back towards the perimeter.

The main purpose of ridging was to improve drainage, although it may have brought other benefits, in helping to define

Figure 8   Ridge and furrow with typical 'reversed S' profile, near Quainton, Buckinghamshire

the individual lands in unenclosed fields. Ridging was unquestionably normal practice in the Middle Ages, and is referred to in a variety of local documents, and by agricultural writers like Walter of Henley (Oschinsky 1971, 321). Yet while archaeologists often rather loosely describe surviving examples of ridge and furrow as 'medieval', in the vast majority of cases this is only true in the widest sense. The ridges we see today may perpetuate medieval land divisions, but are themselves in most cases of post-medieval date, in the sense that this was the period in which the plot of land in question was last ploughed in the fashion described. Midland townships enclosed and put down to grass in the later eighteenth century, as well as those more anciently enclosed, are (or were until recently) usually carpeted with ridge and furrow (Figure 9).

Manorial courts appear to have taken great pains to ensure adequate drainage of the fields. Where the free flow of water was impeded by the banks of soil which accumulated on the 'headland' at the end of a furlong, for example, outlets were cut using a trenching spade or trenching plough. Nevertheless, after protracted rain the water often stood for long periods in the furrows. John Clare described the 'mire and sludgy' winter fields of his native Helpston in Northamptonshire, with the shepherds picking their way across the furlongs and having 'oft to ford the sloughs that nearly meet/Across the lands' (Robinson and Powell 1984, 139).

Figure 9 High-backed ridge and furrow crossed by parliamentary enclosure hedges, at Padbury, Buckinghamshire

Poor drainage was one of the reasons why yields remained comparatively low in eighteenth-century open-field clayland parishes, although a shortage of manure—the consequence of the small number of livestock which could be maintained in the absence of extensive commons—was equally important. Even at the end of the eighteenth century, to judge from a government enquiry of 1795, the average wheat yield of open-field parishes in Northamptonshire was a mere 15.6 bushels an acre—around three-quarters of what might be expected on similar, long-enclosed soils in East Anglia, and perhaps 20 per cent less than in enclosed parishes in the Midlands (Turner 1982b, 498;

1986, 683). Nevertheless, a note of caution should be raised here. Although yields per acre were often low in such parishes, as we noted earlier their land was generally cropped for cereals rather more intensively than was the case in places adopting more 'improved' modes of husbandry. More importantly, the well-documented yields of the late eighteenth century appear to be considerably better than those attained in earlier centuries, and it is clear that open-field farmers were not entirely incapable of making improvements to their farming. Turnips were widely cultivated in Midland open fields in the eighteenth century. In 1801, to judge from Michael Turner's analysis of the Crop Returns, while open parishes grew less of the crop than enclosed ones, the difference was not that great: in Bedfordshire for example an average of 6.7 per cent of the cropped acreage compared with 8.7 per cent. Both, in fact, were rather low figures, and in some Midland districts they were lower still, but this was largely for environmental reasons. As Pitt noted in 1813, most of the Midland soils were 'too strong and too harsh' for turnips to be grown successfully (Pitt 1813b, 97). Other improvements were made. Robert Allen has suggested, in particular, that more careful selection of seed grain may have improved yields significantly in the course of the seventeenth century (Allen 1992, 206–7); while David Hall has argued that, through the post-medieval period, there was a clear trend towards ploughing in higher, steeper ridges. Ridge and furrow in early enclosures has a rather lower profile than that found in places known to have been under the plough in the eighteenth and nineteenth centuries. At Wollaston in Northamptonshire, for example, the manorial demesne was enclosed in two stages, in 1231 and 1583, and contains low-profile ridges which contrast markedly with the more pronounced ridges on the adjacent land, which remained under the plough until 1788 (Hall 1982, Figures 8 and 4; Hall 1999, 33). This trend probably represents an attempt to improve drainage in the absence of other methods (it was, in particular, difficult to install underdrains where land lay in intermingled strips).

The Progress of Enclosure

The 'traditional' landscape of the Midlands

began to decay in the late fourteenth and fifteenth centuries. The population declined dramatically in the wake of the Black Death, the market for arable produce fell, and wage costs rose. In a number of townships the arable fields were laid to grass. Often this followed a phase of voluntary migration, as a proportion of the inhabitants left to find farms elsewhere, with better soil, more reliable water supplies or better access to markets. Faced with communities in decline, landlords often hastened the process, buying up freeholds, terminating insecure copy-holds, and re-letting the land in the form of large capital grazing farms, or setting their own livestock to graze the land (Lewis *et al.* 1997). Such depopulating enclosures cont-inued into the sixteenth century, but they did not affect all parts of the Midlands to the same extent. In particular, because enclosure was easiest where villages were small, and where all the land lay in a single manor and could be acquired by a single owner with relative ease, late medieval enclosures tended to be a particular feature of the higher, clay-covered watersheds, rather than of the major valleys, where larger and more tenurially complex vills could be found on more amenable soils. In Hall's words, late medieval enclosures affected villages which were 'low in population and small in area' (Hall 1998, 351). Thus the belt of high ground running from the Nottinghamshire/Leicester Wolds, through 'High Leicestershire', and on into 'High Northamptonshire' (in the west of that county), had a particularly high incidence of enclosure in the fourteenth and fifteenth centuries, and a marked concentration of deserted settlements can be found here (Fox 1989, 96–100).

Enclosure probably continued at a fairly steady rate through the sixteenth and seventeenth centuries, in spite of the fact that grain prices recovered as population growth resumed once more. In Northamptonshire, probably the most thoroughly researched Midland county, around 28 per cent of vills—around a fifth of the total land area—had been enclosed by the end of the seventeenth century (Hall 1998, 358). Some enclosure occurred piecemeal, but the majority was achieved through the agreement of the principal proprietors. The kind of dramatic, depopulating enclosure familiar from the period before 1550 thus came to an end, in part because most communities holding by the most insecure copyholds had now been eliminated, in part because legal changes ensured greater security of tenure for those copyholders who remained (Allen 1992, 71–2, 54).

The overwhelming majority of sixteenth- and seventeenth-century enclosure was associated with the conversion of arable to grass (Allen 1992, 32). It is impossible to overemphasise this simple point, which was seldom lost on contemporaries. Enclosure brought other benefits but these were seldom so great that landowners were prepared to bear the required legal and other costs to achieve them. Where landowners wanted to create farms suitable for grazing sheep or cattle, however, they had to enclose: it was impossible to run large-scale livestock enterprises in a landscape of scattered, unhedged strips. While enclosure in the sixteenth and seventeenth centuries seldom led to the complete disappearance of villages, there is much evidence for the shrinkage of settlements—grazing farms required fewer labourers than arable enterprises. As in the late Middle Ages, enclosure was concentrated on the high watersheds, although much low-lying 'vale' land was now also affected. The parish of Great Linford in Buckinghamshire was typical. It was enclosed in 1658, by the agreement of its principal proprietors. By 1714, according to a survey, of

the eleven farms in the parish only five seem to have included a farm house, and only three had any land in tilth—and even then, only a few acres. Much of the land was leased to people living outside the village, apparently butchers and graziers supplying the expanding London market (Reed 1983, 142).

Enclosure of this kind continued into the eighteenth century. Thus the Verney family enclosed Middle Claydon in 1654–6, and East Claydon ninety years later: in both cases, the entire parish was laid to grass (Broad 1980, 83). By this time landowners were, once again, responding to obvious economic incentives. Cereal prices were low in the late seventeenth and early eighteenth centuries, because population growth was again sluggish. Arable farms on the Midland clays were hard to let, for it was expensive to work this heavy land and expensive to transport grain to distant markets down the rutted clay roads: much of the area lay far from the main urban centres or coastal ports, and was crossed by few navigable rivers. Ellis, referring to the clays of north Buckinghamshire, thus described how 'Most Arable ground in this Vale lets for but seven or eight shillings an Acre, and the best of all, for but nine shillings. Whereas, when such Plowed-land is got into a right full Sward, it will let for twenty or thirty Shillings an Acre' (Ellis 1750, I, Feb, 112).

It is not surprising, therefore, that many landowners saw the sense of conversion to pasture. Such a move brought other benefits. In particular, it was the landowners' responsibility to maintain the buildings of the farm, and arable enterprises needed more structures—and more expensive ones—than grazing establishments. As Lord Fermanagh wrote to his steward, John Milward, in 1742, concerning a property at Water Stratford in Buckinghamshire: 'Do you think the estate . . . might be turned into Dairy bargains and hold rent, and but a trifle laid down, for surely if near half is ploughed or but a fourth of it, it must needs have many barns and outbuildings to which are great incumbrances, as we see at Adstock and Bierton' (quoted in Broad 1980, 83).

Even where parishes remained unenclosed there is much evidence for the expansion of grassland. Sometimes the ends of strips were hedged off, to form 'green ends', or groups of strips were put down to grass. In many parishes 'cow pastures' were created—in effect, completely new areas of common grazing. Morton, writing in 1712, described how in Northamptonshire

> Many of the lordships, and especially the larger ones, have a common or uninclosed pasture for their cattel in the outskirts of the fields. Most of these have formerly been plowed, but being generally their worst sort of ground, and at so great a distance from the towns, the manuring and culture of them were found so inconvenient that they have been laid down for greensward (quoted in Hall 1995, 22).

Parliamentary enclosure began to replace the various forms of enclosure by agreement in the middle of the eighteenth century. Thanks to the work of Michael Turner and W.O. Tate, we now know that the majority of enclosure acts occurred in two great waves, the first peaking in the 1770s, the second during the Napoleonic Wars (Turner 1980, 63–93). The first peak was strongly concentrated in the Midlands. Parliamentary acts tended to affect those parishes which had resisted earlier enclosure either because the quality of their soils and the nature of their location made the choice between arable and pastoral farming more finely balanced, or—more importantly—because they were more populous and more tenurially complex. The vast majority of Midland enclosures after c.1750 were achieved by parliamentary act, and by the end of the eighteenth century probably less than a fifth of the parishes on the Midland clays remained open.

Given that cereal prices had begun to recover from the 1760s, as population growth began to take off again, it is perhaps surprising that conversion to pasture continued apace. It is certainly more surprising than historians often admit. But there is no doubt that most parliamentary enclosures in the Midland counties did indeed result in the expansion of grazing (Turner 1986, 677). As W.G. Hoskins remarked, 'This conversion of arable to pasture had been the almost invariable effect of parliamentary enclosure in Leicestershire' (Hoskins 1949, 132). The responses made by Midland vicars and rectors to the government enquiry into the likely state of the harvest of 1801 (the Crop Returns) make particularly interesting reading in this context. Typically, the vicar of Breedon on the Hill in Leicestershire remarked how:

> Within the last 30 years almost all the country north-west of Leicester to the extremity of the county has been enclosed: by which means the land is become in a higher state of cultivation than formerly; but on account of a great proportion of it being converted into pasturage much less food is produced than when it was more generally in tillage (Turner 1982a, II, 53).

In many other Leicestershire parishes the incumbents told a similar story. In Kegworth, for example, only 580 acres were under cultivation, around a quarter of the parish, and the vicar noted how this was 'considerably diminished since the Inclosure which took place about twenty-two years ago' (Hoskins 1949, 131). In large parts of Northamptonshire the situation was the same. At Twyell the incumbent reported how 'less corn is grown since the enclosure . . . the land being laid down in grass'; at Ufford, Bainton and Ashton there was 'less corn of all sorts since the enclosure which took place three years ago' (Turner 1982a, II, 151). The 2,000 acres of Clipston parish were now mostly 'good grazing land', but 'before the enclosure most of the field was ploughed' (*ibid.*, 142). The incumbent of Welford similarly reported that the parish had been enclosed in 1778, 'since which time the greater part of it has been laid down to grass' (*ibid.*, 152). Many other Northamptonshire clerics made similar comments.

What is particularly striking is that this expansion of pasture was continuing even during the Napoleonic Wars, when French blockade threatened grain imports and cereal prices rose to dizzy heights. Wilbarston in Northamptonshire, for example, was enclosed in 1798 and was still in 1801 in the process of being 'laid or laying down, for grazing' (Turner 1982a, II, 154). True, there are a few places where the Crop Returns suggest some reversal of the trend. At Church Langton in Leicestershire the incumbent reported how 50 acres had recently been converted to tillage but this represented an increase in arable area of only 10 per cent (*ibid.*, 54). Extension of the cultivated acreage was reported in only two other parishes in the county, a small total—as Hoskins noted—out of 180 surviving returns (Hoskins 1949, 133).

By the end of the eighteenth century pasture land dominated the landscape of the Midlands. J. Wedge in 1794 estimated that some 232,000 acres of Warwickshire were devoted to meadow, pasture and 'feeding ground', and only 154,530 to tillage—and of this, 57,330 acres were rotational grass (Wedge 1794, 11, 50). In Rutland in the same year Crutchley estimated that three-fifths of the farmland was laid to permanent grass, the remaining two-fifths to convertible husbandry featuring long grass leys (Crutchley 1794, 12). In 1801, to judge from the Crop Returns, a mere 22.3 per cent of Northamptonshire (excluding fallow) was devoted to arable crops (Turner 1981, 294). Pitt, writing in 1813, believed that there were 100,000 horses, 100,000 dairy and store cattle, and 200,000 sheep and feeding cattle in the county (Pitt 1813b, 137). A 'very considerable proportion' of its area was under pasture—'the great breadth of upland, laid down, in ancient and modern times, to permanent grass' (Pitt 1813b, 113); and there were many parishes like Fawsley, 'about 3,000 acres, without a single blade of corn' (Pitt 1813b, 131). Leicestershire by 1801 was even more devoted to livestock production, with a mere 80,000 acres or so under arable crops, less than 16 per cent of the total area of the county (Turner 1981, 294). In Burton Overy there were only 93 acres under cultivation out of a total of nearly 1,800, while in the adjacent parish of Carlton Curlieu only 30 acres, out of a total of 1,378, were in tilth (Hoskins 1949, 137–9). Similarly, in north Buckinghamshire—in the clay vales to the north of the Chiltern escarpment—the pastures were extensive, and in 1801 probably less than 20 per cent of the county north of the Chiltern escarpment was under arable cultivation (Turner 1981, 294).

The high water mark of the green tide of pasture probably washed through the Midlands in the first decade of the nineteenth century. Thereafter it was halted, and in some places reversed. The documents called the Tithe Files—drawn up in the mid 1830s in connection with the commutation of tithes—suggest that arable had re-expanded in Leicestershire, Northamptonshire, and the adjacent areas. There are some problems with this source. Tithes were often commuted at the time of parliamentary enclosure, which was particularly prevalent in this region, and so comparatively few files were ever compiled here compared with other parts of England. Nevertheless, the 32 for Leicestershire and the 22 for Northamptonshire suggest that in the former county the area of farmland under arable crops (excluding rotational grass and fallows) had risen from 16 per cent in 1801 to 20.4 per cent in the late 1830s, in the latter from 22.3 to 31 per cent. Even if this reflects a real increase in the extent of arable (rather than differences in the character of the sample taken by each source) grassland still dominated the landscape, with 76.4 per cent of the former county and 64 per cent of the latter still under permanent or rotational grass. Moreover, to judge from the same sources most of the apparent expansion in tillage was due to the substitution of turnips—a fodder crop—for bare fallows. Most areas of the Midlands were thus still mainly concerned with livestock husbandry at the start of Victoria's reign, and there were many districts like the Vale of Aylesbury in Buckinghamshire, which James Caird in 1852 described as 'celebrated for the excellence of its pastures, for which it is better adapted by nature than for tillage. In three parishes which we visited, the proportion of tillage to pasture was very small, there being in the first only 8 acres in 2000 under the plough; in the second 90 acres in 900; and in the third no tillage whatsoever' (Caird 1852, 1).

It was this gradual grassing-down of extensive areas of the Midland 'shires' which created the great swathes of ridge and furrow which were, until relatively recently, so characteristic a feature of the landscape. Recent changes in agriculture have served to remove, wholesale, these earthworks, but in 1946—when the RAF undertook a comprehensive vertical aerial survey of the country—

very extensive areas survived (Figure 10). Historians and archaeologists have normally studied ridge and furrow for what it can tell us about medieval agriculture. But in the present context it has a rather different significance. These earthworks only existed where fields once ploughed in ridges had been laid down to grass, and not ploughed up again. They therefore vividly indicate the extent to which, in the course of the late medieval and post-medieval periods, the English Midlands moved out of arable agriculture and into pasture farming. In fact, the extent of ridge and furrow shown on Figure 10 greatly underestimates the area of land which passed from arable to pasture in this period: in part because of the partial reversal of this trend in the course of the nineteenth century, in part because a substantial proportion of ridge and furrow was destroyed by deliberate levelling to improve drainage, and in part because of short-term shifts back to arable during the First and Second World Wars. Hoskins, writing about Leicestershire in 1949, thus noted how 'modern war time ploughing has wiped out some of the medieval pattern' (Hoskins 1949, frontispiece). Indeed, between 1937 and 1944 the area under arable more than tripled in Leicestershire, and more than doubled in Northamptonshire (Stamp 1950, 420–1).

The New Economy

Eighteenth- and early nineteenth-century writers describe in some detail the farming economy of the new Midland landscape. Some of the pastures were devoted to fattening livestock, some to dairying. Fattening seems to have predominated on the better pastures, often those longest enclosed. The late medieval emphasis on sheep had, in the course of the sixteenth century, been

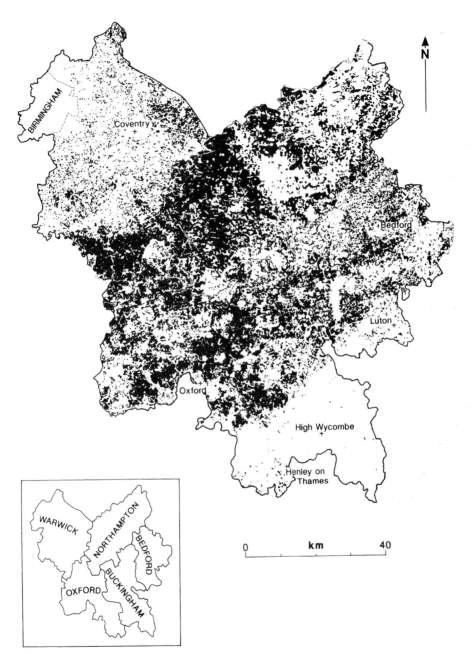

Figure 10   The distribution of ridge and furrow in the south Midlands in 1946. The absence of ridge and furrow from south Buckinghamshire and south Bedfordshire, and to some extent from north Warwickshire, reflects the fact that farmers in these districts seldom ridged their fields. The remarkable density of ridging elsewhere indicates the scale of the shift from arable to pasture, which followed the enclosure of the Midland open fields in the post-medieval period.

replaced by an interest in cattle, but sheep remained important in many areas and sheep and cattle were often grazed together in the same fields. Most of the sheep were locally bred, although a minority were brought in from the Cotswolds and Wiltshire (Pitt 1813a, 113). Throughout the post-medieval period attempts were made to improve sheep breeds (Davis and Beckett 1999), attempts which seem to have intensified in the eighteenth century. The new landscape permitted the development of types of livestock which fattened faster than those which had picked a living from the open-field fallows. Breeding experiments in the middle decades of the century—associated in particular with Robert Bakewell of Leicestershire—produced the New Leicester (Pitt 1813a, 216–17, 245–50), more demanding in its food requirements, but producing a good fleece and better meat, as the less appetising parts of the animals had been systematically bred out. Pitt described the new breed in glowing terms: 'Their offals are small, and their profitable parts are large. Their backs are broad and strait, their breasts are full, bellies tucked up, heads small, necks short, legs thin, pelts light, wool fine of its kind' (Pitt 1813a, 250).

But it was cattle rather than sheep which were now the principal stock, and particular areas—the Northamptonshire uplands, the Welland Valley—gained a national reputation for producing prime, grass-reared beef. In contrast to sheep, only a minority of the Midland cattle were home-reared—around 15 per cent in Northamptonshire, Pitt thought at the end of eighteenth century (Colyer 1973, 45). Most were brought by drovers as young bullocks from distant regions: from Scotland, Wales, Ireland, and the north and west of England. The breeds favoured varied from place to place, and over time. In particular, the longhorn breeds (such as the Welsh black cattle) seem to have declined in most areas in the course of the eighteenth century in favour of shorthorns (Devons, Scots, Welsh 'runts' and Kerrys); while in the nineteenth century the cheaper Irish cattle grew steadily in popularity at the expense of Scots and Welsh breeds (Colyer 1973, 45–6).

The cattle were usually bought by graziers in March and initially kept on the poorer pastures, and fed on hay, until the prime grassland (the 'oxlands' as they were sometimes called) were ready in mid–late April. Most were sold in autumn or early winter, unlike those from East Anglia and the eastern counties, which mainly went in the late winter and spring (Colyer 1973, 47). Both sheep and cattle were sometimes sold locally, but the majority were destined for Birmingham, or for Smithfield in London.

In many Midland districts the extent of grass was such that arable fodder crops played little part in the fattening of livestock. In parts of Leicestershire in 1813, according to Pitt, the sheep were 'bred, reared, and fattened through the whole of the year, upon natural grass, without assistance from turnip, cabbages, or any other food, except a little hay in very severe seasons' (Pitt 1813a, 269). In the Vale of Aylesbury in 1850 'the ewes are fed on the pastures summer and winter, getting, occasionally, corn in troughs in severe winter weather, and about the time of lambing. They receive no turnips during the winter' (Caird 1852, 3). Only where arable played a greater role in the farming economy—often on the pockets of lighter land—might the flocks be wintered on turnips and cabbages. In a similar way, cattle were largely fed in the fields. Stall feeding and the use of fodder were rare, because only in a few districts was it the practice to keep the animals through the winter (Pitt 1813a, 235, 131).

Not all the Midland pastures were devoted to fattening. In Leicestershire there were notable dairying districts around Hinckley, Bosworth, Appleby and Snareston; along the border with Derbyshire and beside the River Trent; in the Vale of Belvoir; and around Melton Mowbray, where the village of Stilton gave its name to a famous cheese (Mingay 1984, 99). Much of central Buckinghamshire was also dairying country, the Tithe Files of the 1830s describing how 'most of the land in the hamlets of Denham, Shipton and Doddershall is pasture for dairying—the dairying in this district, "the Vale of Aylesbury", is confined to butter' (Kain 1986, 411). The pattern of local specialisation was complex, however, for some Midland districts changed their mode of farming over time. Thus in the late seventeenth century the farmers of north Buckinghamshire and south-west Northamptonshire specialised in the production of cheese, but by the end of the eighteenth century they were mainly producing double-skimmed butter for the London market. Similarly, in the course of the eighteenth century, cheese-making re-placed fattening as the main concern of the farmers in east Warwickshire (Broad 1980, 88).

The spread of pasture was certainly the dominant theme in the history of the Midland clays in the period studied here. But as we have seen, even at the end of the eighteenth century some 16 per cent of Leicestershire and 22 per cent of Northamptonshire remained under arable cultivation, and this proportion probably increased slightly in the first three decades of the nineteenth century. The performance of arable farming appears to have improved noticeably in this same period. In Northamptonshire, government enquiries in 1795 suggest that the average yield in a normal year was around 19 bushels an acre, while by the 1830s (according to the Tithe

Files) it was 25.5 bushels (Turner 1982b, 506). Nevertheless, by this time wheat and barley together made up only 40 per cent of the total arable acreage of parishes in Northamptonshire and Leicestershire for which Tithe Files exist; wheat by itself constituted a mere 26 per cent. Even with the re-expansion of arable since 1800, less than 11 per cent of Northamptonshire and a mere 7 per cent of Leicestershire were sown with wheat. Allowing for the extent of open field and the character of open-field rotations in this extensive district, it seems likely that the annual volume of wheat produced in the clayland core of the Midlands fell by considerably more than a half between 1700 and 1830.

The New Landscape

The enclosure of the Midland 'shires' in the seventeenth, eighteenth and nineteenth centuries was not, therefore, associated with the adoption of improved arable husbandry. It was associated instead with a change from cereal farming to grazing and dairying. Yet these areas, too, experienced their own 'agricultural revolution' in the course of the eighteenth and early nineteenth centuries, involving not simply the development of better breeds of sheep and cattle but also improvements in the quality of the pastures on which they grazed. These improvements had begun in the sixteenth and seventeenth centuries (Lane 1980) but were now adopted on a much larger scale.

The writings of eighteenth-century agriculturalists like William Ellis make it clear that the new pastures were often assiduously manured, not only with dung but also with river mud, urban nightsoil, marl, lime and potash (Broad 1980, 85–6). John Broad has noted how, on the north Buckinghamshire estate of the Verneys, potash was in widespread use from the 1680s, 'and grants of considerable quantities are a regular feature of negotiations for new leases and tenancies' (Broad 1980, 86). More important, perhaps, was the gradual blurring in many areas of the old distinction between meadows, cut once a year for hay and only grazed in the late summer and autumn, and pastures, which were not cut, but grazed directly from the early spring. Eighteenth-century writers like Robert Brown advocated mowing all grass, but every third year (Broad 1980, 86–7). Such alternate use of fields for mowing and grazing seems to have been widespread in some districts, although in others the traditional distinction was maintained into the nineteenth century. In some places the practice of convertible husbandry was adopted. William Marshall described in detail the Leicestershire practice of sowing three years of grain crops (oats, wheat, barley) followed by seven or more of grass. Most of the pasture in the region (and especially the best quality grass) was permanent, but long leys like these were frequent in some areas. Lastly, more assiduous efforts were made to drain the pastures. This was an important improvement because excess moisture encourages the growth of coarse grass and rushes, and can reduce grass yields noticeably. One modern study, in Wiltshire, recorded increases of 148 per cent in spring growth as a consequence of improved drainage (Castle *et al.* 1984). In some places, particularly damp areas were treated by making *underdrains*: that is, trenches cut into the surface and backfilled with stones or brushwood, and then covered with soil (Marshall 1796b, I, 141). Alternatively, turfs might simply be removed, shallow slots cut into the ground beneath, and then the turfs replaced. Such simple drains might function effectively for several years, according to Nathaniel Kent, but every effort had to be

made to keep livestock off 'till the drains have time to settle' (Kent 1793, 30). Sub-surface drains never seem to have been much used in Midland grazing districts before the nineteenth century, however, and most improvements seem to have involved paying more attention to surface drainage. This was frequently impeded by the old plough ridges. Water collected in the furrows, no longer regularly liberated by the scouring of gutters and the trenching of headlands. Agricultural writers urged that the ridges should be levelled, or at least that channels should be cut through selected ridges or headlands, in order to allow the water to escape. More important, however, was the provision of additional field ditches: in the course of the seventeenth and eighteenth centuries there was a tendency for average field size to fall, facilitating the removal of water from the surface of the fields (Taylor 1975, 115–17). Reduction in field size was also associated with a shift away from the large-scale sheep ranching characteristic of late medieval times towards more mixed forms of livestock husbandry, as well as reflecting a greater awareness of the need to control grazing more efficiently.

The earliest enclosures had often produced very large fields. At Creslow in Buckinghamshire, enclosed in the early fifteenth century, the Great Field covered no less than 310 acres (Reed 1979, 155–7). Seventeenth- and early eighteenth-century enclosures, in contrast, generally produced rather smaller fields. When Great Linford in the same county was enclosed in 1658, the three great fields (Wood Field, Middle Field and Newport Field) and the small area of common and meadow were replaced by 53 new enclosures. The largest, Great Ground, covered 108 acres, Neath Hill covered 102 acres, but of the remainder 35 were under 20 acres in size and 11 were between 20 and 50 acres (Reed 1979, 177–9). Whereas the enclosures of the fifteenth century had generally created fields with fairly sinuous edges, those created in the seventeenth and eighteenth centuries were more rectilinear in layout, and during this same period the large enclosures created in late medieval times were normally subdivided to create smaller fields, producing a network of short, straight hedges within the older, more sinuous boundaries. The fields produced by parliamentary enclosure were generally smaller still: grazing grounds of more than 70 acres were rare, and in most cases average field size was around 15 acres (Hoskins 1955, 145).

There were other important differences between the landscapes created by enclosures in different periods. Fifteenth- and sixteenth-century enclosures had often been associated with the complete removal of villages and their replacement by single farms. Later enclosures by agreement were less likely to cause massive depopulation, although villages often decreased in size (Reed 1981). In many parts of the Midlands—and especially in central and northern Northamptonshire, and south Leicestershire—there is much evidence for post-medieval shrinkage and desertion: examples in the former county include the shrunken settlements of Rothersthorpe, Passenham, Pytchley, Walgrave, and Foscote, a hamlet in Abthorpe (Royal Commission on Historical Monuments, England 1979, 125, 151; 1982, 110, 128–9). Indeed, in the central parts of Northamptonshire 'Every village . . . has at least two or three places where houses formerly stood, many of which may have been abandoned in relatively recent times' (Royal Commission on Historical Monuments, England 1979, liv). More importantly, new farms were often established away from the old village centre, more conveniently situated in the centre of their pasture fields,

creating a dispersal of settlement which represented, in part, a reversion to the pattern abandoned more than 800 years before when the open fields were first laid out. Parliamentary enclosure, in contrast, while it usually led to some migration of farms out from the village nucleus, was seldom associated with any reduction in the size of settlements. By the 1770s the rural population was rising again.

Different types and periods of enclosure also tended to have different effects upon road patterns. Early depopulating enclosures paid little attention to the layout of roads. Some existing rights of way were maintained while others simply fell out of use. Enclosures by agreement in the post-medieval centuries, however, had by law to consider any impact on public rights of way. These were usually realigned or tidied up, and normally reduced in number, while some entirely new roads and tracks were created. Many were for private use, leading to the new outlying farms. The approach of parliamentary enclosure commissioners was more systematic still. The existing road network was often drastically transformed, with some rights of way being curtailed, and surviving roads narrowed and realigned. The roads created by the majority of parliamentary enclosures on the Midland clays, which took place in the period before c.1790, were rather wide, with ample grass verges (usually 15–20 metres between the hedges): a distinctive feature of the region's landscape. Those created later—mainly in other parts of England—were generally narrower, usually less than 15 metres in width (Turner 1984b, 147). Wide roads allowed for the movement of stock, and also permitted travellers to find a route across the surface churned up by passing sheep and cattle. The reduction in width over time may have resulted from the greater attention paid in later enclosure agreements to the surfacing of public roads, with provision increasingly being made for gravel pits for the use of the Surveyors of Highways (Turner 1984b, 147). It may have been associated with mounting concerns about the use of verges by vagrants and gypsies. It may simply reflect the fact that later enclosures tended (as we shall see) to be in districts in which arable farming predominated, and in which there was less movement of cattle along the roads.

Oliver Rackham has written of the essentially monotonous nature of the 'predominantly planned countryside' of the Midlands (Rackham 1986, 5). But complexities of enclosure history have actually made for a surprisingly varied landscape. In Oxfordshire, for example, Emery has pointed to the contrast between the markedly rectilinear pattern of fields in the parish of Salford, enclosed in 1770, and the rather larger fields and less rigidly rectilinear boundary pattern in the adjacent parish of Rollright, where the village of Little Rollright was enclosed and depopulated in the fifteenth century (Emery 1974, 120). Even within individual parishes, there is—or was—often a contrast between different forms or phases of enclosure. Thus the parish of Raunds in Northamptonshire was partially enclosed in the seventeenth century, and the resultant boundaries have 'long curving sides that follow exactly the ridge and furrow of the earlier open furlongs' (Taylor 1975, 120). These contrast with the dominant field pattern of the parish, created by parliamentary enclosure in 1797. Even where a whole series of adjacent parishes was largely enclosed by parliamentary act, subtle variations in the landscape can occur. For example, because several years might elapse between the enclosure of adjoining parishes, through roads almost invariably change direction slightly where they cross parish boundaries. Parish 'A', enclosing in

1770, would realign its road leading to parish 'B', but only as far as the shared boundary between them. The latter, enclosing five or ten years later, would tidy up and straighten its own section of this road, but only rarely would the two end up in direct alignment.

The Social Landscape

So far I have written as if the grassing down of the Midland shires was entirely a matter of agricultural economics. But it also had social aspects. Enclosure was closely associated with the decline of owner-occupiers, yeoman farmers: it encouraged this process, especially in the case of parliamentary enclosure (the costs generally outweighed any received benefit); and it was itself encouraged by it (agreement to enclose was easier to achieve when fewer proprietors were involved).

As a result of the legal changes of the sixteenth century yeomen farmers could no longer simply be evicted by the gentry. They were instead, in the course of the seventeenth and eighteenth centuries, systematically bought out by them, and more and more of the land on the Midland clays came to be owned by large landowners. This process was never total. Even in 1852 Caird noted that much of the land in Leicestershire was still held by yeomen farmers (Caird 1852, 219). Moreover, in many districts there was a strong spatial component to landownership. 'Closed' villages—owned by a single individual, or a small number of proprietors, and generally enclosed at a relatively early date—were to be found on the heavier land, often on the high interfluves, while late-enclosing 'open' villages, in which ownership was more divided, generally occurred in areas of less intractable soil, often in the major valleys. It ought, however, to be emphasised that while some very large estates existed in the shires—such as those of the Duke of Rutland, based at Belvoir Castle, or Earl Spencer, centred on Althorpe in Northamptonshire (Bateman 1876, 301, 417)—the main beneficiaries of the decline of the yeoman farmer were more modest land-owners, members of the local gentry whose estates extended over no more than two or three parishes, like the Packe family of Prestwold near Loughborough, or the Verneys of Claydon in Buckinghamshire (Broad 1980, 82). This was a region of moderately expensive land, especially when enclosed and put to grass. It was hard for anyone to accumulate a *really* extensive estate here.

The steady expansion of enclosed ground provided more than just economic oppor-tunities for landowners. With communal controls now removed, the landscape could directly reflect their tastes, ideology and leisure interests. Where mansions already stood within extensive parks, these were usually expanded in the course of the eighteenth century. And where a manor house lacked a park, it often gained one. Either process could involve some alteration to the pattern of settlement. Indeed, Taylor has estimated that in Northamptonshire, 8 villages were entirely removed to make way for parks, and no less than 25 had their form significantly altered, in the period 1720–1850 (Taylor 1983, 211). Parks marked, clearly enough, the growing gulf opening up between local elites and communities in the course of the eighteenth century (Williamson 1995). Their clumps and perimeter belts, together with other estate plantations, were in many Midland districts the first areas of woodland to be seen for perhaps a thousand years. Much of this was established to provide cover for pheasants, for the elite's interest in game preservation grew steadily in the course of the eighteenth century, as did

an interest in poaching among other sections of society. Agricultural writers regularly bemoaned the effects on grain yields of large numbers of game birds—a useful corrective to the view that landowners' main interests were in the improvement and rational economic management of their estates. But a more distinctive development in the Midlands in this period was the rise of organised fox-hunting. The grassing down of the shires, and the rise of fox-hunting as an elite pastime, were intimately connected.

Until the end of the seventeenth century fox-hunting had largely been a matter of pest-control, and while the gentry did sporadically hunt the animal, they usually did so by surrounding it within the earth and setting dogs upon it. The classic, modern form of the 'sport', involving a long chase across country, only developed in the course of the eighteenth century, principally in Northamptonshire, Leicestershire and Rutland, counties which always held pride of place in the geography of hunting (Carr 1976, 68). Organised fox-hunting required two things: a countryside characterised by a few large tenant farms, rather than a multiplicity of peasant holdings; and a landscape domin-ated by grass rather than by arable fields. The former circumstance allowed the gentry to pursue their quarry uninterrupted, without the objections of proprietors; the latter ensured that the fox's scent held up well, and permitted the horses to be ridden fast, without damaging standing crops (Carr 1976, 69; Patten 1971). The enclosure and grassing down of the 'shires' produced (in the words of the writer Surtees) a landscape consisting of 'grass, grass, grass, nothing but grass for miles and miles', ideally suited to hunting (Surtees 1929, 90). The emergence of the most notable hunts went hand-in-hand with the spread of enclosure. The famous Grafton hunt began around 1750, the Pytchley in

1761 (Markham 1906, 357, 368–9). Only in such a landscape, uninterrupted save for low-cut hedges, could long chases take place, of the kind enjoyed by the Pytcheley in February 1802, when the unfortunate fox was chased for four and a half hours from Marston Wood to Tilton-on-the-Hill in Leicestershire—a distance of more than 60 kilometres, through 26 parishes (*ibid.*, 357).

Yet hunting did not simply reflect changes in the landscape of the Midlands. It also made its own particular contribution to that landscape. Many landowners established coverts—small areas of gorse and other scrub, often with a few trees for ornamental purposes—where the fox could breed in safety, and where the huntsmen could be sure of finding their quarry. These developed, through natural succession, into the small woods in field corners which are such a characteristic feature of the landscape in parts of Leicestershire and Rutland (Carr 1976, 113–14).

To the fox-hunting squire there was something peculiarly attractive about a prospect over an extensive sea of grass. But a pastoral landscape was appealing in a host of other ways to the landowner wishing to live an uncomplicated and prosperous life. Most elite commentators found grassland a particularly suitable setting for a mansion: this was one of the reasons why the 'landscape parks' of Capability Brown and his ilk became so popular in the course of the eighteenth century. As Humphry Repton put it:

> Labour and hardship attend the operations of agriculture, whether cattle are tearing up the surface of the soil, or man reaping its produce; on the contrary a pasture shows us the same animals enjoying rest after fatigue, while others sporting with liberty and ease excite the pleasing idea of happiness and comfort annexed to a pastoral life. Consequently such a scene must be more in harmony with the residence of elegance and comfort, and marks a degree of affluence . . . (*Red Book for Honing in Norfolk*: quoted in Williamson 1995, 122).

Moreover, grazing required less labour than arable farming, and this was an important consideration at a time when the local indigent were supported by local rates, paid for in large measure by the landowner himself. Where a village was 'closed'—that is, when it was largely or entirely in the hands of a single proprietor—he or she might thus limit or reduce its size, through selective demolition, thereby limiting the number of people who, through age, ill-health or illegitimacy, might become a potential burden (Holderness 1972; Short 1992; but see Banks 1988 for a critique of these views). Where grazing farms predominated over ploughland, this was clearly much easier to achieve. In addition, as we have seen, replacing a plethora of small arable farms with a number of large grazing enterprises simplified estate administration and reduced the amount which needed to be spent on the repair and maintenance of farm buildings, etc. Such matters were not, in themselves, sufficient reason for landowners to enclose their lands and turn them over to pasture. But they may have tipped the balance in some places, and in some districts.

Estate policy and social attitudes moulded the development of the landscape in other ways. Large landowners needed to attract tenants with sufficient capital, and not only the provision of the farm buildings and the character of the farm house, but also its location, might weigh heavily with prospective tenants. Large graziers might be men with social aspirations: they and their wives might not be keen to rub shoulders with local labourers, or live in a house with a view across the village street to the ale house. The migration of farms out of Midland villages after enclosure is usually interpreted in terms of the practicalities of agriculture— the farm was placed centrally and conveniently within its new fields. But it also constituted a radical reshaping of social geography, changing the patterns of human interaction, emphasising class divisions and markedly reducing any notion of 'community'. Indeed, in a whole host of ways the enclosure of the Midland open fields transformed social experience. Where once the majority of the land in a township or parish had been open to all its inhabitants, now movement was limited to a small number of defined rights of way. Enclosure made for a new landscape, but also for a new kind of landscape, experienced from a smaller number of viewpoints. In *The Mores* John Clare contrasted with passion the freedom of movement enjoyed by the inhabitants of Helpston before enclosure, and the new landscape, in which:

> Fence now meets fence in owners little bounds
> Of field and meadow large as garden grounds
> In little parcels little minds to please
> With men and flocks imprisoned ill at ease
> (Robinson and Powell 1984, 168).

The Forests

So far I have discussed the Midlands as if every parish conformed to that by now familiar model: nucleated village surrounded by arable open fields, and with only small areas of common meadow and pasture. While most of the Midlands did indeed look like this—before enclosure and conversion to pasture—there were exceptions. A string of forests, islands of wooded countryside in the champion landscape of the Midlands, ran through the centre of Northamptonshire and into Buckinghamshire (Rockingham, Salcey, Whittlewood and Bernwood); while to the east, in Rutland, lay the much-reduced remains of the forest of Leighwood (Mingay 1984, 106–8). These occupied areas of particularly poorly-draining boulder clay, Lias clay or Oxford clay soils, although Rockingham lay partly on a deposit of infertile sand. In all these areas, the slow progress of clearance and settlement resulting from the poor or intractable character of the local soils had been compounded by their legal designation in medieval times as 'forests'—areas subject to forest law, a bundle of legislation designed to conserve deer and their habitats for the king's hunt (Steane 1974, 193–4). Such legislation covered not only the 'core' areas of the forests—large tracts of wooded common land of which the king, rather than any local lord, was the legal owner—but also a wider penumbra of more settled countryside containing fields and villages. The latter, generally rather loosely nucleated, were clustered on the better soils, usually in the principal valleys. Their open fields were often complex and irregular, sometimes featuring areas of sporadically cropped 'outfield' land. They often lacked a resident landlord, and their extensive commons attracted squatters. They thus absorbed, to some extent, the surplus population of the neighbouring districts. Moreover, the economies of forest districts were generally rather different from those of the neighbouring champion lands, being based not primarily on arable farming but around stock-rearing, dairying, and woodland industries—the production of wood from enclosed coppices or woodpasture pollards, timber, and bark for tanning (Pettit 1968; Mingay 1984, 108).

By the start of the period under consideration here royal rights had been alienated from large sections of forest land, and many of the woods had passed into private ownership, especially towards the edges of the forests, some being turned into private parks (Pettit 1968). The commons meanwhile had lost much of their timber, degenerating—as poorly managed woodpastures were wont to do— into open grazing. But they remained extensive, often shared between several parishes. As late as 1790 fifteen parishes enjoyed common rights over some 4,486 acres of Whittlewood (Mingay 1984, 107). Large stands of timber and coppice did, however, survive within the enclosed woods. In 1790 the crown woods in Salcey Forest were still 5 kilometres long and 3 broad; in Rockingham, there were still 9,482 acres of woodland; and in Whittlewood 5,424 acres, much of it in the hands of the Dukes of Grafton (Mingay 1984, 107; Steane 1974, 194; Pettit 1968).

Some forests disappeared in the seventeenth century—Bernwood was deforested in 1632 by Chancery decree—but attempts under the Commonwealth to sell and improve the royal forests proved largely abortive and did not affect any Midland examples (Thirsk 1985, 374–8). It was only in the late eighteenth century that the forests came once more under the scrutiny of a government keen to discover whether the value of the timber produced in them and the income from the forest courts were equal to the amount of money which might be raised through their enclosure and conversion to farmland. A Commission, set up to examine the Northamptonshire forests, concluded in 1792 that:

Though the ancient forest laws, and the courts, when regularly held, have been found by experience to conduce very much to the increase and preservation of

timber in forests thinly inhabited . . . yet in Rockingham Forest, where the Crown has little property left, where a considerable part of the land is already in tillage or pasture, and the country pretty fully inhabited, it cannot be desirable that those laws should be continued (Lambert 1977, 18).

An act of 1795, and another of 1796, divided the ownership of Rockingham between four great landowners—the Earl of Upper Orrey, the Earl of Westmoreland, the Earl of Exeter and Mr George Finch Hatton. By a further act of 1812 royal lands in the forest, intermixed with other land, were sold. In 1824 Whittlewood Forest was enclosed, and the following year the same fate befell Salcey (Nisbet 1906, 349).

Enclosure and disafforestation had dramatic effects. In Bernwood most of the woodland which remained at the time of disafforestation in 1632 was cleared soon afterwards (Broad 1997, 76–9). The open fields in the vicinity of the various villages were enclosed, and the extensive commons disappeared. They were initially put to the plough but subsequently went the same way as the rest of the Midlands, and tillage gave way to pasture, which was used to feed dairy cows supplying butter or cheese for the London market. Typical was a farm in Boarstall which was put on the market in 1769. It consisted of a compact holding of 144 acres; there were only 10 acres under the plough, 'for the convenience of the tenant' (Broad 1997, 81). Later disafforestations followed a similar path: commons and residual open fields were removed, massive fellings took place, and new ring-fence farms were laid out. As in the rest of the Midlands, most became grazing farms, or mixed farming enterprises with a strong bias towards livestock production.

The Costs of Enclosure

From the fifteenth to the nineteenth century many commentators expressed concern about the effects of enclosure and the expansion of pasture in the Midland counties. Worries that food supplies were being threatened were sharpened at times of particularly rapid population growth in the sixteenth and again in the later eighteenth century. People understandably associated high grain prices with the contraction in ploughland which they witnessed all around them. The vicar of Clapham in Bedfordshire observed in 1801 that 'the numerous enclosures that are rapidly increasing, and the converting of many acres to pasturage, which used to be in tillage, are very inimical to the production of bread and other kinds of grain' (Turner 1982a, I, 34); while in Dean in the same county the incumbent believed that 'Many parishes before enclosed were great sellers of grain, after enclosed not enough for parish consumption' (*ibid.*, 35). Of more general concern, in all periods, were the effects of enclosure and conversion to pasture on small farmers and the poor. In the south Midlands nearly a third of the arable land was already farmed in holdings of 100 or more acres at the start of the seventeenth century; by the start of the eighteenth century this figure had risen to 54 per cent and by *c.*1800 to 84.7 per cent (Allen 1992, 73–4). The decline of small owner-occupiers may well have been hastened by parliamentary enclosure, for the allotment of land received in lieu of field land and common rights was seldom equal in value to what had formerly been enjoyed, especially when the legal costs and the costs of fencing the allotment were taken into account. Many small proprietors sold out immediately to their more prosperous neighbours (Snell 1985; Neeson 1993; Hammond and Hammond 1911). Cottagers and labourers fared worse,

however. Many received no compensation at all at enclosure, other than perhaps the opportunity to benefit from some small 'fuel allotment' administered by a committee comprising the lord of the manor, the vicar, and members of the local middle class (Birtles 1999). Many of the poor had enjoyed the commons without having any strictly legal right to do so. Common rights, in the Midlands as elsewhere, were generally attached to specific properties—ancient commonable tenements. With the gradual engrossment of small farms by large estates in the course of the post-medieval period, many of these had become cottages rented by the poor, and the attached rights, strictly speaking, were in the hands of the owner, not the occupier (Birtles 1999). Others lived in cottages which, added to the tenurial core of the village at a relatively late date, had never enjoyed common rights. Leigh Shaw-Taylor, studying a sample of parishes in the south Midlands, discovered that at the time of parliamentary enclosure 'about one labourer in 20 owned a cottage to which common rights were attached and only one labourer in seven rented such a cottage . . . Eighty per cent of common-right cottages were owned by large landowners and farmers. Traders and artisans owned most of the rest' (Shaw Taylor 2000, 509).

The effects of enclosure were perhaps most keenly felt in the forest areas, where commons had been most extensive (Neeson 1993). But even in the champion districts, where common grazing was often of limited extent, the impact was generally disastrous. The poor lost the opportunity to glean over the fields after harvest or to graze livestock on the fallow fields, practices which might save them from having to fall back upon the meagre assistance provided by parish poor relief. In the Northamptonshire village of Raunds, for example, there was—typically—

little common ground, the ploughlands running to the parish boundaries in all directions, but the enclosure of 1797 was fiercely opposed by the cottagers and others on the grounds that they would be 'deprived of an inestimable Privilege, which they now enjoy, of turning a certain Number of their Cows, Calves, and Sheep, on and over the said lands; a Privilege that enables them not only to maintain themselves and their families in the Depth of Winter . . . but in addition to this they can now supply Graziers with young or lean stock . . .' (Snell 1985, 178).

Some modern historians—generally those of a right-wing persuasion—have suggested that the enclosure of open fields also brought benefits to the poor, not least because it provided employment opportunities. New hedges and ditches had to be established and then maintained, and the new techniques of the 'agricultural revolution' were, in general, labour-intensive—turnips needed to be hoed, muck needed to be transported from farmyards and assiduously spread upon the fields (Chambers and Mingay 1966, 99–100). The proponents of such views have paid little attention to the changes in land use which usually followed the enclosure of the open fields in their Midland heartlands. Grazing farms required much less labour than arable farms, a point seldom lost on contemporaries. Eden, discussing Kibworth Harcourt in Leicester in his *State of the Poor* of 1797, noted how the poor rates were 'not one-third of their present figure before the enclosure'. The explanation for this was simple:

Before the fields were enclosed they were solely applied to the production of corn; the Poor had then plenty of employment in weeding, reaping, thrashing etc., and would also collect a great deal of cash by gleaning, but . . . the fields being now in pasturage, the farmers have little occasion

for labourers and the Poor being thereby thrown out of employment, must of course be supported by the parish (quoted in Hoskins 1949, 134).

Such contemporary claims are firmly supported by the findings of modern historians. Keith Snell, in his monumental study *Annals of the Labouring Poor*, showed how enclosure in Midland counties led to a marked increase in unemployment, especially during the summer months, when labour was no longer in demand for hoeing, weeding and harvest work (Snell 1985, 152–4).

A social audit has often been made on the enclosure of the Midlands. An *ecological* audit has seldom been attempted. If the former was largely negative, the latter would perhaps be more balanced. In forest areas, ploughing and re-seeding of ancient commons and the destruction of hundreds of acres of ancient, semi-natural woodland amounted to a substantial environmental disaster. But in the more extensive champion areas the changes of the long eighteenth century were largely beneficial. Before enclosure, as we have seen, most parishes had few hedges or trees and little permanent pasture. Their ecology was characterized by arable weeds—common poppy (*Papaver rhoeas*), corn marigold (*Chrysanthemum segetun*) and the like—and by the fauna that lived off these and was able to survive in a fairly bleak and open landscape. Enclosure, first and foremost, produced areas of permanent grassland in which, in time, a far wider range of flora and fauna came to be established. Despite the strictures of agricultural improvers, many Midland pastures were poorly drained and only sporadically re-seeded. The range of available niches was made particularly wide by the fossilised remains of the plough ridges which, within a limited area, ensured considerable variation in soil water content. On the heaviest clays, especially where the land was level, drainage was often poor and the pastures coarse and waterlogged. The Tithe Files for Standhill in Oxfordshire, for example, described how 'the land might be made fine rich pasture and support large dairies. But it is in a miserable condition—no underdraining. The fields covered with rushes—the roads next to impassable and parts of the pasture so full of anthills that a person could walk from one end of a field to the other on the tops of them' (Kain 1986, 398). Long-established, unimproved grassland like this might make for poor grazing, but it provided a wealth of habitats. Within a few decades ridge-and-furrow pastures came to be characterised by 'a large number of grass species, similar to those encountered in flood meadows . . . and [by] a great number of herbs', including such plants as betony (*Betonica officinalis*), cowslip (*Primula veris*), yellow rattle (*Rhinanthus minor*), black knapweed (*Centaurea nigra*) and green-winged orchid (*Orchis morio)* (Duffey

1974, 60). Equally important were the many thousands of kilometres of hedgerow established in this period. Although initially planted with one species (usually hawthorn or blackthorn) and still, even today, generally species-poor, they nevertheless provided shelter for a wide range of wildlife, especially birds. So, too, did the plantations and coverts widely established in this period by the gentry.

The landscape history of the Midland clays in the course of the 'long eighteenth century' is thus tolerably clear. The dominant theme was a steady drift into pasture, a process with profound social and environmental, as well as agrarian, implications. But here we are at once faced with a paradox, or at least with a puzzle. In the later eighteenth and nineteenth centuries England's population, and hence demand for grain, grew inexorably. And yet the region which had for centuries been the most intensively cultivated in the country was steadily laid to grass.

CHAPTER 3

The Light Land Revolution

The Sheep-Corn Countries

It is not in the damp clay vales of Midland England that we must look to find the classic agricultural revolution of the textbooks. This was instead a phenomenon of the light lands of southern and eastern England, of the wolds and downs and heathlands. At the start of the period studied here these, too, were open 'champion' landscapes, largely devoid of hedges and trees. But instead of heavy clays, these districts had subsoils of chalk or sand; and instead of poor drainage, the principal problems faced by farmers were the infertility and, in many districts, the inherent acidity of the soils. Moreover, whereas in the Midlands the arable open fields were extensive and the areas of common grazing were comparatively small, in these districts the arable was more limited and the commons often very extensive, taking the form of tracts of heathland on the more acidic soils, and downs on the more calcareous soils.

Because their soils were comparatively easy to cultivate, many of these districts had been extensively settled in prehistoric times. On the higher ground large numbers of Bronze Age burial mounds and various types of early prehistoric enclosure survived on the heaths and pastures; while on the chalk soils in particular the earthwork remains of ancient field systems testify to the extent to which the later Roman and early Saxon periods had seen some retreat from the margins of cultivation. Such ancient remains

survived, in a way that they seldom did in Midland districts, because for centuries the pastures and heaths had remained largely unploughed. Large flocks of sheep were grazed on them by day and folded by night on the arable fields, thus ensuring a constant flow of nutrients from the one to the other which allowed the poor, leached soils to be kept in heart. The sheep were primarily valued as 'mobile muck-spreaders' and the open sheepwalks, far from being under-utilised 'wastes', were essential for keeping the poor, thin soils in cultivation (Kerridge 1967, 42–5; Jones 1960, 5–6).

The chalklands of Wiltshire, Berkshire, Dorset and Hampshire, and their extension along the South Downs into Sussex, were the classic sheep-corn districts (Kerridge 1967, 42–56). All had landscapes of nucleated villages and open fields which were usually of 'regular' type, similar to those of the Midland shires, although on these light lands the ploughlands were seldom ridged to any significant extent. The chalk soils varied considerably in quality, but everywhere made better barley than wheat land: these were the two main crops, although by the start of the seventeenth century oats, tares, peas and beans were also grown, and together made up perhaps a quarter of the sown acreage (Kerridge 1967, 46–7). Parishes were often long and thin, with the villages located where regular supplies of water were available, in the principal river valleys or along the spring line at the foot of escarpments. It was here that the meadows, so vital for the supply of hay which provided the principal winter fodder for the flocks, were located. The main arable land usually lay on the slopes above the village, with the extensive tracts of open downland above this: distinctive, close-cropped turf containing a range of characteristic species including horseshoe vetch (*Hippocrepis comosa*), gentian (*Gentianella*) and milkwort (*Polygala vulgaris*). The distinction between permanent pasture and arable was fairly firm, although blurred somewhat by the practice of sporadically breaking up parts of the downland and bringing it into cultivation for a few years, before allowing it to revert once more to pasture.

The fold was crucial and the movement of the flocks was controlled by strict rules. The sheep manure was applied to the fallow preceding the barley during the winter and spring, when the dung was at its best; indeed, the sheep might be kept there even when the crop began to grow through. By May, however, the flocks were moved on to the fallows waiting to receive the wheat, and here they generally stayed until October. They were often then pastured on the downs for a month or so, before the whole cycle began again. The principal breeds—the 'Old Wiltshire', the 'Berkshire Nott', and the 'Western'—were all hardy animals, able to thrive on the thin upland pastures, and to walk long distances each night from down to fold. They were not, in other words, bred to stand around in one place, putting on weight, and their value as meat animals was therefore limited, although farmers derived some income from this, and more from their fleeces (Kerridge 1967, 43–51).

To the north of the Wessex downlands, and separated from them by a relatively narrow band of heavier soils, was another sheep-corn region, the Cotswolds, which extended across much of Gloucestershire, through north Wiltshire and into north

Oxfordshire. The soils here were not based on chalk but on limestone, mixed in places with sand and clay. Like Wessex, this was village country; and here, too, the arable lay largely open, although often organised into two great fields rather than three. Only limited amounts of enclosure had taken place here at the end of the seventeenth century. Cotswold farming operated along broadly similar lines to that in Wessex, but the soils were often more mixed and the pastures less extensive. The climate was also wetter, so that for part of the year the sheep might be protected from the elements by shelters—'cotes'—erected on the high pastures.

Not all sheep-corn areas were in the south of England. The wolds of Yorkshire and Lincolnshire were also chalk uplands, although the soils here were often mixed, especially towards the peripheries of the chalk masses, where the underlying deposits of clay gave rise to more fertile loams. Villages were closely clustered in these areas, but elsewhere they were often thinly scattered, their parishes again often of attenuated shape, sometimes extending down on to the more amenable soils of the neighbouring lowlands. The pastures could be very extensive, in part because rather more settlements had formerly existed on the uplands, sustained by water from unreliable springs: small, often late-settled villages which, like the famous Wharram Percy, had been abandoned during the fifteenth and sixteenth centuries and their lands put down to grass. Indeed, some of the high wold pastures were grazed not only by sheep, but also by rabbits, for large commercial warrens had become an increasingly important feature of the area in the course of the seventeenth century (A. Harris 1961, 29–31). Deliberate depopulation of settlements to create warrens and sheep-walks seems to have experienced something of a revival in the late seventeenth century when grain prices were particularly low (A. Harris 1958, 97–8).

Where the soils were deeper open fields were of normal, 'Midland' form. But on the higher wolds more idiosyncratic arrangements often prevailed. The areas close to the village were cropped regularly, the unit of rotation usually being the bundle of strips—the furlong—rather than the field. The more distant areas were ploughed up and cropped for a few years, then allowed to revert to grass for a while. As the Georgical Committee was informed in 1674, the Yorkshire Wolds farmers had 'in many townes 7 feilds and the swarth of one is every yeare broken for oates and lett ly fallow till itts turne att 7 yeares end, and these seven are outffeilds' (A. Harris 1961, 25). Hedgeless arable and extensive upland pastures once again made for open and somewhat bleak scenery. At the start of the eighteenth century one commentator described the landscape around Wetwang in Yorkshire as having 'scarce a bush or tree for several miles' (Hey 1984, 74). The local sheep-breeds—the Old Lincolnshire and the Wolds—were hardy animals, able to thrive on these open pastures throughout the year.

There were several extensive sheep-corn regions in East Anglia: the 'Good Sands' area of west Norfolk; the Norfolk and Suffolk Breckland; the heathlands of north Norfolk; and the Suffolk Sandlings. All were areas of predominantly sandy rather than chalky soils, although in all districts except the last some areas of calcareous soils could also be found, and chalk often underlay the acid sands. Here the field systems were normally less 'regular' than in the Midlands. Often the holdings of individual farmers were clustered in particular areas of the open fields, rather than being scattered throughout the territory of the vill; sometimes there were numerous 'fields', rather than two or three; and temp-

orary outfields were a frequent feature (Postgate 1973). A Parliamentary Survey of the Norwich Dean and Chapter manors in Sedgeford in north-west Norfolk, made in 1649, typically described how the arable lay in strips 'intermixed and undivided with customary and other lands', which were divided between the 'infield lands' and the temporarily cropped 'brecks' which occupied the higher and more acid ground. The survey also informs us that there was a *foldcourse* for 1,200 sheep belonging to the manor, 'which are to be kept in this manner, viz partly upon the common . . . partly upon the shack of all the arrable ground whether they be customary, freehold or demesne lands . . . and partly on the lands or unplowed ground of the said Brecks whereof five parts of the whole into eight being divided are every year to lye and lay for pasture . . .' (NRO LeStrange OC1: DCN 51/91). Under this version of sheep-corn husbandry—widespread across Norfolk, Suffolk and parts of Cambridgeshire—folding arrangements were tightly controlled by the manorial lord (Allison 1957; Bailey 1989). The tenants benefited from the manure dropped by the sheep as they roamed over the fallows but the intensive night-folding or 'tathing' was the monopoly of the manorial lord, which tenants could only enjoy in return for a cash payment. The sheep were organised into communal flocks, dominated by the stock of the manorial lord (or his lessee), and under the care of a manorial shepherd. Originally devised as a way of ensuring that the manorial demesne received more than its fair share of manure, in post-medieval times the essence of the institution changed (Bailey 1990). The fold course became a way of keeping large commercial flocks, from which the lord or his lessee excluded the sheep of the tenants. Nevertheless, although the sheep might be valued for their meat and wool, they remained the cornerstone of arable husbandry, and the principal local breed—the black-faced Norfolk Horn—was a slow maturing, leggy animal which could 'breed and thrive upon open heath and barren sheep walks, where nine tenths of the breeds in the kingdom would starve' (Marshall 1787, I, 365).

All the East Anglian sheep-corn regions differed one from another in ways sometimes dramatic, sometimes subtle. In north-west Norfolk relatively thin layers of sandy, acid drift masked the chalk. As on the northern wolds, the landscape here was dominated by the contrast between small parishes on the drift-covered uplands—with poor soils and unreliable supplies of water—and the larger, more populous places on the lower ground, on the calcareous soils of the valleys and the coastal strip (Wade Martins and Williamson 1999a, 9–12). Many of the 'upland' settlements had declined drastically between the fourteenth and the seventeenth centuries: places like Waterden, a separate if small vill in medieval times but which, by the time it was mapped in 1713, was only a single farm of 805 acres (NRO Ms 21130 179X4). Much of the heathland in this district had, by the seventeenth century, been converted into sporadically cropped outfield 'breaks', but the area of regularly cultivated arable often remained of limited extent.

To the south of this extensive district lies Breckland, the most agriculturally marginal region in south-eastern England. Here acid sands and gravels lie directly on the ice-weathered surface of the chalk and the resultant problems of acidity and drought-iness are accentuated by climatic factors: sharp late frosts and very low rainfall. Even the better soils, those within the major valleys, were poor by East Anglian standards and prone to wind erosion. Thus an agreement made in 1782 between George Foxe,

tenant of a farm near Merton Park, and the Walsingham estate noted: 'In consideration of Lord Walsingham's permission to break up the north part of Mill Hill Break, I do hereby promise to pay all expenses of clearing land that may blow from the said piece of land into the park' (NRO WLS LXI/1/7, 430X5). The area of arable in each village was generally smaller than in north-west Norfolk, and much of it was farmed as the outfield 'brecks' which have given the district its modern name (Postgate 1962). The heaths were also more extensive. Even at the end of the eighteenth century, to judge from the county maps published by Faden (for Norfolk in 1797) and Hodskinson (for Suffolk in 1783), well over 40 per cent of the district was still occupied by heathland. Settlement, already fairly sparse in medieval times, had dwindled still further from the fifteenth century (Bailey 1989). There were many places like Wordwell in Suffolk, a distinct vill in medieval times, but by 1736 a single farm, 'the chief profits whereof arise from a flock of sheep, the soil being for the most part a barren dry heath, a very bleak place' (Paine 1993, 23). Large areas of the poorest soils had, since late medieval times, been given over to rabbit warrens.

The other sheep-corn areas of East Anglia—the stretch of poor heathlands extending north from Norwich to the coast, and the Sandlings on the coast of Suffolk— were on the whole less hostile environments. In the former there were numerous ribbons of more loamy land in the principal valleys, which also contained lush meadow and pasture; while the Sandlings contained only a narrow strip of appalling soil and most parishes here contained areas of more fertile land. To the east lay rich coastal marshes, progressively improved in the course of the post-medieval period, while to the west were heavier and more fertile soils on the edge of the East Anglian boulder clay plateau. In both districts, in marked contrast to the areas so far described, settlement was sometimes fairly dispersed and open fields were already in decay by the start of the seventeenth century. Moreover, in both these somewhat atypical sheep-corn areas cattle as well as sheep formed a major part of the local economy, grazed on the valley pastures or coastal marsh—a fact, as we shall see, of some importance in their later agrarian development. Both dairying and bullock-rearing were carried out, often on a large scale. Between Easter and Michaelmas 1601, 1,200 barrels of butter and 1,198 cheeses were shipped to London from Walberswick and Southwold alone, the produce of the rich Suffolk coastal marshes (Burrell 1960, 52).

These were not the only sheep-corn districts which deviated from the extreme 'champion' model exemplified by the Wessex Downs or the northern Wolds. In the Chilterns and the North Downs the chalk was extensively capped with clay on the higher ground, and here there were—probably always had been—hedged fields and woods. Field systems were highly irregular, with numerous open fields interspersed with enclosed land, and the settlement pattern was often fairly dispersed, with many small hamlets and isolated farms as well as villages: these were, essentially, areas of 'ancient countryside', and in Kerridge's words, 'the landscape was often a chequer board of champion and woodland' (Kerridge 1967, 56).

Their arable character and, in most cases, comparatively poor soils ensured that by the start of the eighteenth century most sheep-corn districts were dominated by large landed estates. These continued to expand and by the 1870s properties of 10,000 acres were not uncommon in such districts, and some truly enormous estates existed. That of

the Earl of Leicester in north-west Norfolk, for example, covered some 43,000 acres (17,400 hectares); the Earl of Yarborough's in the Lincolnshire Wolds extended over 54,000 acres (21,850 hectares); while that of Sir Tatton Sykes in the Yorkshire Wolds covered 34,000 acres (13,760 hectares) (Bateman 1876, 263, 493, 432). Poor land, economic factors, and the active policy of estate owners combined to ensure that these were also, by the nineteenth century, landscapes of large farms. On the Wolds, and in parts of west Norfolk, farms of 500 or even 1,000 acres (200 or 400 hectares) were by no means uncommon by the start of the nineteenth century. This situation had developed gradually over time. A survey made in 1689 of the open fields of Hunstanton in west Norfolk suggests that the average size of farms was a mere 17 acres, and that only two farms held more than 100 acres (NRO Lestrange BH1). By 1819, the average size of farm was 223 acres, and three of the farms held well in excess of this amount (NRO Lestrange BH9). A map of the Wolterton estate on the poor heathy soils of north Norfolk, surveyed in 1732, suggests that the average size of farms was around 56 acres; by 1809 it was 236 acres, and over 80 per cent of the estate was farmed in units of over 200 acres (Wade Martins and Williamson 1999, 78–79). On the Somerleyton estate, on the northern fringes of the Sandlings region, a survey of 1663 can be compared with a sales catalogue of 1851 (ESRO 194/A11/11; ESRO 749/2/165). Between these two dates the average size of farms virtually doubled, from 56 acres to 106. In the former period 62 per cent of the tenanted land had been farmed in units of more than 150 acres; by the mid-nineteenth century the figure was 83 per cent. The same process continued in all sheep-corn districts. On the Monson estate on the Lincolnshire Wolds, for example, 'there was from the 1720s to about 1830 a long term trend towards larger farms' (Beastall 1978, 21).

The Limits to Output

The sheep-corn areas of seventeenth-century England were thus very varied in character but in all, agricultural output was limited by two main factors. Firstly, cereal yields were generally meagre, especially in heathland districts. In some places they were so awful that it is a puzzle why anyone bothered to crop the land at all—presumably low farm incomes were offset by even lower rents. Wheat yields of less than 8 bushels per acre were common on the East Anglian heaths at the end of the seventeenth century; barley yields were only slightly higher (Wade Martins and Williamson 1999a, 162–5). Even on the more calcareous soils crop yields, while significantly higher than this, were low by later standards—more or less comparable with those attained in Midland open-field parishes, around 18 bushels per acre for wheat, slightly less for barley (Wade Martins and Williamson 1999a, 165–7).

In part, yields were low for the simple reason that there was seldom enough manure available to keep the soil in good heart, for although the sheepwalks might be extensive, the size of the flocks was limited by the availability of winter feed, which in traditional systems was principally derived from comparatively small areas of riverside meadow. In addition, nutrients were rapidly leached out of these thin, porous soils. So too was lime, ensuring that soil acidity steadily increased. The easily exchangeable bases held by soil colloids were removed in solution by rainwater, which is slightly acid due both to the CO_2 in the atmosphere and to the various decay products of humus, compounding the loss of lime which occurs in all soils through repeated cropping. Although the problem was most acute on heathland soils, even those of the calcareous wolds and downs were often—somewhat surprisingly—at least mildly acidic (Beastall 1978, 174).

In addition to all this, the quantity of grain which these districts produced was limited by the simple fact that the area under cultivation was often small. The situation varied from place to place, depending on soils and topography, but everywhere pastures, heaths or outfields occupied a substantial portion of the land. In a few places the extent of permanently cultivated land might reach 80 per cent of parish area but in most the proportion was much less. In the Yorkshire Wolds, for example, while there were some parishes with very little grass, there were many like Riplingham in which there were, prior to enclosure, 750 acres of arable but 400 of sheepwalk and 250 of other common pasture; or West Lutton, with 450 acres of arable but 1,200 of grass (A. Harris 1961, 28). Strickland, writing in 1812, believed that before the improvements of the eighteenth century two-thirds of the Yorkshire Wolds had been under pasture (Strickland 1812, 106). He perhaps exaggerated, and estimates by modern historians have been slightly lower. Nevertheless, 'pastures and outfields together formed at least two-fifths of the total area of many townships' (Sheppard 1973, 158–9).

Such extensive tracts of grazing survived unploughed for two reasons. The first was that any significant reduction in their area, and any commensurate expansion of the arable acreage, would have reduced the numbers of sheep available for the fold, and thus the amounts of manure available to maintain the precarious fertility of the open fields. In addition, however, the thin poor soils which the sheepwalks occupied could not, in many cases, have been successfully cultivated, at least on a regular basis. In districts characterised by thin and infertile soils, the downs and heaths always occupied the thinnest and most infertile.

The Floating of the Meadows

One important step towards raising the productivity of sheep-corn districts had been initiated before the start of the period under consideration here: the 'floating' of water meadows. The artificial inundation of grassland during the winter with continually flowing water raised the ground temperature above 5 degrees centigrade and stimulated early growth, thus reducing the need for winter fodder. Irrigation began before Christmas and stock were put onto the fresh grass in early March. After the flock had been moved on to summer pastures in May, moreover, the meadows would again be irrigated and substantial crops of hay taken in June or July (Kerridge 1953; Bettey 1977 and 1999; Bowie 1987b; Cutting and Cummings 1999). The increase in feed resulting from both summer and winter irrigation ensured that larger flocks could be kept and, as a result, that more manure was available for the arable land. Not surprisingly, irrigated meadows were worth far more than unwatered ones. At Compton in Hampshire in 1738 the rent of unwatered meadow was 20 shillings per acre while watered meadows went for 40 shillings (Bowden 1985, 68). Irrigated meadows on the Itchen near Winchester were said in 1808 to be worth three times an equivalent area of unwatered land (Bowie 1987b, 156). According to Thomas Davis, writing in the 1790s about the Wiltshire meadows, 'the improvement in the value of the land is astonishing', their contribution to sheep husbandry 'almost beyond comprehension' (T. Davis 1794, 34–5).

There were two main forms of irrigation. In 'catchwork' floating, channels were cut along the contours of the valley side, the uppermost being fed from a leat taken off the river at a higher level, or from nearby springs or minor watercourses. The water simply flowed down the natural slope from one ditch or 'gutter' to the next: the system was best suited to steep-sided valleys (Cutting and Cummings 1999, 159–60). More expensive, and leaving more obvious archaeological traces, were 'bedwork' systems, which were employed wherever valley floors were wide and flat and where, in consequence, water could not otherwise be induced to flow continuously (which was essential: stagnant water damaged the grass). A leat taken off the river some distance upstream fed water into channels ('carriers' or 'carriages') which ran along the tops of parallel ridges, superficially resembling the 'ridge and furrow' of former arable fields. The water flowed smoothly down their sides and into drains (located in the 'furrows') which directly or indirectly returned it to the river (Wade Martins and Williamson 1994, 20–1) (Figures 11 and 12).

Although some of the earliest examples are recorded, in the sixteenth century, in Herefordshire and Staffordshire, floating was quintessentially a practice of the Wessex chalklands. Irrigated meadows were already common in Wiltshire by the middle of the seventeenth century; thereafter they began to spread into Hampshire, Dorset and Berkshire. By 1750 almost all the main river valleys in Wessex were being 'floated' (Jones 1960, 7–8; Bettey 1999, 184–5). By the end of the eighteenth century there were said to be between 15,000 and 20,000 acres (6,000–8,000 hectares) of watered meadow in south Wiltshire alone (T. Davis 1794, 34); while in Hampshire it has been suggested that 'during the eighteenth century, in particular,

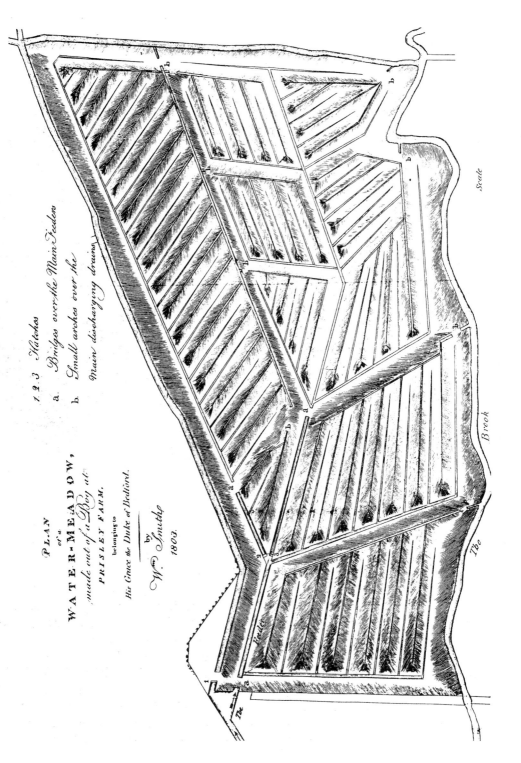

PLAN
of a
WATER-MEADOW,
made out of a Bog at
PRISLEY FARM.
belonging to
His Grace the Duke of Bedford.
by
Wm Smith
1803.

1. 2. 3   Hatches
a.   Bridges over the Main Feeders
b.   Small arches over the
     Main discharging drains

Figure 11   Plan of a water meadow at Prisley, Bedfordshire, from Smith 1806

water meadows must have been pushed to the limits of areas where it was possible to construct them' (Moon and Green 1940, 377). The elaborate systems then established— usually of 'bedwork' type—remained in widespread use well into the nineteenth and, in many cases, the twentieth century. They have left impressive archaeological traces over many thousands of hectares of valley floor. A handful of examples, including that at Britford near Salisbury, are still in use.

During the late seventeenth and early eighteenth centuries floating was widely adopted in other sheep-corn areas of western

Figure 12   Irrigating water meadows at Charlton-all-Saints, Wiltshire, c.1935

and southern England, notably the Cotswolds. The spread of the technique into eastern districts, however, was slow, in spite of the publication of a number of texts on the subject (Boswell 1779; Wright 1792; W. Smith 1806). On the Wolds of Lincolnshire and Yorkshire, in the Chilterns, on the North and South Downs, and in the sheep-corn districts of East Anglia, floating had made little headway even at the end of the eighteenth century. Young asserted in 1804 that the practice was 'Of very late standing in Norfolk: the experiments made are few, but they are interesting enough to promise a speedy extension'; while in Suffolk he noted that 'Of all the improvements wanted in this county, there is none so obvious, and of such importance, as watering meadows' (Young 1804a, 395; Young 1795, 196). Similarly in Kent in 1813 it was reported that 'the practise as yet has few friends' (Boys 1813, 164), while in the same year there were said to be no irrigated meadows at all in Lincolnshire (Young 1813b, 312–14). The Napoleonic War years saw a brief flurry of activity in these regions, mostly the work of a handful of prominent improvers and large tenant farmers; but few of the systems then created (often at considerable expense) remained in use by the middle decades of the century. Copland in 1866 was thus able to claim that while in Wessex the practice of floating had been employed 'time out of mind', a 'want of knowledge' had prevented its widespread adoption elsewhere (Copland 1866, 172). Archaeological investigations provide firm support for this contention: the distinctive earthworks of floated meadows, while by no means unknown, are certainly rare in eastern England (Bowie 1990; Wade Martins and Williamson 1994).

In reality, of course, the reasons for the late and limited adoption of water meadows in the east are more complex than Copland suggested. In many eastern sheep-corn districts the gentle gradient of most valleys not only precluded the institution of cheap 'catchwork' systems but also made the creation of successful bedworks dependent on the construction of long, elaborate leats, without which the fall of water would be insufficient for successful floating. Long leats were both expensive to construct and likely to interfere with the water supply to mills (W. Smith 1806, 120). The peaty soils which naturally formed in such valleys were unsuitable for watering. But climate was probably the most significant factor. The east was drier than the west and supplies of water in the smaller valleys were often less reliable. More importantly, in the west of England mild winters and early springs made the early forcing of grass feasible on a regular basis. In the more Continental east, in contrast, sharp late frosts made the early 'bite' less dependable (Wade Martins and Williamson 1999b, 205–6). As Pusey noted in 1849, the practice of floating was less well suited to the drier and colder areas of the country (Pusey 1849, 477). The impracticality of floating in the east of England may explain why the next key innovation in light land husbandry was first taken up here: the new turnip-based rotations.

The New Rotations

By the 1720s and 1730s agricultural writers were singing the praises of the new crop rotations being employed in eastern sheep-corn districts, rotations which combined cereal crops with regular courses of clover and turnips. Several modern historians and soil scientists have described their benefits (Chorley 1981; Sheil 1991). Clover and other 'artificial grasses' provided high, nutritious yields of fodder, allowing more livestock to be kept. In addition, they had the useful characteristic of fixing atmospheric nitrogen directly in the soil. Turnips did not fix atmospheric nitrogen in this way, but they did provide an excellent source of winter fodder, increasing the amount of animals which could be kept through the winter and thus the quantities of nitrogen recycled.

The most famous form of 'improved' rotation, endlessly championed by propagandists like Arthur Young, was the so-called 'Norfolk four-course': a recurrent four-year cycle of wheat, turnips, barley, and clover or other 'artificial grasses', such as sainfoin. Wheat was sown in September or October, and harvested in August or September the following year. The stubbles were then grazed by stock into the winter, and in spring the soil was ploughed and harrowed, both to destroy weeds and to provide the fine seed-bed necessary for turnip seeds. These were planted around midsummer, usually in regular rows, allowing for repeated hoeing during the late summer and autumn. This not only benefited the plants but also provided a more general measure of weed control, a role also fulfilled by the dense foliage of the plants themselves as they came to maturity. The turnip course thus fulfilled one role of the old year-round fallow—weed control. The turnips might be fed off in the field, usually by sheep. But they were often 'pulled' and taken back to the farmstead and fed to fattening bullocks, kept in yards—the roots make excellent cattle feed. The yards, surrounded by shelter sheds, were usually placed next to the barn so that straw from the threshed crop could be conveniently moved there, providing bedding for the cattle, and rotting to a fine manure as it mixed with their dung and soaked up their urine. The resultant fertile but smelly mass was laboriously carted back to the fields and applied, in particular, to the fallow preceding the turnip course.

The field was free of turnips by February or March, so that the preparation of the seed-bed for barley could begin. This was sown around April, and under-sown with clover or some other 'artificial' grass. The barley was harvested in August or September but the 'seeds' continued to grow through the stubbles, on into the following year. The next spring they would be grazed by livestock,

and in summer cut for hay. In late summer the field would be ploughed and harrowed, ready to receive wheat, and thus the whole cycle began again. Not all turnip-based rotations worked quite like this, as we shall see. Where the soils were particularly fertile it was common to take a second barley crop after the wheat; where they were less fertile, the clover was often left in the ground for a second or third year. Such rotations had become, by the end of the eighteenth century, the normal mode of 'improved' farming on all the thin, light soils of England (Low 1838, 205).

Such rotations did not emerge, fully formed, at the start of the century. They seem to have developed gradually and the uptake of the new crops was uneven. Clover was the first to be widely grown. From the middle of the seventeenth century agricultural writers like Andrew Yarranton were enthusiastically advocating its cultivation, together with sainfoin (*Onobrychis sativa*) and nonsuch (*Medicago lupulina*) (Yarranton 1663). By 1700 these 'artificial grasses' were being widely integrated into arable rotations in the sheep-corn districts, sometimes in the form of long leys of five, six or more years—that is, in a form of up-and-down or 'convertible' husbandry. They acted as a substitute for 'bare' fallows and their use was especially prominent on the more calcareous soils. At Hunstanton in north-west Norfolk the crop was a standard part of rotations by the early eighteenth century. A detailed tithe book spanning the years 1705–11 shows that the most common rotation consisted of a basic sequence of wheat > barley > peas > barley, followed by one or two years of clover, and then a fallow (NRO LeStrange KA9 BHC7). Early eighteenth-century leases from East Anglian sheep-corn areas frequently mention the crop. Similarly, on the Massingberds' estate of South Ormesby on the Lincolnshire

Wolds sainfoin was being sown by 1672; by the 1690s between 12 and 20 acres of the crop were being mown annually on the estate. By the second decade of the eighteenth century, between 150 and 200 acres were being grown here each year (Beastall 1978, 18).

It was long thought that the cultivation of turnips as a field crop was first pioneered in the 1730s and 1740s by East Anglian aristocrats like 'Turnip' Townshend (Riches 1937, 81–92). But research in the 1960s and 1970s revealed that they were being grown in many parts of eastern England by the end of the seventeenth century (Kerridge 1956). It is often assumed that they were initially grown with the conscious intention of increasing the amounts of manure available and thus the quantity of grain being produced. It is doubtful, however, whether farmers would have looked at things quite like this: turnips (and, indeed, clover) were fodder for livestock, and their cultivation probably represents an attempt by arable farmers in the decades either side of 1700 to diversify into beef production at a time when grain prices were low but meat prices were comparatively buoyant. Like the farmers on the Midland clays, those in sheep-corn districts began to purchase bullocks brought by drovers from Scotland, Ireland and the north of England, fattening them for a year or two before consigning them to market. But bullocks could not thrive on the meagre grass sward, ling and broom of the sheepwalks, and the area of meadow available for winter hay in sheep-corn districts was often limited. Turnips were a godsend, the ideal crop for this new form of light land enterprise.

Looked at in this way, it is not surprising that turnips were first grown on a large scale in those rather anomalous sheep-corn areas— north Norfolk and the Suffolk Sandlings—in which cattle production had always formed a

significant part of the economy. Some historians have doubted the impact of turnip cultivation in East Anglia in the period before the late eighteenth century (Overton 1991, 312), but detailed documentary research suggests that, in some districts at least, the crop was already of considerable importance by the 1720s (Wade Martins and Williamson 1999a, 102–15). As early as 1666 a lease for a farm in Horsham St Faiths in the heathlands of north Norfolk bound the tenant to leave 20 acres sown with the crop at the end of the tenancy, while a tithe account for Thorpe St Andrew in the same district lists the crops growing on six farms in 1706 (NRO MSS 16.023; NRO PD 228/51 (W)). Of these, five were growing turnips in quantities ranging from 6 per cent to 34 per cent of their cropped acreage. On average, turnips accounted for some 13 per cent of the total area under crops. But it may have been in the Suffolk Sandlings that the crop first came to be grown on a large scale. Certainly, in 1722 Daniel Defoe was able to describe how 'This part of England is remarkable for being the first where the feeding and fattening of cattle, both sheep as well as black cattle, with turnips, was first practised in England, which is made a very great part of the improvement of their land to this day' (Defoe 1976 [1724], 86–7).

In the decades around 1700 turnips began to be grown in substantial numbers in other eastern sheep-corn areas. On the Houghton estate in north-west Norfolk they were being cultivated in small quantities as early as 1673, but the correspondence of John Wrott, agent for the Walpole family, suggests that they became more important as a crop around the end of the seventeenth century. On 3 March 1701 he complained that 'wee have had a very tedious winter for Bullocks and Sheep in Turnips, that they are nothing so forward as they used to be other years'. On 14 March

1701 he commented: 'As to the ploughing concerned this yeare, it will be thus: wee shall sow about 40 acres of Turnips, & about 70 acres of Barley, which is more than we used to sow, and shall therefore sow the lesser quantity of oates, not above 12 or 14 acres of oates . . .'. (Plumb 1952, 87, 88). By the 1720s and 1730s their cultivation, together with that of clover, was being stipulated in leases for the tenant farms on the estate, often in large acreages—up to a fifth of the total area of the farm for each crop (Plumb 1952, 63). On the nearby Raynham estate a series of letters dating from the period 1661–86 makes no mention of turnips, but the next run of estate correspondence, from 1706, shows that they were by then a well-established part of the farming regime. On 16 February, for example, Lord Townshend's agent informed him: 'As I remember your Ldship intended the new enclosure called Girdhill, which is next the new pond, for turneps', but added that he considered that 'ye close by the wind mill more fitt for turnips this yeare' (Saunders 1916, 41–2). The surviving accounts from other estates in north-west Norfolk present a similar picture. Turnips were being widely cultivated as a field crop on the Holkham estate by 1710, while on the Hunstanton estate's Downs Farm in Barret Ringstead the crop featured as part of the rotation in almost every field covered by a cropping account covering the period 1715–19 (NRO LeStrange OA3).

Even on the marginal soils of Breckland turnips were being cultivated on some scale. In evidence submitted in a court case in 1723 they were said to have been grown in the fields of Thetford 'for 25 years past' (NRO Petre Box 9/1), and they are mentioned in a number of leases for Breckland farms from the 1720s and 1730s (NRO WLS XIX/27/2; ESRO HA £/3/286). By this time they were

becoming established in other sheep-corn areas of eastern England. On the Wolds of Lincolnshire their cultivation is recorded as early as 1696 (Beastall 1978, 15), and they were widely grown by the 1730s: probably, as in Norfolk, to feed the Scottish cattle which were increasingly being fattened in the region. By 1754 both turnips and clover were standard crops on the Massingberd estates, often combined in a regular, four-course rotation (Beastall 1978, 18).

Although turnips and clover were regularly cultivated in many sheep-corn districts in the early eighteenth century, even in East Anglia uptake was patchy. While they were a standard aspect of husbandry at Raynham or Houghton by 1710, in the nearby parish of Hunstanton tithe accounts for the years 1705–11 show that they were grown only in small closes near the village, and comprised a mere 0.8 per cent of the total cropped acreage (NRO LeStrange BCH7). Similarly, in Barsham, some 25 kilometres to the east, tithe accounts covering the period 1671–1735 make no mention of the crop before 1701, and only twice thereafter, in small quantities (NRO PD117/3). Thus in 1713 the accounts recorded payments from one farmer for 'ye Tith of his *patch* of peas and turnips'. In the Yorkshire Wolds some farms were growing turnips as early as 1745 but Young was able to describe their cultivation as a novelty in 1769 (although their spread thereafter must have been rapid, for Marshall described them in 1788 as 'the most solid basis of Wold husbandry') (A. Harris 1961, 65–6; Young 1771, I, 181; Marshall 1788, 12). On the Lincolnshire Wolds cultivation was widespread, but again many parishes grew few if any, even at the end of the century. On the Wessex chalklands they were virtually unknown as a field crop before 1730, and rare before 1760 (Wordie 1984, 331–2). As late as 1801, in Wiltshire parishes like

Avebury, Tilshead, Berwick or Collingbourne Ducis, turnips generally occupied between 2 per cent and 4 per cent of the cropped acreage. In some parishes they were hardly grown at all, with only one acre out of 521 occupied by the crop at Durrington, for example (Turner 1982a, III). As late as 1815 turnips were described as a 'comparatively late introduction' on the chalklands of Dorset, while in Hampshire in 1813 they were still 'gaining ground among the most respectable farmers' (W. Stevenson 1815, 251; Vancouver 1813a 175).

There were a number of reasons for the remarkably gradual and uneven adoption of this, the key improvement of the light land revolution. The most important was that it was difficult to integrate the cultivation of turnips (and to a lesser extent clover) into open-field rotations. Turnips could only be planted as a substitute for bare fallows where the right to graze across the fallow fields had been limited or abolished. Otherwise, any farmer planting his strips with turnips would simply have to watch them being eaten by the communal flocks. It is clear that open-field communities were, on occasions, able to alter radically their system of farming—even change the essential layout of their fields—in order to incorporate the new crops. On the light soils at Ashley near Scunthorpe, for example, the landowners and occupiers drew up an agreement in 1784 'for Improvement of Lands in the several open Arable fields there by sowing of Turnips and Clover'. The farmers agreed to fence off some of their strips in the East Field, which were to be 'sown with Turnips or Clover this present year'. The north side of the North Field was to be 'taken in and enclosed the second year of the said term and sown with Clover and Turnips'; while West Field was to be divided into three parts and farmed according to a four-course rotation. Rights of common

grazing were terminated on all the land sown with the new crops, and cottagers with common rights were to be compensated (LRO Misc Dep 77/16). Such a transformation of ancient customary arrangements was no simple matter, however, and more common was the less complicated procedure of simply fencing off the strips on which the turnips grew, to protect them from the sheep. But if the land was fenced in order to keep out the sheep, it was also deprived of their dung. Moreover, even this limited move required the consent of fellow cultivators. As late as 1837 the compilers of the Tithe File for Great Milton in Oxfordshire bemoaned how:

> The arbitrary and antiquated customs of open field husbandry present here as they do universally a bar to improved cultivation and check the enterprise of the farmer. The . . . occupiers on the lighter soils venture upon the innovations of turnips and artificial grasses. They do so however on sufferance as the nonconformity of any one of the open field farmers would place them in peril of a return to the old course of crops (Kain 1986, 398).

Indeed, even when turnips were cultivated in open fields the plants did not always remain there throughout the winter, in order to produce the roots. In some cases fellow-cultivators would not allow fences to remain for this long, or the farmer himself had no wish to forgo the dung of the communal flock: having planted the seeds at the usual time, around Midsummer Day, only the summer foliage was grazed, and then ploughed in as green manure. As Stevenson noted in Dorset in 1815: 'In the open fields, turnips are often sown in the fallow season, merely for the purpose of ploughing them in, before wheat is sown on the same land' (W. Stevenson 1815, 263).

In many western sheep-corn areas the widespread adoption of 'floating' in the course of the seventeenth and eighteenth centuries lessened the need for the new crop, and thus avoided the institutional upheavals which its cultivation involved; while in some eastern districts traditional arrangements were particularly inimicable to the innovators. Where fold courses existed landowners often zealously guarded the rights of the manorial flocks to range freely over the fields. Thus in Thetford in Norfolk in the 1720s the lord of the manor still retained his fold course for 1,000 sheep across Magdelen Field from 14 September to 3 May. Witnesses to a dispute in 1724 claimed that some occupiers of the field had been sowing turnips for 25 years, and that the shepherds had kept the sheep off them, treating them as if they were growing corn, 'until last year when the sheep ate up the defendants turnips' (NRO Petre Box 9/1–4). The spread of the crops was, in such circumstances, essentially dependent on the whim of the manorial lord. At Ashill, also in the Norfolk Breckland, undated mid-eighteenth-century documents relating to a similar dispute detail the lord of the manor's claim that the farmers deliberately planted crops in positions that prevented the sheep moving through the fields, 'By which Means the sheeps feed hath been and still is nearly precarious'. The farmers wanted to continue growing turnips and clover

> Which in this parish are become a great improvement and infact Sir Henry Bedingfield descendants and his daughter who lived near the said parish and were well acquainted with the customs of the said manor did for more than 40 years ackuiesse and no way oppose the landowners inclosing and sowing the said new enclosures with turnips. (NRO Pete Box 17/1)

It does, therefore, seem clear that while turnips and clover certainly were cultivated in open fields, their widespread adoption depended upon enclosure; and it is evident that in most sheep-corn districts large-scale enclosure was indeed followed by the more general adoption of the new crops. On the Yorkshire Wolds, for example, the old two-crops-and-a-fallow rotation, while by no means universal, was 'still widely practised' until the open fields were enclosed in the decades around 1800 (A. Harris 1961, 23). Yet it was not only institutional arrangements which discouraged the cultivation of turnips. Environmental factors were also important. In many places the soil, in its native state, was simply too acidic for them. It had first to be altered, by the practice of *claying* or *marling*.

Marling and Reclamation

Marling involved digging pits through the acidic topsoil to reach a more alkaline subsoil beneath. This was brought to the surface and assiduously spread and mixed with the former, thus neutralising acidity (Mathew 1993). The practice was employed in many districts but was, quintessentially, a practice of heathland farming. By great good fortune most of the principal heathland districts overlay chalk at no great depth, the marly upper layers of which could almost have been created for the purpose. Marling has not always received a great deal of attention from historians, and what it actually achieved is not always fully understood. Its most important benefit, as already intimated, was that it allowed the cultivation of turnips on otherwise unsuitable soils. Turnips do not thrive in acid conditions: they are liable to fail completely on sour land and are prone to attack by finger-and-toe disease (Hanley 1949, I, 138; D.H. Robinson 1949, 232). In addition, red clover is susceptible to acidity, and usually fails to reach the seedling stage in particularly base-poor soils (D.H. Robinson 1949, 109). In many districts, the adoption of the new rotations thus depended on significant alterations to soil chemistry. But soil acidity limited productivity in more general ways. Cereal yields are badly affected, especially those of barley: under acid conditions the roots become stunted and discoloured. High soil acidity enhances the solubility (and hence the availability) of certain harmful elements, such as aluminium and manganese, again adversely affecting the growth of cereals. Of course, contemporaries would not have understood the precise ways in which soil chemistry affected crop growth; nor would they have employed the same terms as modern agricultural scientists. Nevertheless, years of observation and experience ensured that they were well aware of the problems of farming 'sour' land, and of the benefits to be gained from marling on such soils.

In addition to all this, nitrogen is converted into nitrites by soil bacteria which are highly susceptible to acidity. The pH of the soil was thus of crucial importance in the adoption of the new rotations, for without a healthy microbe population any increased applications of farmyard manure resulting from the cultivation of turnips and clover would have been pointless: they could simply not have been broken down. The absence of such bacteria also affects the extent to which clover is able to fix atmospheric nitrogen in the soil. In short, not only could the key crops of the agricultural revolution not have been successfully cultivated on untreated acid soils, even if they could have been, few of their principal benefits would have been realised. Apt indeed was Richard Bacon's description of the 'new husbandry' as a 'union of high manuring and an appropriate application of the calcareous soils' (Bacon 1844, 267).

Marling had been practised since at least medieval times (Prince 1964), but its scale increased massively in the course of the eighteenth century, and in western East Anglia, in particular, the ground is still peppered with abandoned pits, although many more have been filled in (Figure 13). By 1752 the anonymous individual writing as 'N' in the *Gentleman's Magazine* put marling at the head of his list of the practices which typified the 'improved' husbandry of Norfolk (Anon. 1752). But routine marling was difficult where land lay in a myriad of small intermingled parcels. Individual landowners would have found it hard to excavate a sizeable pit within the confines of a single strip, or even within a bundle of contiguous consolidated strips. Moreover, the complex intermixture and widely scattered character of farms made the movement and spread of the marl uneconomic. Communal marl pits had certainly existed in the old landscape but they were few in number. A map of Lodge Farm in Castle Acre, west Norfolk, surveyed in 1715 shows only one marl pit, 'No Mans Pit', situated among the open-field strips of West Field. A map surveyed *c.*1840 shows no less than seven 'old pits' and sixteen 'new pits' within this same area (Prince 1964, 22; Bacon 1844, 267–8).

Not all heathland areas in the east of England overlay chalk. In some, rafts of chalky material occurred within the glacial drift, and were extensively quarried; but in others no 'calcareous earth' was locally available and chalk—mined in extensive quarries—was brought considerable distances, usually by boat. In Norfolk, major workings had developed by the 1770s at Whittlingham near Norwich and at Horstead and Coltishall, their produce disseminated by wherry along the Broadland rivers (by the following century the Horstead workings had become a local tourist attraction with the fanciful name

Figure 13   Abandoned marl pits, west Norfolk

'Little Switzerland') (Williamson 1997, 147). In a similar way, Sandlings farmers acquired their chalk by sea from large commercial workings located on the coast of Kent and Sussex.

Marling was thus of critical importance in the improvement of existing arable land in heathland districts, and was inextricably linked with enclosure. But the two processes together had another role in the 'light land revolution'—in the extension of the cultivated acreage. As we have seen, between a quarter and a half of the land of most sheep-corn villages lay under heath or pasture. The adoption of the new rotations allowed large numbers of livestock to be kept on fodder crops growing in rotation in the arable fields; and as a result, the role of the heaths and downs as 'nutrient reservoirs' was rendered redundant. These areas could now be re-claimed and farmed, along with the rest of the parish, under some form of 'improved' rotation. But much of this land was common land, and reclamation could therefore only take place after its legal status had been changed by enclosure—after common rights had been curtailed and it had been divided, as hedged allotments, between those who had formerly shared rights in its exploitation. And where such sheepwalks occupied acid land, and took the form of heaths, they could only be brought into cultivation after particularly assiduous marling.

The largest applications of marl always seem to have been associated with heathland reclamation. A letter written in 1739 by Thomas Marsham, the agent for Thomas Barret, typically described how a 'vast tract of land' at Horsford in north Norfolk could be reclaimed—but only 'if marl and clay be easily had' (ERO D/DL/C8/1). Even in areas of chalk downland and wold the upper layers of the soil were often acidic, lime having been leached down to lower levels, and measures had to be taken to remedy this when land was brought into cultivation. On the Lincolnshire Wolds, for example, following enclosure the turf was 'pared and burnt' by gangs using breast ploughs. This destroyed pests such as wireworms, and also provided large inputs of potash. Next, the land was often dressed with a mixture of clay and sand, and then chalked, usually with 80 cubic feet per acre. The most enthusiastic improvers then supplied 60 bushels of bone per acre (Beastall 1978, 174). Every twenty years or so further dressings of chalk were applied, the need for chalking being indicated by the appearance of finger-and-toe disease in the turnip crop (Caird 1852, 190). Marling and chalking, facilitated by enclosure, were central to the light land revolution. They raised yields on existing arable land; they allowed the reclamation of heaths and sheepwalks; and they permitted the adoption of the new rotations on land which would otherwise have been unsuitable for them.

The Progress of Enclosure

As on the Midland clays, enclosure in light land districts had begun in late medieval times. Many small vills in the most marginal locations had been deserted in the fifteenth century and turned into grazing grounds or warrens. In the following two centuries further townships similarly located—often on the high, infertile watersheds, away from the principal valleys—were acquired by large estates and their open fields removed. This kind of enclosure probably increased during the agricultural recession of the late seventeenth and early eighteenth centuries, when many small owner-occupiers were forced to sell up. As a consequence of such steady engrossment a marked distinction had developed in many sheep-corn districts by the early eighteenth century, paralleling that already noted in the Midlands, between enclosed 'estate' parishes—often on the poorer soils of the 'uplands'—and larger 'open' villages more favourably located, where enclosure had made less progress. Most of the places where the cultivation of turnips was widespread at the start of the century seem to have been in the former locations: hence the contrast, noted above, between farming practices on the enclosed land of the Raynham or Houghton estates, and in the open fields of nearby Hunstanton.

Nevertheless, although enclosure made some headway before the eighteenth century, vast areas of light land remained unenclosed. In the Yorkshire Wolds, for example, two-thirds of the parishes were still almost entirely open as late as 1730 (A. Harris 1961, 23). In the second half of the eighteenth century enclosure proceeded apace. In some districts much was still achieved by the old expedient of simply buying up all the properties in a parish. This was especially true in eastern heathland areas, such as the East Anglian Breckland. Between 1760 and 1798 Lord Cornwallis set out to buy the Breckland parishes of Culford, Ingham, Timworth and West Stow. By 1800 the Culford estate controlled their entire area, which was surveyed and then divided into nine new farms, mostly covering more than 1,000 acres each (Paine 1993, 23–7). On William Faden's map of the county of Norfolk, published in 1797, the words 'common fields' are emblazoned prominently across a number of Breckland parishes, implying that open arable was here a particularly noticeable and prominent feature of the landscape. The neighbouring parishes of East Wretham, Brettenham, Kilverstone, Riddlesworth, Gasthorpe, West Harling and Bridgeham are all distinguished in this way. By 1840, all had been enclosed, but in only one—Bridgeham—was this achieved by parliamentary act (in 1804). Yet it was not only in highly marginal environments like this that non-parliamentary enclosure occurred on a substantial scale, as Chapman and Seeliger's work in Hampshire has shown. In this county the heaths did not overlie calcareous chalk and were therefore less susceptible to improvement than those in East Anglia, remaining largely unenclosed until the mid-nineteenth century. But numerous enclosures by agreement took place on the chalk downland in the north of the county, throughout the eighteenth and nineteenth centuries. The affected parishes were interspersed fairly evenly amongst those enclosed by more 'normal', parliamentary means (Chapman and Seeliger 1995).

Most light land enclosure in the period after 1760 was, nevertheless, achieved by parliamentary acts: most parishes which could be enclosed by other means had already been so, leaving a rump of more popular, and tenurially complex, places. Some, especially on the Wolds of Lincolnshire and Yorkshire, on the limestone cliff and heath of Lincolnshire, and in north-west Norfolk, were enclosed in the first great wave of enclosure, peaking in the late 1770s. But most had to wait until the Napoleonic War years, when grain prices soared to unprecedented heights. By the end of the War, the vast majority of light land parishes had been enclosed.

Enclosure was almost invariably associated with the extension of the area in tilth.

Indeed, even in the early years of the eighteenth century, when grain prices were low, there was some ploughing of heath and down. In part this was to grow more grain, as light land farmers expanded production in the face of falling prices: 'By putting a bigger volume of produce on the market, even at reduced prices, they could at least maintain their incomes' (Jones 1967, 166). In some places, however, it was to grow turnips and clover as farmers diversified into beef production. The expansion of ploughland was particularly marked on the downlands of the south of England, where the adoption of clover and sainfoin, and of meadow irrigation, enhanced manure supplies and thus allowed the thinner, poorer soils of the higher downs to be cultivated (Jones 1960, 8). Daniel Defoe in 1722 noted how large areas of the Wessex downs had recently been ploughed, something which had 'increased the quantity of corn produced . . . in a prodigious manner' (Defoe 1976 [1724], 193, 265). On the Houghton and Raynham estates in north-west Norfolk, similarly, heaths were being ploughed and reclaimed on some scale, and outfields brought into more regular cultivation, in the 1720s and 1730s. But the rising grain prices in the period after 1750, and especially the extraordinary prices of the Napoleonic War years, saw a much more sustained onslaught on the heaths, wolds and downs; and by the first decades of the nineteenth century there had been a real revolution in land use here. Strickland, writing in 1812, believed that whereas at the start of the eighteenth century two-thirds of the Yorkshire Wolds had been under pasture, that figure had since been halved (Strickland 1812, 106). By the 1830s, to judge from the Tithe Files, most parishes had less than 30 per cent of their land under permanent pasture. On the Lincolnshire Wolds, similarly, the ancient grass pastures fell to the plough wholesale, and by the 1850s it was said that 'the highest points are all in tillage, and the whole length of the Wolds is intersected by neat hawthorn hedges'. In west Norfolk, by the 1840s, virtually no permanent grassland survived, except along the floors of the principal valleys, or as closes in the immediate vicinity of farmsteads (Figure 14).

Everywhere, as enclosed pastures replaced open heaths and downs, new breeds of sheep appeared: 'long-wool' breeds, no longer valued primarily for their ability to survive on the bleak commons and endure the nightly walk to the fold, as the old 'short-wools' had been, but rather for their ability to fatten quickly on turnips and clover (Ryder 1964, 7). In East Anglia, the old Norfolk Horn was steadily replaced, first by Bakewell's New Leicester, subsequently by Southdowns and Southdown crosses ('Suffolks') (Wade Martins and Williamson 1999a, 128–9). On the Lincolnshire Wolds the Old Lincolnshire flocks were crossed with New Leicesters to produce the Improved Lincoln (Beastall 1978, 164–8), while in Yorkshire the old Wolds breed was replaced by Improved Lincolns and then by Leicesters (A. Harris 1961, 54). Similar changes occurred on the downs of southern England (Bowie 1987a, 1990).

The New Landscape

Today the Lincolnshire and Yorkshire Wolds and the more gently rolling lands of north-west Norfolk are classic examples of Rackham's 'planned countrysides', land-scapes of 'thin hawthorn hedges, windswept brick farms, and ivied clumps of trees in corners of fields: a predictable landscape of wide views, sweeping sameness, and straight lines' (Rackham 1986, 5). Whether created by parliamentary surveyors and commissioners,

or by the agents of large landed estates, these are indeed landscapes of straight-sided rectangular fields, usually much larger than those created by eighteenth-century enclosure in the Midlands (Figure 15). Those on the Yorkshire chalk generally covered between 30 and 70 acres (Caird 1852, 310); on the Lincolnshire Wolds they were generally '30 to 100 acres, presenting to the eye of the stranger the aspect of open-field lands' because the hedges were often concealed by the rolling topography (Jennings 2000, 71). Not all the new hedges came into existence at precisely the same time. As the Russells remind us, in their remarkable examination of Lincolnshire enclosures, in some parishes 'few people were awarded land. Therefore some of the plots awarded were very large, and were quickly subdivided into the size of field considered appropriate' (Russell and Russell 1985, 9).

The roads in these light land districts are frequently narrower than those laid out by parliamentary enclosure in the Midlands, lacking the latter's wide verges, largely because most were created later, in the decades around 1800 (Turner 1984b, 147). The hedges established at this time are still noticeably species-poor, usually consisting of hawthorn with small amounts of blackthorn, ash, elder and dog rose—rather different from the more mixed, species-rich hedges of anciently enclosed districts. In part the contrast reflects the fact that the former are relatively new features of the landscape, and have not had much time to be colonised by a wider variety of trees and shrubs; many, of course, were planted in very open country, far from woods or older hedges from whence new species could infiltrate. But it also reflects important changes in planting fashions.

Single-species planting was now easier on a large scale due to the development of the substantial commercial nurseries which, by

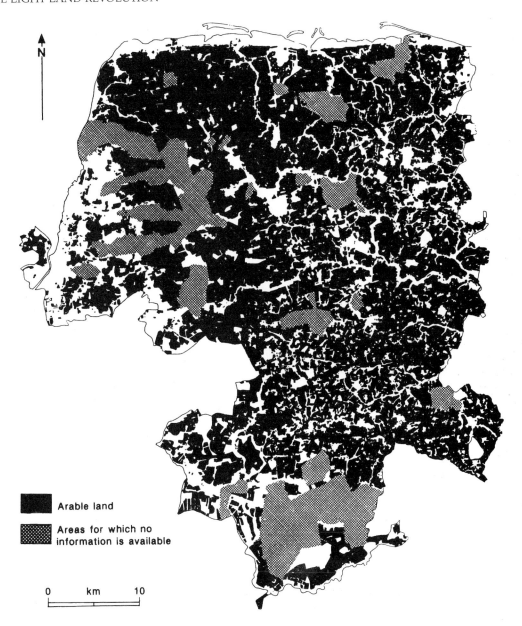

Figure 14 *The extent of arable land use in west Norfolk, c.1840 (mapped from the Tithe Award maps in Mosby 1938)*

Arable land

Areas for which no information is available

0   km   10

the second half of the eighteenth century, were appearing in most major provincial towns. But landowners and enclosure commissioners favoured neat hedges of hawthorn or sloe for another reason. Most of the hedges planted before *c.*1700 had supplied a range of products required by what was still effectively a peasant economy—fuel and wood, to some extent nuts and fruit—as well

Figure 15   Typical late parliamentary enclosure on light land: large fields and straight, species-poor hedges, Strethall and Ickleton, north Essex/south Cambridgeshire borders

as serving as barriers to contain livestock. But Georgian and Victorian landowners and farmers made rather simpler demands on their hedges, and in particular did not see them as major repositories of fuel, not least because coal was now coming into wide-spread use (Williamson 2002). Blackthorn and hawthorn made poor firewood and provided few other benefits, but did provide an impenetrable barrier in a short space of time. Similar reasons help explain why few new pollards were established in hedges after the 1780s; indeed, in many districts, after the 1820s, few trees of any kind were planted there. Most agricultural improvers advocated concentrating timber in plantations, rather than scattering trees along the field boundaries.

Straight, flimsy hedges of hawthorn or (more rarely) blackthorn were thus the normal form of enclosure in the eighteenth and nineteenth centuries not only on the light lands but also, as we have seen, on the Midland clays. The most striking exceptions to this general dominance are to be found in the Breckland of Norfolk and Suffolk, and sporadically in other heathland areas. Here, some landowners planted hedges of Scots pine—a plant able to thrive in particularly harsh conditions—most of which have now grown into lines of mature, romantically twisted trees. Only in the Cotswolds, and in the narrow 'heath' area in Lincolnshire, were stone walls used to enclose the new fields in sheep-corn districts.

As in the Midlands, the enclosure of open fields and commons was often accompanied by changes in the pattern of settlement. Before enclosure, large tracts of sheepwalk, especially on the high wolds and downs, had been entirely devoid of human habitation. In 1768 Arthur Young journeyed across Salisbury Plain and described how 'in twenty miles I met with only one habitation, which was a hut' (Bettey 2000, 44). By the early nineteenth century, however, numerous new farms had been created, their remote locations often reflected in their names: Botany Bay, Quebec, New Zealand, Waterloo. Most were neat, symmetrical, double-pile brick-built structures, sometimes with roofs of slate, sometimes (in the east of England) of pantiles. The new farms were equipped with large barns and—increasingly—regular rows of cattle sheds, enclosing a yard in which bullocks could be over-wintered. Indeed, even where farms remained on the same sites in sheep-corn areas they were often comprehensively rebuilt. In part this was because the older buildings were unsuited to the needs of the new husbandry in which farms functioned, in effect, as 'manure factories'. In part it reflected the inadequate size of barns, in particular, as the area under cultivation was expanded in these districts, and as landlords continued to engross farms to make larger and larger units. Smart new farms, with fashionable farmhouses, were here—as in the Midland shires—needed to attract tenants of sufficient capital. Indeed, the need was greater here, because of the great schemes of reclamation which were taking place: for while the landlord supplied the fixed capital, the farmer supplied the working capital and the flocks and herds necessary to provide the

manure required to keep the ploughlands in heart.

The migration of farmsteads out of the village was not the only change in settlement to occur in these light land districts during the eighteenth and nineteenth centuries. In the period before c.1750, in particular, some places shrank markedly in size, for the kinds of reasons already described in the previous chapter. Not only were landlords eager to reduce the number of farms. Where villages were closed or 'close', they were also keen to restrict the number of cottages. Susan Neave's important study of east Yorkshire has shown how 'Many settlements decreased in size between the mid-seventeenth and mid-eighteenth centuries, and a large number of 'shrunken village' earthworks date from this period of contraction' (Neave 1993, 135). The Penningtons of Warter Hall thus systematically bought out all the other freeholders in Warter in the first half of the eighteenth century. As farms were purchased their land was often divided amongst existing tenants. In 1673 there were 85 households in the parish; by 1743 this had dropped to 58 (Neave 1993, 134). The population of many townships increased once again in the late eighteenth and early nineteenth centuries but, as Neave makes clear, 'this was largely due to the establishment of post-enclosure farmsteads away from village centres' (ibid., 135).

Similar patterns of change—and in particular, the shrinkage of some closed villages—are evident in the Lincolnshire Wolds, in some parts of Wessex, and in the western districts of East Anglia. But there is an implied paradox here: for whereas in the grass shires a reduction in the size of the local population was possible because a grazing economy required less labour, in these light land districts not only did arable farming continue but the area under the plough expanded. Moreover, the new forms of husbandry—involving the repeated hoeing of turnips, the digging and carting of marl, and the assiduous spreading of manure—required significantly greater inputs of labour than traditional farming methods, which had depended primarily on the movement of the *flocks* (Trimmer 1969). In these districts, therefore, even more than in the Midlands, closed villages were net importers of labour from neighbouring 'open' ones, often located several miles away. By the nineteenth century the distances which labourers had to walk to their place of work in these arable areas had become a major social scandal.

Some closed villages were rebuilt, in whole or part, in fashionable 'model' form, often when removed to make way for a new park around a mansion. Notable examples include Houghton and Holkham in Norfolk, Lockinge in Berkshire, and New Sledmere and Horsham in the East Riding of Yorkshire (Darley 1978, 291, 295, 301–2). The layout and design of such settlements proclaimed both the taste and the paternalistic concern of the landowner. Devoid of Nonconformist chapels, and in many cases of public houses, they represented controlled spaces, the homes of a deferential and superficially contented estate population. And in innumerable other ways the new landscapes reflected the beliefs, aspirations and pastimes of their owners. The light land estates were not simply factories of agricultural production. Landowners were actively involved in large-scale tree-planting, and in the creation of elaborate and extensive parks and gardens. Some of the largest and most elaborate of English parks are found in these districts: places like Holkham, with its vast perimeter belt, planted with 4 million trees between 1783 and 1805 (Williamson 1998b, 101–2). Sledmere Park, in the heart of the Yorkshire Wolds, was 'an island of woodland in the

middle of a rather bare countryside' (A. Harris 1961, 74). The Earls of Yarborough planted 17.5 million trees on the Lincolnshire Wolds between 1787 and 1889; by the end of the nineteenth century the estate contained 8,000 acres of woodland (Figure 16) (Clemenson 1982, 76). Innumerable lesser landowners made a smaller, but often visually impressive, contribution, establishing belts, clumps and plantations in formerly open country. Conifers, especially Scots pine, were commonly planted on the sandier soils, beech on the Cotswolds, Chilterns, Downs and Wolds—like the great wall of beech trees established by Lord Chedworth at Stowell near Northleach in Gloucestershire.

New plantations were normally most extensive in the immediate vicinity of great houses, but by the early nineteenth century they were being established on some scale in more remote parts. Planting was an activity deeply imbued with symbolic meaning in the eighteenth and nineteenth centuries, especially in areas as devoid of trees as these (Daniels 1988; Williamson 1995, 124–30). It asserted both the ownership of land and confidence in the family's continued enjoyment of possession: for why plant trees if your progeny will not enjoy the benefits, financial or otherwise? Planting proclaimed the fact that land was enclosed—for it was impossible to establish trees successfully where rights of common grazing still existed. It demonstrated patriotism, at least in the case of oak plantations, because throughout the eighteenth century, and into the nineteenth, there was recurrent concern that the nation possessed insufficient timber reserves to maintain the fleets upon which its security depended. Plantations also provided shelter for stock and, in particular, for game: in the course of the eighteenth century landowners took an increasing interest in preserving and shooting the pheasant, a bird which—unlike

Figure 16 Some of the 17.5 million trees planted on the Yarborough estate, Brocklesby, Lincolnshire, between 1787 and 1889

the partridge—thrives in a wooded environment. The planting of woods and plantations was, above all, a prime symbol of gentility, for the simple reason that only large landowners possessed sufficient land to take tens or hundreds of acres out of cultivation in this way. For all these varied reasons, converting the bleak, open prospects of the vernacular countryside to the sylvan scenes demanded by polite taste was an activity loaded with significance.

Landscapes of improvement were, indeed, important instruments of legitimation at a time when the social and political hegemony of the landed classes was being increasingly challenged by an expanding and vociferous middle class. They demonstrated patriotism, social responsibility, and a commitment to produce the food necessary to feed the teaming millions of the cities. But they also expressed the world-view of the traditional elite in more fundamental ways. They embodied the very spirit of improvement in an age of rationality: the idea that existing arrangements were provisional, rather than God-given, and could be changed where the resources and the will existed. Owners and their families were not shy about proclaiming their achievements. A memorial tablet in West Heslerton church proudly proclaims: 'Whoever now traverses the Wolds of Yorkshire and contrasts their present appearance with what they were cannot but extol the name of Sykes'—the family whose estates embraced much of the surrounding countryside.

Landowners employed two key weapons in their war on the traditional landscape: enclosure and the lease, that is, the legal document drawn up between owner and tenant which stipulated the respective responsibilities of each. Leases might, for example, allow a tenant to break up a portion of sheepwalk, letting him farm it at a low rent for several years and, perhaps, subsidising the costs of its reclamation in other ways. They often stipulated how the farm should be managed, including the courses of cropping to be pursued. In the first half of the eighteenth century, when prices were low and farms hard to let, the terms set out in leases were generally lax and generous. But as grain prices rose and competition increased landlords could make greater demands. Leases became more prescriptive and detailed. The tenant's interest, naturally enough, was to maximise the production of food, and therefore his income. The landlord's, in contrast, was to maintain or enhance the value of his property. As the balance of power shifted, there were important implications for farming practice, in all areas, but perhaps especially here, on the thin, hungry lands of England.

The turnip-based rotations followed by light land farmers in the early eighteenth century—such as those recorded at Downs Farm in Barret Ringstead in north-west Norfolk in the period 1715–19—were often irregular by later standards, with the various elements of the rotation following each other in changing and apparently random order. This was probably because the new crops were regarded by farmers simply as a way of providing fodder for livestock, rather than as a way of enhancing soil fertility. In the second half of the century rotations tended to become more regular, increasingly approximating to the 'Norfolk four-course'. This was partly because, with rising grain prices,

farmers were more interested in producing grain and in adopting rotations which would best achieve this aim. But it was also because landlords and their agents were now in a better position to dictate the terms of leases. Strict adherence to the 'four-course' or some less intensive variant ensured that half or more of the farm was, at any one time, under 'restorative' rather than 'exhaustive' crops, and thus assured the long-term fertility of the land. Tenants, left to their own devices, would often have pursued more intensive courses of cropping, especially towards the end of a lease. The elite's obsession with the four-course arguably expressed something more: that desire for regularity and symmetry which was embodied in other aspects of what Deetz has termed the 'Georgian Order', most notably in the elegant façades of their homes (Deetz 1977). Changes in the character of crop rotations in light land areas illustrate clearly the complex factors and conflicting interests which might underlie the development of farming practice in the eighteenth and nineteenth centuries.

The Achievement

The sheer scale of enclosure and reclamation in sheep-corn districts mesmerised contemporaries. Arthur Young typically described the changes in north-west Norfolk.

All the country from Holkham to Houghton was a wild sheep walk before the spirit of improvement seized the inhabitants . . . Instead of boundless wilds and uncultivated wastes inhabited by scarce anything but sheep, the country is all cut up into enclosures, cultivated in a most husbandlike manner, well peopled, and yielding an hundred times the produce that it did in its former state (Young 1771, II, 1).

The extension of cultivation on these light lands did indeed increase the production of grain significantly. But the extent of reclamation varied from district to district. On the Yorkshire and Lincolnshire Wolds, and in north-west Norfolk, the area under cultivation often expanded by 50 per cent or more. But in the downlands of the south many parishes still had 30 per cent, and some over 50 per cent, of their area under pasture in the 1830s (Kain 1986, 195, 205). The thin nature of the chalk soils on the higher downs, their high, exposed character, and in some cases their significantly damper climate all made them less attractive for arable cultivation and, in particular, for the cultivation of turnips. In Sussex the high chalk was 'still largely grazing land' in the 1840s, to judge from the Tithe Award maps: only the lower slopes were under the plough. The 'thinner and more exposed soils' on the higher ground were still 'near the margin of profitable arable cultivation' (Briault 1942, 490).

On the poorer heaths, especially in East Anglia, the transformation of the landscape was also often limited. Much of the land was so poor that extensive tracts of permanent grazing had to be maintained, in order to keep the necessary numbers of sheep required to sustain the arable in good heart, and the practice of cultivating outfield 'breaks' often persisted in the new, enclosed landscape. Some of the land was so bad that in places rabbit warrens continued to be viable enterprises throughout the agricultural revolution period. The warren at Stanford in Norfolk, for example, covered more than 537 acres in the 1820s, and to judge from the details in a lease agreement, it was stocked with 7,200 rabbits (NRO WLS LXI/23 436 X 6). Estate owners often preserved areas of open heathland for another reason: to maintain cover for hares and partridges.

One of the complaints made in 1786 about Abel Smith, a troublesome tenant of the Walsingham estate in Norfolk, was that he had 'cleared all the furze off Wether heath, which leaves it as naked as Lincolns Inn Fields for the protection of game, and threatens to plough up the whole heath unless he is given permission to plough 30 acres' (NRO Petre Box 17, bundle 1).

Even where the more marginal heaths and downs were reclaimed they were often rapidly abandoned at the end of the Napoleonic Wars, as prices fell back once more. William Cobbett, crossing the high chalk downs between Winchester and Wherwell in 1822, 'Came by some hundreds of acres of ground, that was formerly most beautiful down, which was broken up in dear-corn times, and which is now a district of thistles and other weeds' (Cobbett 1830, 56). To the south-east of Winchester, in the following year, he met with similar scenes:

> These hills are amongst the most barren of the Downs of England: yet a part of them was broken up during the rage for improvements; during the rage for what empty men think was an augmenting of the *capital* of the country. . . . A man must be mad, or nearly mad, to sow wheat upon such a spot. However, a large part of what was enclosed has been thrown out again already, and the rest will be thrown out in a very few years. The Down itself was poor; what then must it be as corn-land! Think of the destruction which has taken place . . . (Cobbett 1830, 139).

Much of the reclamation activity of the poorest soils probably had less to do with a careful consideration of profit and loss than with a fashionable enthusiasm for 'improvement' on the part of aristocratic owners. It is worth noting, once again, how the word 'improvement' was applied indiscriminately in the eighteenth century to both land reclamation and agricultural innovation, *and* to such things as landscape gardening and tree-planting. Some forms of 'improvement' fall uncomfortably between the two, notably the architect-designed 'model farms', erected in some fashionable or whimsical style (J.M. Robinson 1980). When the great agricultural improver Thomas William Coke expanded Holkham Park in the 1780s and 1790s, the centre-piece of the landscape was the Great Barn, designed by the country house architect Samuel Wyatt as a setting for Coke's agricultural shows, the famous sheep-shearings. The surrounding parkland consisted of a mixture of sweeping turf, arable land, and tree clumps, the latter carefully positioned both for aesthetic effect and for the benefit of the game (Williamson 1998b, 100–4): 'What can be more beautiful than the diversified scenery which there presents itself? . . . The effects of order and industry, combined with abundance, must be gratifying to every spectator' (Curwen 1809, 238).

The generally unsuccessful experiments with meadow irrigation made by large landowners and gentlemen farmers in eastern England in the decades either side of 1800 also fall into this category. Many examples were located within landscape parks: they were objects of fashionable display as much as aspects of practical agriculture (Wade Martins and Williamson 1999b, 206–9). The more perceptive were well aware that reclamation schemes often had complex motives. When in 1774 Thomas de Grey bemoaned the costs of enclosing the heaths at Tottington in Breckland, he observed candidly in a letter that the 'great expense . . . would but ill answer, unless there was a real satisfaction in employing the labourers and bringing forth a ragged dirty parish to a neatness of cultivation' (NRO WLS XXLVII/19 415 X 5).

These kinds of argument should not be carried too far. The expansion of cultivation at the expense of 'waste' may not have been an unqualified success, but it did increase significantly the amount of land under arable crops, especially in the east of England. There is rather less evidence that the new husbandry served to raise output on *existing* arable land to quite the extent that contemporaries and modern historians have suggested. Yields certainly did increase, but not to the same extent everywhere, and improvements were often unspectacular. On the 'Good Sands' of north-west Norfolk average yields of wheat rose from around 20 bushels per acre in the early eighteenth century to perhaps 22 in the 1750s and around 25 in the 1830s, although barley yields increased more markedly, from around 12 bushels per acre in the early eighteenth century to around 30 in the mid-1830s (Wade Martins and Williamson 1999a, 167–9). On the chalk soils of southern England, increases seem to have been of a similar order. In Dorset, for example, Young implies that wheat yields from chalkland farms were around 20 bushels per acre in 1770 (Young 1771); they were thought to be about the same in 1815 (W. Stevenson 1815, 222); and were only slightly higher, at *c*.22 bushels, in the 1830s, to judge from the Tithe Files. It was in areas of acid soils that the real improvements occurred. On the heathlands of East Anglia the average yields for wheat rose from less than 12 bushels per acre in the early eighteenth century, to around 22 or 23 by the 1830s, while those for barley virtually tripled (Wade Martins and Williamson 1999a, 162–5). Yet changes in crop rotations, to less intensive modes of cereal cropping, ensured that real increases in the production of grain were not quite as great as this. In most heathland districts in the seventeenth century cereals occupied between 45 and 55 per cent of the arable land, the rest being fallows or crops like peas or beans. By the 1830s they generally accounted for less than 45 per cent and in some districts—where the new rotations featured long leys of two or three years—as little as a third. Nevertheless, such was the scale of the increases in yields in heathland districts that even wheat output must have risen appreciably during the 'long eighteenth century'. The message here is simple: the light land revolution brought the greatest benefits to the poorest land.

Most historians have assumed that such improvements were mainly achieved through the adoption of the new rotations, which allowed more animals to be kept and thus more manure to be produced. Yet on the light lands of East Anglia, certainly, the available evidence suggests, at best, a fairly modest increase in livestock numbers—and this during a period in which, in many districts, the area of cultivated land had increased by a third or more (Wade Martins and Williamson 1999a, 171–2). Indeed, in most sheep-corn districts the expansion of arable must have outstripped any increases in manure resulting from the adoption of the new crops, and their real significance was probably that they allowed a growth in the cultivated area without any concomitant diminution in the numbers of livestock. Of more importance than stocking densities, perhaps, was the fact that much of the manure was now being produced more efficiently, rotting with organic matter in yards, rather than lying around on the surface of fields, in the rain, rapidly losing its most important elements (L.S. Thompson 1957). But increases in yields were probably at least as much a consequence of the sustained war against soil acidity, carried out through marling and chalking. The most dramatic improvements were, as I have said, on the most acidic land.

But other factors were also significant in raising yields. The classic light land revolution, as already noted, was very labour-intensive. Turnips required regular hoeing, farmyard manure needed to be moved long distances. Marl was dug and spread manually and vast amounts of labour were deployed when sheepwalks were pared and burnt and converted to tillage. There was little attempt to use machines of any kind: the surplus of labour in most light land districts made it unnecessary, and any displaced labour would simply have become a burden on the poor rate. Threshing machines, although well developed by the end of the century, thus remained rare (except to some extent in the Yorkshire Wolds), and seed drills were only sparingly used (Hutton 1976; MacDonald 1975; Collins 1987). There was instead a shift from broadcast sowing to 'dibbling' seed in rows, something which again reflected the availability and low cost of labour. This, and other labour-intensive improvements in the preparation of the seed-bed and the aftercare of crops, were probably major factors in the improvement of yields in light land districts, especially in the south where wages were generally low.

Much was achieved by the light land revolution. But much was lost. Small proprietors were almost extinguished as a class in most chalk and heathland districts by the 1840s; while the enclosure of open fields and the commons had, once again, an adverse effect upon the labouring population. Nor should we forget that this was essentially an *environmental* revolution, involving large-scale alterations to the soil chemistry. Even in the nineteenth century some observers worried about the side-effects. Some reported how intensive marling had led to an increase in the incidence of 'warping' or spontaneous abortion among sheep. The Raynbirds, writing of recent developments in the East Anglian

Breckland in 1849, noted that 'Although marl has been found . . . most excellent for wheat, yet a sad mortality in the sheep has been observed whilst feeding on land that has recently been marled' (Raynbird and Raynbird 1849, 118). Moreover, the destruction of thousands upon thousands of acres of ancient, semi-natural habitats—acid heath, chalk heath, and downland—was an ecological disaster on an awesome scale. The nineteenth-century botanist Claridge Druce was told how the soldier and monkey orchids had been 'tolerably plentiful' on the chalk around Whitchurch in Oxfordshire until the 1830s when, according to his informant, the steep slopes were pared and burnt, 'roasting alive' both types of plant (Druce 1886). In Breckland the great bustard declined rapidly in numbers and by the 1840s was extinct. The bird made its nest in the fields of rye, sown broadcast, but following enclosure and soil improvement, wheat was more widely grown. It was sown in drills and weeded by gangs of labourers: few nests survived. In addition, the Breckland was increasingly subdivided by hawthorn hedges, pine rows, and tree belts, 'not only entirely changing its aspect but rendering it entirely unsuitable to the wary habits of the bustard, which soon learned to become as jealous as any strategist of what

might afford an enemy harbour' (H. Stevenson 1870, 17).

Of course, the environmental effects of enclosure were not entirely negative. The network of new hedges provided a measure of compensation for the loss of heath and down, and what was bad for open-country birds like the bustard might be a boon for those which preferred a more scrubby environment, such as the wren or the blackbird. But what Charles Babington wrote in 1860 of the south Cambridgeshire chalklands must have been true of many other light land districts. Until the turn of the nineteenth century the hills had been

open and covered with a beautiful coating of turf, profusely decorated with *Anemone Pulsatilla* [Pasqueflower], *Astragolus hypoglottis* [Purple milk-vetch], and other interesting plants. It is now converted into arable land, and its peculiar plants mostly confined to small waste plots . . . Even the tumuli, entrenchments, and other interesting works of the ancient inhabitants have seldom escaped the rapacity of the modern agriculturalist, who too frequently looks upon the native plants of the country as weeds, and its antiquities as deformities (Babington 1860).

CHAPTER 4

Ploughing Up the East

The Forgotten Revolution

Modern historians, like contemporary agricultural writers, have focused their attention on the light land revolution of the sheep-corn countries: on turnips, marling, and the reclamation of sheepwalks. But these were districts of, at best, only moderately fertile soils. They never became the prime wheat-growing regions of England. By the middle of the nineteenth century—as, indeed, today—these were to be found in very different terrain: in the wet fenlands of Lincolnshire, Cambridgeshire and Norfolk, and on the heavy clays of East Anglia and the Home Counties. In the early nineteenth century arable cultivation was even more extensive in these eastern districts than it is today, for extensive areas of the Weald of Kent and Sussex were then under the plough. Yet if we turned the clock back to 1700, things would have appeared very different. Far from being arable lands, most of these were *pastoral* districts, in which animals were fattened, or butter, cheese and milk produced. The expansion and intensification of grain production in these fertile areas was, arguably, the *real* agricultural revolution of the eighteenth and nineteenth centuries.

One of the reasons why eighteenth-century commentators were obsessed with the light land revolution was that leading landowners like Thomas William Coke were closely involved in it. Men like Arthur Young

felt at home in the company of such men, and in that of the large capitalist farmers of north-west Norfolk or the Lincolnshire or Yorkshire Wolds. The regions discussed in this chapter were rather different. They were not, for the most part, characterised by large landed estates, but by smaller gentry properties, absentee owners, and—albeit to a small extent, by 1700—owner-occupiers. And while some large capitalist farms could be found in most districts, by and large they were characterised by smaller farming enterprises. In part these characteristics were a consequence of the fact that dairying and stock-rearing had encouraged the survival of units of production of relatively modest size—dairying, in particular, was suitable for small family farms, whether tenanted or owner-occupied. In part it reflected the fertile nature of many of these soils. And in part it was a hangover from the deep, medieval past, for these areas had often been poorly manorialised in the early Middle Ages, and characterised by a high density of free tenures.

Young and his ilk had little interest in the small farmers or splintered estates of these regions. To a large extent they failed to understand the nature of farming here or the ways in which it could be best improved. Although certain elements of the 'light land revolution' were adopted in these districts, other kinds of improvement proved much more important, both in raising yields and in expanding the arable acreage.

The Clayland Countrysides

The largest and most important of these eastern districts were located on the heavy but fertile boulder clay soils of the south-east Midlands and East Anglia. Firstly, there was a relatively small area lying well within the champion belt, embracing much of Bedfordshire, west Cambridgeshire and Huntingdonshire (Figure 7, p. 30). This 'south-east Midland, arable district' was one of 'regular', extensive open fields and nucleated villages, like that to the west whose history was discussed in Chapter 2. But the development of the two districts diverged steadily in the agricultural revolution period. Most of the Midlands, as we have seen, was laid to grass after enclosure. In this eastern champion district, in contrast, enclosure was not usually followed by conversion to pasture, but by more intensive arable land use.

The other, and far larger, boulder clay district lay to the south and east, separated from that just described by the sheep-corn lands of the Chilterns (Figure 7). It extended across southern East Anglia, Essex, south-east Cambridgeshire and into east Hertfordshire. This was not a 'champion' district but a tract of classic 'ancient countryside', already largely enclosed by the seventeenth century, generally well-wooded, and with a fairly dispersed pattern of settlement. In medieval times it had been among the most densely settled and most intensively arable areas of England. In the sixteenth and seventeenth centuries, however, while remaining well-populated—and becoming increasingly industrialised, with a flourishing textile industry—its farmers had turned to dairying and bullock-fattening, and much land was laid to grass. The key change of the eighteenth and nineteenth centuries was the reversal of this development.

This extensive block of countryside can itself be divided into two, roughly along the line of the Gipping valley which runs through the middle of Suffolk. To the north, in south Norfolk and north Suffolk, pasture predominated greatly over tillage at the start of the period studied here: few farms had more than a quarter of their land under the plough. To the south, grass and grain were more evenly balanced. This difference reflected, in large measure, aspects of soil and topography, for north of the Gipping the clay plateau was only infrequently cut by major valleys, whereas to the south it was much more dissected.

There were other districts of heavy soil in the south and east of England and these likewise saw a significant expansion of tillage, although they were, for the most part, less suitable for arable agriculture. The London clays and associated Tertiary deposits in south Hertfordshire, Middlesex and south Essex, and the complex clays and sands in the Weald of Kent, Sussex and Surrey, both carried less fertile, more acidic soils. Population levels had always been relatively low here, pasture had generally predominated over tillage, and large areas were under grass and devoted to cattle farming in the seventeenth century. Here, too, industry often flourished in early modern times, most notably iron production in the Weald, while the proximity of London impacted on the local economy in complex and diverse ways. Like the claylands of East Anglia, these were (and are) classic 'ancient countrysides'. By the late seventeenth century open fields were absent or of limited extent, the settlement pattern was highly dispersed, and the landscape was well-wooded and densely hedged except where areas of common land existed.

One last area should perhaps be mentioned here, although in some ways rather different from the 'true' claylands of the south and east. In west Hertfordshire, south Buckinghamshire and south-eastern Oxfordshire the chalk which forms the long dipslope of the Chiltern Hills is blanketed by an Eocene deposit which, although technically known as 'clay with flints', gives rise to soils which are less tenacious, more freely draining, and easier to cultivate than any of the 'true' clays so far discussed, albeit soils which are leached and only moderately fertile. This once again was essentially an area of 'ancient countryside', with numerous isolated farms and small hamlets, winding lanes, and ancient hedges. But it was, at the start of the period studied here, a mainly arable region and areas of open fields (of 'irregular' form) often survived where the valleys cutting through to the underlying chalk were most extensive.

The districts under discussion were thus very varied in character at the end of the seventeenth century. But all displayed at least one of the following characteristics: heavy clay soils, a landscape densely treed and hedged, and a preponderance of pasture over tillage. By the middle of the nineteenth century they had been transformed by a revolution in farming. Where cereal farming had already been of importance yields had been increased and the land was cultivated more efficiently. Where—more usually—pasture had dominated, arable had now expanded, often to an astonishing extent. Even the tenacious Wealden clays were, by the end of the eighteenth century, coming under the plough. As Marshall, writing of the Sussex Weald in 1798, put it: 'Excepting the commons and some narrow strips of brookland there is scarcely an acre of natural herbage or old grassland in a township' (Marshall 1798, II, 126). We must now examine how this revolution in farming was

achieved, and the nature of its effects upon the landscape.

The Clayland Revolution: Changing the Soil

Across most of the south and east of England the main problem facing arable farmers was not a shortage of soil nutrients—nitrogen and phosphates were not rapidly leached away as they were on the poor 'hungry' lands of down, wold and heath—but seasonal waterlogging. This was 'cold' land: fields which lie wet for much of the winter do not warm up so rapidly in the spring as those on drier soils; implements cannot be got on to them so quickly; and, more importantly, germination and therefore plant growth are delayed. In addition, waterlogged crops do not take up nutrients well, and their root structure is poorly developed. The removal of stagnant surface water allows root systems to develop to a greater depth (D.H. Robinson 1949, 36–7). Drainage also helps soil structure: the pore space within the soil is increased, and aeration improved. Paradoxically, this increases the amount of water which can be taken up by the plant because the roots can derive moisture from a greater depth (D.H. Robinson 1949, 37). Contemporaries would not have known or understood all the reasons why waterlogging adversely affected the growth of cereal crops, but they could see clearly enough that it did.

Not only did improved drainage benefit cereal crops directly. It was also a necessary precondition for the successful adoption of the new rotations, for turnips are particularly susceptible to waterlogging, while the tightly packed nature of seasonally waterlogged clay soils makes it difficult to 'pull' the crop, so that it has to be fed off in the field. Yet this in turn can increase problems with structure and drainage, for large numbers of animals (especially if closely folded) serve to compact clay soil (Cook 1999). For all these reasons, the transformation of the eastern claylands into productive arable land was dependent on the adoption of effective modes of drainage.

Traditionally, arable farmers in clayland districts had drained their land in two ways. Where open fields persisted they used ridge and furrow, in the manner already described (above, p. 31). Where the fields were enclosed they relied on the deep ditches which, together with hedgebanks, surrounded and defined each field (Hall 1999, 38–9). Surface drainage was sometimes assisted by a particular mode of ploughing, in narrow impermanent ridges which were ploughed out and replaced by new ridges, in different places, every year or every few years (Williamson 1999, 41–2). This was a practice known as 'stitching' or 'stetching' and was, according to William Folkingham in 1610, a particular feature of East Anglia and Hertfordshire (Folkingham 1610, 48).

The crucial development in the course of the eighteenth century was the widespread adoption of *underdrainage*: that is, the practice of cutting drains beneath the surface of the soil which removed water first downwards, beyond the root zone, and then laterally, away from the field. Although described by Kent in 1793 as 'the most effectual way of draining ploughed ground' (Kent 1793, 23), the importance of underdrainage before the middle decades of the nineteenth century has been consistently underestimated by historians. Typical is the assertion of Chambers and Mingay that 'The problem of heavy land drainage remained unsolved until the introduction of cheap tile drainage in the 1840s, leaving the high-cost and inefficient farming of heavy claylands as the most obvious weakness in the progress of

eighteenth century farming' (Chambers and Mingay 1966, 65; Sheil 1991, 53). In fact, underdraining was employed on some scale before *c*.1840 and was of considerable importance both in raising yields and in expanding the area under cultivation on the heavy soils of southern and eastern England.

Before the adoption of earthenware tiles and pipes in the nineteenth century drainage was usually carried out using 'bush' drains. As their name implies, these were trenches cut across fields which were filled with brushwood and/or various other materials, capped with straw or furze, and then backfilled with soil (Figure 17). The drains either emptied directly into the ditches surrounding the field, or into a larger underground drain which did so. Field drains of this kind would commonly last between ten and fifteen years, although they could survive for longer: Arthur Young in 1804 reported some at Redenhall in Norfolk which were still serviceable after 27 years (Young 1804a, 392).

Although faggots cut from woods or pollards, or trimmings from hedges, were the usual 'fill' employed by drainers, other materials were sporadically employed. In Kent in the early nineteenth century it was reported that 'Some lay flints or stones at the bottom, others green brushwood; and some make the trench with shoulders towards the bottom, and lay thereon a tuft of grass, with the grass-side downwards, thereby leaving an entire cavity for the passage of the water' (Boys 1813, 152). Historians often imply that bush drainage was primitive and ineffectual compared with pipe drainage (Harvey 1980, 72). But eighteenth-century agricultural writers understood well the techniques of underdraining, especially the need to align the drains carefully with regard to the natural slope of the ground; and while earthenware drains lasted longer there is no real evidence that they were any more efficient. In the middle of the nineteenth century some prominent agriculturalists could still recommend the old method in preference to the new (Evans 1845). This was partly on grounds of cost, but it was also argued that tile drains would become clogged with soil, and that the process of renewing bush drains every fifteen years or so, and the breaking up of the soil which this entailed, helped the water to descend more rapidly after rain (Raynbird and Raynbird 1849, 116). Either way, because they usually only lasted for the duration of a lease the installation of bush drains was seen as the tenant's business rather than the estate's responsibility. As such the practice is seldom referred to in lease agreements. This is one of the reasons why most historians have failed to note the key importance of this improvement in the eighteenth and early nineteenth centuries.

So far as the evidence goes, the idea of laying single drains, or small groups of drains, to improve particularly damp areas of ground had been known since at least the early seventeenth century. In contrast, the practice of 'thorough' drainage—filling a clay field with a dense network of drains—seems only to have developed in the eighteenth

Figure 17   Men digging bush drains on a Norfolk farm in the 1890s, from Haggard, 1899

century. Most agricultural writers believed that it was first employed in Essex at the start of the century—hence its alternative name, the 'Essex method' (Evans 1845). Bradley in 1727 described the practice as 'but a late invention' on the claylands of north Essex (Bradley 1727), while in 1728 Henry Salmon described how the 'cold and wet lands' of Hertfordshire—the clay soils which occupy much of the south and east of the county—had been 'greatly improved' by the use of underdrains, an innovation which had been introduced 'within twenty years' from the neighbouring parts of Essex (Salmon 1728, 1; Bradley 1727, 23).

The subsequent diffusion of the technique was gradual. In 1845 Henry Evans was informed that it had been in use 'for a century and a half' in East Anglia, but estate surveys present a different picture. One describing the farms of the Hobart estate in Wymondham in south Norfolk typically commented that the tenants 'like all others in the woodland or dairy part of Norfolk are slovenly and don't endeavour to drain their land in a husbandlike manner—heavy strong land, but could be improved' (NRO, MC 3/59/252 468 X 4). The 1780s and 1790s, however, saw the rapid spread of the practice throughout the East Anglian boulder clays. One of the contributors to the Raynbirds' *Suffolk Agriculture* of 1849 reported:

> The statement of old farmers, who allege that sixty or seventy years ago the practice was just being introduced into the parish in which they had been brought up, and that previous to that time the system of *thorough* drainage by placing drains at regular and close intervals throughout a whole field was not practised, but merely drains put in here and there to carry water from a particular wet spot (Raynbird and Raynbird 1849, 112).

Various farming journals and diaries confirm that underdrainage was being carried out on a large scale by the last decades of the century. Randall Burroughes, that energetic improver on the Norfolk clays near Wymondham, was draining around 25 acres of his large (*c*.300 acre) farm each year in the 1790s. His drains were generally spaced at intervals of 12 yards (*c*.12 metres) and dug to a depth of 24 or 26 inches (*c*.0.6 metres). They fed into main drains dug to a depth of 28 inches (Wade Martins and Williamson 1995, 27). These dimensions were typical—similar, for example, to those quoted by Arthur Young in his *General Views* of Norfolk and Suffolk (Young 1804a, 389–93; Young 1795, 172–3). Burroughes described drainage as 'an expensive improvement', and careful analysis of his journal suggests that it cost around £2 per acre—more or less the figure suggested by Phillip Pusey in his remarks following Henry Evans's article 'Norfolk Draining' in the *Journal of the Royal Agricultural Society* for 1845 (Wade Martins and Williamson 1995, 27–8; Evans 1845).

By the early years of the nineteenth century underdrainage was becoming standard practice on the boulder clays of Hertfordshire, Essex and East Anglia. Vancouver in 1813 believed that there was no district in Essex in which it was 'not well-understood and practised'; while Young, writing of Suffolk in the following year, simply remarked that 'This most excellent practice is general on all the wet lands of the county; it is too well known to need a particular description' (Vancouver 1813b; Young 1804a, 392; Young 1795, 172–3). The Tithe Files of the late 1830s refer to the practice on a number of occasions, that for the north Suffolk parishes of South Elmham All Saints and St Nicholas, for example, commenting on how 'There is a great spirit of improvement pervading this part of the county and that by means of underdraining which is now in very general practice the produce of these heavy lands will be very much increased' (PRO, IR 18 9736).

By the 1840s one of the contributors to the Raynbirds' survey of Suffolk agriculture went so far as to assert that 'At the present time nearly every piece of land in the heavy land district of this county has been drained, and many pieces several times' (Raynbird and Raynbird 1849, 115). By this time, such was the importance of drainage that the need for capping materials could have important knock-on effects upon other aspects of farming practice. Thus the agent for the Ashburnham estate in Suffolk described in his survey of 1830 how the wheat stubble was 'left standing in the fields of consider- able length having been reaped with a sickle in that manner' so that it could be used in the fill of drains. Interestingly, the Tithe File for Earsham in south Norfolk noted with approval that the farmers there used furze and ling for their drains, 'knowing too well the use of straw for manure to bury it in this shape' (ESRO, HB 4/2; PRO, IR 18 6336 5896).

By combining the various references to places where drainage was being practised in the Tithe Files, and in the various volumes of the *General Views*, we can obtain a very partial and rather crude impression of the distribution of drainage activity in England in the early nineteenth centuries (Figure 18). This confirms the more general observations of agricultural writers like Pusey, that it was essentially a practice of the boulder clay soils 'in the large and well-farmed counties of Essex, Suffolk and Norfolk, as well as in Hertfordshire' (Pusey 1845), but was also adopted in the boulder clay arable districts of Cambridgeshire and Bedfordshire. It seems to have spread, to some extent, onto the London clays of south Hertfordshire and

Essex, and into the Weald, although the extent of its adoption is less clear here and uptake may have been patchy. In 1813 John Boys claimed that it was practised in Kent on 'all land having a porous soil on the surface, and a retentive clay-soil a little below it' (Boys 1813, 151–2); and it has been claimed that by the 1830s 'the extension of drainage had occasioned the virtual disappearance of the traditional Wealden three-course of wheat, beans, fallow' (Kain 1986, 113). Nevertheless, James Caird as late as 1852 lamented the paucity of hollow drains in the Sussex Weald, and the overall impression is that until the Victorian period drainage had made rather less headway to the south of the Thames than to the north. In the late eighteenth century new sorts of drainage 'fill', more durable in character, were being devised. Horseshoe tiles, set upside down on a flat 'sole' tile, were increasingly used. But it was not until the 1840s, 1850s and 1860s, as we shall see, that the use of ceramic tiles and pipes became common in England.

Draining was the main way in which the character of the soil in the south and east was changed in the course of the agricultural revolution. But marling and liming were also important in certain districts. Marling was seldom practised on any scale on the boulder clays, even though these often overlay chalk marl at no great depth. These soils were, for the most part, at least moderately calcareous and were normally only marled when pastures were being broken up and brought into cultivation for the first time. The Raynbirds for example reported in 1849 that in Suffolk 'on heavy land it [marl] is used on freshly broken-up pasture land, and mixed with farmyard manure in the formation of compost heaps' (Raynbird and Raynbird 1849, 52). But, in contrast, on the 'wet, stiff soils' of the Weald, on the London clays of south Essex and south Hertfordshire, and on the clay-with-flints of the Chiltern dipslope, marling and 'chalking' were much more important. These soils were generally acidic and benefited greatly from applications of 'calcareous earths'. In Kent, according to Boys in 1813, chalk was used 'to great advantage . . . on some wet, stiff soils, having no calcareous earth: in quantity, from fifty to eighty cart-loads per acre. Its beneficial effects are said to last twenty years' (Boys 181,

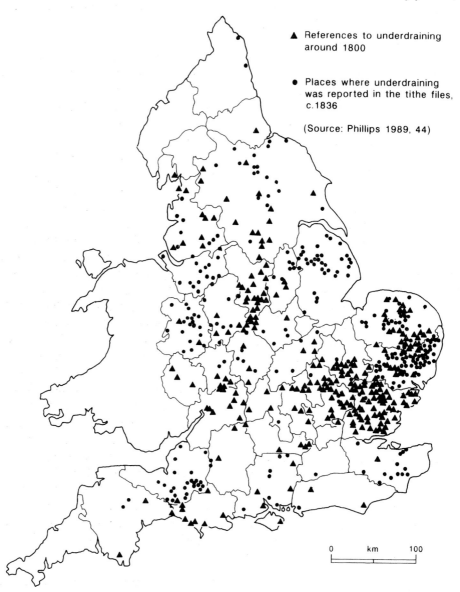

▲ References to underdraining around 1800

● Places where underdraining was reported in the tithe files, c.1836

(Source: Phillips 1989, 44)

Figure 18   The distribution of drainage activity in late eighteenth-century and early nineteenth-century England (after Phillips 1999, Figures 5.2 and 5.3)

pastoral husbandry. One typically noted that 'The county of Hertfordshire consists chiefly of Land in Tillage, and by clearing the Hedges of all kinds of Trees they admit of plowing to the utmost Bounds of their Land' (Lambert 1977, 748). Thomas Preston from Suffolk had firm views on the subject. He baldly stated that 'Much Timber and the Improvement of Arable Land are incompatible. Arable land in Suffolk is improved, and therefore timber is lessened' (Lambert 1977, 749). He responded with gusto to the request for 'any other Observations or Information on the Subject':

> Underwood, particularly Blackthorn Bushes, in Hedge Rows that spread Two or Three Rods wide, is the true nursery of Oak Timber, but such Rows are a dead Loss and Nuisance in a well cultivated Country. England possessed in the past Age a great Plenty of Oak. Why? Because Cultivation was in a barbarous State. It is the Improvement of the Kingdom . . . that has brought about the very good and proper Diminution of Oaks; and it is to be hoped that the Diminution will continue, for if it does not, the Improvement of our Soil will not advance (Lambert 1977, 776).

Although the removal of woods and hedges and the reduction of hedgerow trees were the main features of landscape change on these heavy soils, there were some additions. Where gentlemen's mansions existed—especially numerous on the clays around London—belts and plantations were often planted in (usually diminutive) parks, and small areas of woodland might be established on occasions elsewhere. And, as well as the hedges planted when commons were removed by parliamentary enclosure, others appeared where the large upland grazing grounds—a particular feature of the East Anglian clays, but sporadically found else-

where—were broken up into more manageable units. Nevertheless, such additions did little to compensate for the massive losses sustained. In 1801 one observer of the Essex countryside was able to declare: 'what immense quantities of timber have fallen before the axe and mattock to make way for corn' (Brown 1996, 34). The term 'ancient countryside' so often used by landscape historians for these areas should not blind us to the extent of the changes which have occurred within them in the relatively recent past. As Everitt noted of Kent, 'the whole period from 1750 to 1830 or 40 probably saw greater changes in the rural landscape than at any comparable time since the colonisation of the Weald' (Everitt 1976, 22).

The Practice of Clayland Farming

Removal and realignment of hedges, felling of trees, chalking and liming, and above all the installation of underdrains were in some areas accompanied by the adoption of the new crops and rotations of the 'light land revolution'. In the early seventeenth century most clayland farmers in the south and east of England, like their fellows in the Midlands, grew some combination of wheat, barley, beans and oats, usually fallowing their fields every third year—regular weed control was particularly necessary on these strong lands. A common rotation—practised, for example, at Finningham in Suffolk in the 1680s—was fallow, winter corn (wheat), barley; but elsewhere barley might follow the fallow, and oats or beans were often taken as the second or 'aftercrop' (ESRO HB 405/C2/1). In different districts rye and peas might be important, and documents such as tithe accounts also mention the cultivation, albeit in much smaller quantities, of buckwheat, tares, hemp and coleseed.

As in the regions already discussed, clover was the first of the new crops to be adopted on a wide scale, and by the 1680s it was frequently grown by farmers, often as long 'leys' of two, three or more years. Turnips were more gradually and sparingly cultivated, perhaps first on the East Anglian boulder clays. They are mentioned as a field crop as early as 1624 at Framlingham and Saxtead in Suffolk (ESRO JC 1/25/1) and by the 1680s they were widely established. At Cavendish in Suffolk 1683, for example, a note in the rector's tithe book stated that 'if any of the said fields or closes be at any time seeded or sown with turnip seed' then the tithe was to be assessed at 2 shillings per acre (WSRO FL 540/3/13). Two years later Nathaniel Bisbie, rector of the Suffolk parish of Long Melford, described in his memoranda book how many of his parishioners 'convert their arable . . . into Clover grass; and often sow their fallows with Turnips for the depasturing their sheep and cattle' (WSRO FL 509/3/15, 526). Nevertheless, farmers at this time were generally growing only small quantities of turnips—in the 1680s and 1690s at Walsham le Willows in Suffolk most seem to have had between 3 and 7 acres on farms of 50 acres or more (WSRO FL 646/3/6–13)—and they were probably regarded as a useful source of fodder by men whose livelihoods depended more on their herds than their ploughs. Turnips were also cultivated from an early date on the clay-with-flints soils of the Chiltern dipslope in west Hertfordshire and south Buckinghamshire, an area in which arable and pastoral pursuits were more evenly balanced. William Ellis, writing in 1736, believed that they were being grown here as early as the 1690s, and there are numerous references to both clover and turnips in probate inventories from the decades either side of 1700 (Richardson 1984, 254–5).

During the first half of the eighteenth century the new crops were grown on an increasing scale, and rotations tended to become more regular. At Shotesham in south Norfolk remarkably detailed tithe documents show how the practice of clayland farming developed in the course of the eighteenth century (NRO FEL 480 553). Turnips were already widely cultivated on the lighter loams of the parish by the late 1720s—Edward Ollyets's farm, for example, had an average of 19 per cent of its cropped acreage under the crop—although where the soils were particularly heavy the older forms of rotation persisted. Overall, bare fallows were already comparatively rare, accounting for only around 12 per cent of the arable acreage. Some farmers in the parish grew vast quantities of turnips, taking two or even three crops successively: they seem to have been involved in intensive bullock-fattening. They also grew large amounts of barley— around a third of the cropped area was devoted to the crop, much of which was also probably being used as cattle feed—together with small amounts of oats, beans, peas, buckwheat, vetches, rye, coleseed and hemp. Rotations were generally highly irregular, by later standards, and clover was often used to lay land down for several years. As the years passed the pattern of farming gradually changed in the parish. Long clover leys were replaced by single courses and the frequency of bare fallows declined. By the late 1740s year-long 'summerleys' accounted for only c.4 per cent of the arable area, turnips now accounted for c.16 per cent of the cropped area, more wheat was grown and rotations had become much more regular. Although on some of the smaller holdings, in particular, courses of cropping remained chaotic, by the 1750s most farmers had abandoned the practice of growing successive crops of barley or turnips, and more and more were following some form of 'improved' rotation, mainly wheat > barley > turnips > barley > clover, with variations including the substitution of oats for wheat or peas for clover (NRO FEL 480 553).

Other parishes on the East Anglian boulder clays were embracing the new crops with equal enthusiasm in the middle decades of the eighteenth century. At Kirstead and Langhale in south Norfolk in 1742 turnips made up 16 per cent of the crops on the Hall Farm and clover another 16 per cent, while six years later, on 'Mr Rayners Farm' in the same parish, 21.5 per cent of the cropped acreage was under turnips and 18.3 per cent under clover (NRO PD 300/14). By 1783 at Mattishall in Norfolk the rector estimated that farmers grew the following proportions of crops: 22 per cent turnips; 30 per cent barley and oats; 26 per cent clover, nonsuch or peas; and 22 per cent wheat. Analysis of the tithe accounts for the parish suggests that various forms of 'improved' rotation were employed in more than 80 per cent of the fields (Gonville and Caius College archives, Cambridge).

Nevertheless, the spread of the new rotations on the boulder clays was by no means uniform. On a farm at Earl Stonham in Suffolk 10 of the 26 fields (46.5 out of 126 acres) between 1788 and 1792 had rotations featuring bare fallows and no turnips (ESRO HD 305/1); while at Hill Farm, Rushmere, 25 per cent (6 out of 24) fields were still being regularly fallowed in the period 1806–9 (ESRO HA 2/A2/1/23). Elsewhere turnips were shunned altogether, as on a farm in Dallinghoo—of 42 acres in 7 fields—during the same period (ESRO GB1/13c/1). Things had changed little in this parish half a century later, to judge from a cropping account for a different farm, running from 1808 to 1813: year-long fallows were recorded 15 times in the 18 fields covered by

the account, and turnips were completely absent (ESRO HB 10/427/437). No turnips were grown on any of 7 farms at Henley, Suffolk, during 1787 and 1788; nor on the Home Farm at Hasketon, 74 acres of arable land, in the years 1797, 1798 and 1801 (ESRO HA 93/3/235; ESRO HA 24 50/19/3.26); nor in the fields described in a cropping account for a farm at Wetherden, running from 1797 to as late as 1842 (ESRO HA 87 C2/2; C1/1/5). Instead the fields were fallowed every fifth year, with courses of clover sometimes (although not always) interspersed with wheat, barley and oats.

All these farms were located on the heaviest boulder clay soils, those of the Beccles Association. As Young emphasised in 1794, the stronger clay loams of Suffolk were 'Much too wet for turnips, though some are found on it' (Young 1795, 48). Although bush drains could go some way to ameliorate this problem, where the plateau clays were most level drainage by this method was never very effective. Even in the late 1830s, to judge from the Tithe Files, turnips were principally grown in the more dissected areas. As many as 10 per cent of the parishes in Suffolk, mainly located on the more level and intractable clay soils, grew none at all, and bare fallowing was still widely practised.

Further to the west, in Hertfordshire, the situation was the same. Arthur Young believed (correctly) that turnips had been cultivated 'very early . . . as a general article of husbandry . . . before they were commonly introduced in Norfolk'. Yet while they were widely grown on the Chiltern dipslope, and in the more dissected parts of the boulder clay plateau which covers the eastern half of the county, they remained rare on the 'clays and strong loams' around Sawbridgeworth near the border with Essex, and in the south, on the London clays towards Middlesex (Young 1804b). They were still rare in the latter region in the 1830s, to judge from the Tithe Files, and bare fallows were frequent, although in the east they were now more widely planted, presumably because of the spread of underdrainage. Nevertheless here, as in several other boulder clay districts in the 1830s, less than 10 per cent and in many cases less than 5 per cent of the arable acreage was sown with the crop. To the south of the Thames, in Kent, Sussex and Surrey, the story was similar. Where the soils were more sandy, especially on the Hastings Beds of the Low Weald, turnips were sporadically grown, even in the early eighteenth century. But for the most part, while clover and other 'artificial grasses' were commonly cultivated, turnips remained rare even in the 1830s, and bare fallows widespread (Kain 1986, 102, 103, 166). While turnips were widely cultivated on the arable claylands of the south and east, in other words, they never really constituted a key feature of husbandry here during the agricultural revolution period.

The Clayland Revolution: The Achievement

By the start of Victoria's reign the open fields of west Cambridgeshire, Bedfordshire and Huntingdonshire had disappeared and most of the commons and heaths of the south-east had been enclosed; many hundreds of kilometres of hedgerow in the Home Counties and East Anglia had been removed or realigned; thousands of hedgerow trees had been felled; and an unknown, but very extensive, area of land had been drained and marled. Above all, vast areas of ancient pasture had fallen to the plough. On the boulder clays of Hertfordshire, Essex, Norfolk and Suffolk, more than two-thirds, and in some places more than three-quarters, of the land area was now given over to crops. Much of the London clay remained under pasture,

it is true, supplying the capital with hay and used for finishing livestock for the markets of the metropolis (Longman 1977, I,16). Indeed, the extent of grass may even have increased here in the course of the eighteenth century. But on the Wealden clays the extent of tillage was often considerable, far in excess of anything seen before or since. The end of the Napoleonic Wars saw some contraction in the area under the plough, but writers like William Cobbett nevertheless describe the Weald in the 1820s and 1830s as a mixed farming district, its landscape dominated by ploughland: 'The corn here consists chiefly of *wheat* and *oats*. There are some bean-fields, and some few fields of peas; but very little barley along here. The corn is very good all along the Weald . . .' (Cobbett 1830, 115). Extensive areas were in tilth when the tithe maps were surveyed in the late 1830s. On the sandier soils of the Hastings Beds, the proportion of arable was well in excess of pasture, while most of the stiff Weald clays were also predominantly arable. Only in some districts, to the west of the River Ouse, were grass and tillage more evenly balanced (Briault 1942, 83–4).

In addition to this phenomenal extension of the arable acreage, output was enhanced by some improvements in yields, although not to the same extent everywhere. Yields in the Weald remained fairly low—even in the 1830s, if we can believe the information in the Tithe Files, most parishes averaged around 20 bushels of wheat per acre, meagre by any standards, although higher (to judge from the descriptions of a 'normal' crop made by respondents to the 1801 Crop Returns) than the 16–18 bushels per acre generally achieved at the turn of the century (Turner 1982a, II). On the fertile boulder clays of East Anglia and Essex, in contrast, yields for wheat increased from around 20 bushels an acre in the 1750s to around 26 in the 1830s, those for barley from perhaps 24 to 38: rises significant enough to have made for an increase in output, even allowing for the fact that the widespread cultivation of clover, and in some districts of turnips, often meant less intensive courses of cereal cropping (Wade Martins and Williamson 1999a, 158–62).

The usual explanation for improvements in yields—that they resulted from higher stocking densities, achieved through the cultivation of the new fodder crops—does not really seem to apply in these districts. In many places turnips were only sparingly adopted and in few of these districts can the ratio of livestock to cropped acres have increased to any significant extent in the late eighteenth and early nineteenth centuries. The cultivation of clover and (to a lesser extent) turnips can hardly have compensated for the phenomenal reduction in the area of pasture, and such evidence as there is suggests, once again, that they did little more than maintain existing stocking densities (and thus manure inputs) in an increasingly arable landscape. Tithe records for Stansfield in Suffolk, for example, dating from *c.*1760 and *c.*1808, suggest if anything a *fall* in the ratio of livestock to sown acres (WSRO FL 627/3/18; WSRO FL 627/3/19; Wade Martins and Williamson 1999a, 172–3).

Of much more importance were the wider changes to the farming environment already described: the onslaught on outgrown hedges and pollards, underdrainage, and liming or marling. Different techniques were evidently important in different areas. On the boulder clays of east Hertfordshire, Essex, Suffolk and Norfolk, and perhaps in the Midland arable areas, underdrainage was the most important improvement. 'Draining has been effected at enormous outlay', wrote Glyde of the East Anglian claylands in 1856, 'but from the great increase in production, no one questions the propriety of the expenditure' (Glyde 1856, 338). He believed that this improvement

alone was responsible for increasing wheat yields on the Suffolk clays by around a third in the period between 1770 and 1850. According to Caird, 'The chief characteristic of Suffolk agriculture is the success with which heavy land farming is carried on . . . Drainage is of course the primary improvement on this description of land' (Caird 1852, 152). And it was not just agricultural writers who voiced such a view. The rector of Stansfield in Suffolk in 1808, for example, commenting on the local farming population, remarked favourably of one young man that he had 'at great expense' installed land drains on his farm, 'which is the most effective method in this country to get good crops' (ESRO FL 627/3/21). The improvement was a particularly attractive one because, although the cost was high, the benefits were almost immediately apparent. As the agent for the Ashburnham estate in Suffolk asserted in 1830, those who undertook to underdrain their land were 'reimbursed by the first crop' (ESRO HB4/2).

As we have seen, the East Anglian boulder clays were not significantly deficient in lime and so marling was not an improvement of any great importance here, although common practice when pastures were first being broken up. Thinning or removal of hedges, and the felling of pollards, however, must have contributed significantly to enhanced yields. While a muted affair when compared with the appalling 'prairification' of the eastern counties which occurred in the 1960s, 1970s and 1980s, the nature of the benefits would have been similar, reducing the effects of overshadowing and nutrient loss, and also perhaps bringing improvements in vermin and weed control. In 1750 it was thought that marling and cutting down trees would together raise the rental value of Flixton Park Farm in Suffolk from £156 to £200 (ESRO HA 12/E1/5/86).

On the Wealden clays and sands, and on the London clays and associated Tertiary deposits, similarly, the more meagre improvements in yields can have been only partly the consequence of the new rotations. Clover was widely cultivated but turnips were hard to grow on these stiff soils. Underdrainage seems to have been widely adopted, although probably on a limited scale before the 1840s, and simplification of the bosky landscape and, in particular, the large applications of chalk and lime must have been the main improvements on these acid soils.

As a result of expanding the cultivated acreage, and of raising yields per acre, production of grain in these southern and eastern districts may have doubled between *c*.1750 and 1830. Yet it is important to emphasise that this achievement was largely the work of relatively small farmers. Some polarisation in landownership and some increases in farm size occurred in these districts (Wade Martins and Williamson 1999a, 79–80), but they never came to be dominated by large unitary estates to the same extent as light land regions. Farms were generally much smaller, and 'closed' villages were rare. Moreover, estate owners, large or small, seem to have made relatively little contribution to the expansion of production in these districts, at least in the period before *c*.1830. Indeed, the evidence suggests that investment levels were generally low, in part because there was little difficulty in finding tenants for small farms on what were, for the most part, relatively fertile soils with reasonable access to the London market. Moreover, many proprietors owned fairly small acreages, were absentees, or both. As a result, farmhouses survived here *en masse* from an earlier age of yeoman prosperity—these districts still boast the highest density of late medieval and early modern vernacular houses in England. So too did farm buildings which

were sometimes, rather unusually, erected by the tenants themselves. James Caird thus described in 1852 how on the clay soils of Essex 'The farm buildings are usually of wood and thatch, old, and in warm weather as dry as tinder . . . the common practice in the county is for the proprietor to give the wood, very frequently grown at his tenant's cost, and for the farmer to erect the buildings and provide the thatch at his own expense' (Caird 1852, 135). Even where more normal practice was followed and landowners took full responsibility for houses and buildings, they often neglected their duties, and estate surveys from the mid nineteenth century frequently paint a picture of decay. That made for the Ashburnham estate in Suffolk in 1830 typically described the buildings as generally of a 'very inferior description, mostly being very old and having been neglected for a great many years, there are now considerable repairs wanting' (ESRO HB 4/2). Clayland farmers often improvised cattle yards and provided makeshift shelters in lean-tos erected against the adjacent barn (Wade Martins and Williamson 1999a, 123–4). The investment necessary for the most important improvements—underdrainage, marling and liming, and the removal of excess trees and hedges—seems almost invariably to have come from the tenants, rather than the owners. The agricultural revolution in the south-east was very much a *farmers'* revolution. As one commentator, writing in the 1840s about the changes on the Suffolk clays, noted: 'I cannot but look with surprise at the altered state of the country when I pass through and consider the enormous amount of labour which has been expended *by the tenantry* in clearing, draining and breaking up pastures etc.' (Raynbird and Raynbird 1849, 127). The Raynbirds' correspondent italicised the words *the tenantry*. An equally important emphasis, however, could be placed on the words *enormous amount of labour.* The clayland revolution, perhaps even more than the classic revolution of the light lands of England, was highly labour-intensive and, once again, made very little use of machines.

Ploughing the Fens

The intensification of arable production on the claylands of the Home Counties and East Anglia was remarkable. But more dramatic still were the changes taking place in the Fens of Lincolnshire, Cambridgeshire, Suffolk and Norfolk. This region hardly figures in most accounts of the agricultural revolution, in part because of a widely shared misconception about the history of fenland reclamation. Many people assume that the Fens were an under-exploited quagmire before the mid-seventeenth century, and that they were then successfully reclaimed. As a result of the General Drainage Act of 1600 it was possible for large landowners to overrule local proprietors and suppress any common rights which obstructed the path of drainage schemes, and to reward independent financiers of such schemes with a share of the reclaimed land. Earlier drainage attempts had been made, but these were limited in scope compared with what was now undertaken. A group of wealthy businessmen, in association with the Earl of Bedford, employed the Dutch engineer Vermuyden to formulate a comprehensive scheme for fen drainage (Darby 1983; Taylor 1973, 188–205; Taylor 1999, 146–9). The idea was to speed up the flow of the principal watercourses draining across the fens, by scouring their outfalls, straightening their courses, and embanking them to prevent inundation of the surrounding land during times of spate. The most dramatic achievement was the construction of the Old and New Bedford Rivers, running ruler-

straight for some 3.4 kilometres from Earith in Huntingdonshire to Denver in Norfolk (Figure 21). The project, begun in 1631, was completed by 1652, although it met with considerable local opposition from commoners who feared the destruction of their traditional way of life. The fens were divided, and the 'adventurers' (investors) and 'undertakers' (contractors) rewarded, as agreed, with allotments of fen land (Taylor 1999, 147). Similar schemes were undertaken further north in the Lincolnshire Fens. Dutch engineers were engaged by the Earl of Lindsey and his associates to drain parts of the Lindsey and Lower Witham Fens. The North Holland Fens, to the north-east of Spalding, were drained in the 1630s: the main feature of this scheme was the construction of the 38-kilometre long South Forty Foot Drain (Taylor 1999, 142). Attempts were made to drain Deeping Fen, north-west of Crowland, from the 1630s, but little real progress was made until 1666, when an act of parliament allowed the Earl of Manchester and a consortium of landowners to drain the area (Taylor 2000, 12).

As a consequence of all this activity, according to Overton, 'The fenland, which in the early seventeenth century had supported an economy based on fishing and fowling, had, by the second half of the eighteenth century, become some of the most fertile arable land in the country' (Overton 1996a, 90). According to such a chronology, the draining of the fens was essentially a phenomenon of the period before that under consideration here, and indeed fen drainage formed a major plank of Eric Kerridge's agricultural revolution of the seventeenth century. But in reality the landscape and economy of this extensive region did change dramatically in the eighteenth and nineteenth centuries: for the account presented above is misleading in a number of ways.

Figure 21   The Old Bedford and New Bedford Rivers: Vermuyden's great drains run relentlessly across the Cambridgeshire Fens. The surrounding fields, defined by drainage dykes, are of varying ages.

Firstly, it is important to emphasise that much of the area that we call 'The Fens' had, in fact, been drained and settled since early medieval times. Fenland was, and is, two distinct regions. The *peat fens*, which extend over an area of some 1,700 square kilometres, comprise those areas furthest from the North Sea and consist of deposits of peat, overlying silts and marine clays. Until the seventeenth century this was indeed a vast damp common, exploited by communities living on its margins (or on islands of older rock within it). Grazing occurred for some of the year but large areas were principally mown for hay or litter, or cut for thatching materials (Darby 1940). Some sections were also cut for peat, while the reserves of fish and wildfowl were systematically exploited. The area was not a wilderness, in any meaningful sense of the word—thousands of years of intensive exploitation had fundamentally altered its ecology—but it was almost unbelievably rich in wildlife: 'the local population unwittingly sustained and managed the Fens in what would be regarded today as a large nature reserve' (Newbold 1999, 211). The peat fens were the principal target of the improvers: hence the name now generally given to the largest of the drained areas, the Bedford Level, which extends across a vast tract of Cambridgeshire, into adjacent counties.

The northern and eastern *silt fens*, or Marshland, occupy around 1,500 square kilometres in Lincolnshire and Norfolk and have a very different history. Much of this was higher, firmer ground, on the drier parts of which settlements had been established in Saxon times. Subsequently, expansion occurred inland, onto the lower silt ground, with the new fields being protected by 'walls' or banks. The oldest fields, concentrated around the principal villages, were of irregular shape, but later ones took the form of long strips, seldom more than 20 metres in width

yet in some cases as much as 2 kilometres in length (Silvester 1988 and 1999). Only limited rights of common grazing, and few communal controls, existed over this land in the Middle Ages. Some of it was pasture, but most was under arable cultivation (Silvester 1988, 164–5). In post-medieval times, in contrast, the relative extent of grazing and arable fluctuated in accordance with market conditions, but grassland generally predominated. Certainly, at the start of the period studied here the majority of the area seems to have been under pasture. Thomas Cox in 1700 thought that the farms of the district 'turn to more Profit by Grazing than Ploughing', and tithe books, like those for the Norfolk parishes of North Runcton and West Winch dating to 1713, suggest that virtually all the silt soils were under grass (Darby 1983, 138; NRO PD 332/20). This whole area was little affected by seventeenth-century drainage activity: it was already adequately drained.

The seventeenth-century reclamation of the peat fens was an impressive achievement and the great drains created by Vermuyden must rank as one of the greatest engineering feats of the seventeenth century. Nevertheless, these endeavours did *not* lead to the creation of a landscape of enclosed arable fields. This was partly because the reclaimed land was not all divided up into individual allotments. On the contrary: only around half the fen was actually *enclosed* at this time—those portions allotted to the undertakers and adventurers and to a few leading landowners, or divided into 'severals' by the agreement of the commoners. The majority remained as open common grazing, although now often allocated to specific parishes rather than shared between many and, as a result of Vermuyden's drainage works, less liable to serious inundation than before (Figure 22). Some areas lay entirely unre-

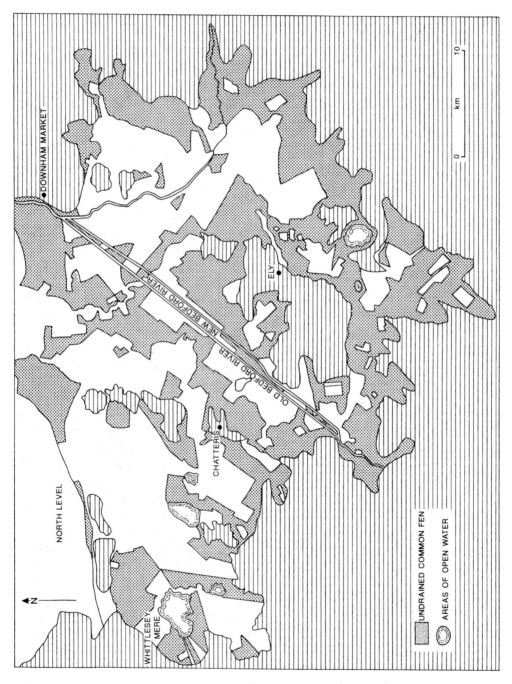

Figure 22 'As it is now drained.' The extent of unenclosed and undrained fen in the southern and middle levels of the Bedford Level, c.1700

rose from around 20 to around 30 bushels an acre (Pusey 1841, 406), although some farmers reported a doubling or even tripling of yields (*ibid.*, 407). The land was very intensively cropped, often with numerous courses of wheat interspersed with crops of oats, beans, coleseed, and roots.

The reclamation of the peat fens was thus a more protracted and complex process than is sometimes assumed, and as a consequence the landscape itself is more varied and intricate than appears at first sight, with numerous different blocks of dyked fields orientated in different directions (Taylor 1973, 196–205). Some represent enclosures of fen ground dating to before the great schemes of Vermuyden; others represent allotments given to adventurers, undertakers and wealthy landowners in the seventeenth century; most are portions of fen which were only enclosed and divided in the eighteenth and nineteenth centuries. Whatever their origins, almost all have farms within them, usually erected soon after enclosure, often many kilometres from the 'upland'. These usually occupy the long, low ridges called 'roddons'—silt and gravel beds of lost rivers, now standing proud of the shrinking peat (Taylor 1973, 204).

Although by the start of Victoria's reign a number of undrained areas still remained in the Fens, most of the area had been

Figure 24   Stretham Engine, Stretham, near Ely, Cambridgeshire. Built in 1831 and still retaining most of its original equipment, this is the best-preserved steam pump in the Fens

reclaimed, and much had been put to the plough; indeed, the Tithe Files of *c.*1836 suggest that around 55 per cent of both peat and silt soils were in tilth. It was a technological and an agricultural triumph, but an ecological disaster. Before drainage, vast areas of rich fen meadow had supported complex, diverse communities, dominated by such plants as blunt flowered rush (*Juncus subnodulosus*), marsh thistle (*Cirsium palustre*) and marsh orchid (*Gymnadenia densiflora*). There were extensive reed beds and sedge beds which were regularly cropped by the commoners. In damper areas, bog myrtle (*Myrica gale*) grew, interspersed with areas of *Sphagnum* moss, fringed by areas of heather and grass of parnassus (*Parnassia palustre*); while peat cuttings harboured a large number of wetland plants, including insectivorous butterworts (*Pinguicula sp.*) and, on the drier ridges between, yellow loosestrife (*Lysimachia vulgaris*) and marsh pea (*Latyrus palustris*). Sluggish rivers, pools and meres would have contained an even more diverse range of plant species. A similarly diverse range of fauna—terrestrial, amphibious and aquatic—occupied this range of rich habitats: the bird life alone included hobbies, sparrow hawks, red kites, coot, moorhen, bittern, water rail, spotted crake, corncrake, mallard, teal, redshank, godwit, lapwing and heron (Newbold 1999).

By 1840 this unbelievably rich environment had been largely replaced by improved pastures and arable fields; and the latter were expanding steadily at the expense of the former. Witnesses to a parliamentary commission in 1836 were unanimous in their belief that the area of ploughland had greatly expanded throughout the Fens over the previous decades, and that wheat rather than oats was now the main crop. Indeed, George Calthrop, a corn merchant from Spalding, believed in 1836 that the price of wheat in England was being adversely effected by the 'immense tracts of land brought into cultivation in the fens of Lincolnshire, Cambridgeshire and Norfolk' (BPP 1836 VIII, 1, 236).

The North-East

The ploughing of the Fens and the intensification of arable farming on the clays of East Anglia and the south-east was mirrored by an expansion of tillage in the north and east of England: in the long strip of lowland country running through the west of Lincolnshire, the Vale of York, and into the coastal plain of Durham and Northumberland. In the northern parts of this extensive area, open fields had largely disappeared by the start of the eighteenth century and the economy was dominated by a mixture of cattle-farming (rearing, fattening and dairying) and arable, often combined in forms of 'convertible husbandry' (Brassley 1984, 31–41; Butlin 1973). Further south—in the southern Vale of York—arable farming was more prominent and here many open fields survived until the parliamentary enclosure period, although many early-enclosed townships, laid largely to pasture, could be found on the heavier land. In 1799 Robert Brown believed that 'In the Vale of York, one-third of the ground is in tillage, and two-thirds in grass. This is the common proportion; but where there are extensive open-fields, and in some places where the soil is light, the proportion of tillage is larger and may amount to about one half' (Brown 1799, 101).

In the late eighteenth century, and the early nineteenth, the area of arable appears to have expanded throughout these north-eastern lowlands. In Northumberland the cropped acreage was said to be 'rather upon the increase' in 1805 (Bailey and Culley 1805, 121). In 1801, to judge from the Crop Returns, *c.*17 per cent of Durham and Northumberland were under arable crops; but by *c.*1836 the Tithe Files suggest that around 46 per cent of the former county and 54 per cent of the latter were in tilth. While this figure is certainly distorted by the over-representation in the Tithe Files of lowland areas (as opposed to the uplands of the Cheviots and Pennines, where comparatively little expansion of arable seems to have taken place), and while the former figure excludes fallow land and rotational grass, it is nevertheless clear that a major shift in land use had taken place in the first three decades of the nineteenth century (Turner 1981, 294; Kain 1986, 319, 331). Turnips were widely adopted on the lighter land, combined with wheat and barley, long clover leys and oats.

In this district much of the land lay in large estates, and landowners were more involved in agrarian change than in the clayland regions of the south (indeed, more of Northumberland was occupied by large estates than any other county of England except Rutland: Newton 1972, 118). In particular, many new farms were erected, ranged around cattle yards. Some were supplied with threshing machines, usually driven by horse gins set in circular or octagonal buildings called wheelhouses, although some were powered by steam and a few—like that at Chollerton Farm near Hexham in Northumberland—by windmill (Wade Martins 1995, 88). Wheelhouses are more common in the north-east than in any other part of England (Hellen 1972; Hutton 1976). Mechanical threshing was evidently much commoner here than in the south (where few farms were supplied with this kind of plant), probably because wages were generally higher in these more industrialised districts.

As in the south-east of England, expansion and intensification of arable farming were associated with the enclosure of the remaining open land, and with some simplification of the field pattern in places long enclosed, although this was here a less marked feature. Respondents to the government enquiry of 1792 noted that some hedge removal was taking place in Yorkshire, but that the practice was 'not much adopted' in Durham and Northumberland (Lambert 1977, 748). Nor does underdrainage seem to have been a particularly common practice in these districts before the 1830s. The most important improvement adopted was the large-scale application of lime—a long-established practice, but one which increased significantly in scale in this period. An examination of this topic, however, moves us away from the arable revolution of eastern England, and brings us to a broader consideration of the changes taking place in the north and west of the country.

CHAPTER 5

Moor and Vale

The North and West

The history of the English landscape is often written from a southern perspective, and the 'north and west' are often lumped together as a single region—one of high hills, high winds and heavy rainfall. In a volume as short as this it is difficult to do more than generalise about what are, in reality, the highly diverse landscapes which occupy the vast area lying to the north and west of the Midland Plain. But we can, at the very least, begin by differentiating two broad types of countryside.

In the west of England—from Lancashire and Cheshire, through southern Shropshire, central and eastern Herefordshire, south Staffordshire, north Wiltshire, and on into Somerset and Devon—lies a broad band of generally low-lying landscape (mostly below 250 metres OD) which, by the start of the eighteenth century, lay largely in enclosed fields. The pattern of settlement was, as it had been since at least the Middle Ages, characterised by scattered hamlets and farms as well as—in many areas, instead of—the nucleated villages which characterised the Midland Plain to the east. These are still today, for the most part, well-hedged, 'ancient countrysides' of winding lanes, thick hedges, and scattered farms and hamlets (Dyer 2000, 97–9; 117–21).

The soils of these western districts are often derived from heavy clays and this, combined with high levels of precipitation and a generally mild climate, ensured that most were characterised by pasture farming in the early modern period—by dairying, cattle-rearing and grazing (Mingay 1984, 129). There were, it is true, many exceptions to this general rule. The central Herefordshire Plain, with its deep rich soils and comparatively low summer rainfall (sheltered by the high Welsh uplands to the west), was an arable district, and corn fields were a prominent feature of the landscape in many parts of south Shropshire and south Staffordshire (Hey 1984, 129–31; Thirsk 1984, 172–7). Nevertheless, grass generally predominated over grain in these western lands, as it had done since late medieval times. Earlier in the Middle Ages, in contrast, arable had been more prominent. The archaeological evidence for this—in the form of ridge and furrow—was noted by Pitt in 1796, when he described how in most parts of Staffordshire there were 'Evident marks of a cultivation far more extended than any thing known in modern times' (Pitt 1796, 233). Indeed, in many of these vale lands open fields, albeit of 'irregular' form, had once been widespread (Roberts 1973; Dyer 2000, 108–9). These had largely disappeared by the start of the eighteenth century—mainly through gradual, piecemeal enclosure—but numerous areas of common grazing remained, ranging from small greens and commons to extensive low-lying heaths, moors and wetlands, like the great Levels in the area around Glastonbury in Somerset, or the 'mosses' of Cheshire, Lancashire and Shropshire.

To the north and west of these green low-lands lay the 'highland zone' proper, where the majority of the land lay above 300 metres OD. Although the different upland masses displayed a great deal of variation, they had much in common. Apart from obvious aspects of topography (these were all areas of elevated terrain) and climate (their height, combined with the location of most towards the western side of England, generally ensured high levels of precipitation), all were characterised by relatively thin, poor soils, infertile and acid because lime and other minerals were constantly being leached from them (Stamp 1950, 145–56; Coppock 1971, 41–4; Brassley 1984, 30–1). These factors (combined in more northerly areas with a short growing season) again ensured that livestock rather than arable husbandry formed the basis of the agrarian economy at the start of the period studied here. These were not primarily fattening but rearing districts: they were reservoirs which supplied young sheep and cattle to the farms of the adjacent lowlands, or to lands still further afield.

The uplands seldom form a continuous, uninterrupted mass. The higher land is generally dissected by vales of lower, more hospitable ground, often of considerable extent. In these, and on the lower margins of the main hill ranges, arable land had often been extensive in medieval times—as the remains of ridge and furrow, and strip lyn-chets, climbing high up the sides of the Yorkshire Dales vividly demonstrate. The fifteenth and sixteenth centuries had seen a steady reduction in the area under culti-vation, however, and by the seventeenth century most of this lower ground was under grass. In Wensleydale in Yorkshire, for example, inventories from the period 1670–1700 show that one in seven farmers in the lower dale grew some crops, but only one in twenty in the upper dale (Hey 1984, 69).

Oats and biggin (coarse barley) were the most important crops on the poorer land, although on the deeper soils of the major valleys these might be accompanied by wheat, rye and peas.

The most noticeable feature of the 'upland' landscapes—even more prominent at the start of the eighteenth century than today—were the moors. Arthur Young in 1773 com-mented: 'you may draw a line from the north point of Derbyshire to the extremity of Northumberland of 150 miles as the crow flies, which shall be entirely across waste-lands; the exceptions of small cultivated plots, very trifling' (Young 1773, 37). Moors took, and still take, a variety of forms, related in part to climate, in part to systems of management, and in part to the nature of the underlying soils and geology. Some are formed over podzols or brown earths, espec-ially those located on lower ground, on more dissected terrain, or towards the eastern side of the country. Such moors are dominated by heather—mainly ling (*Calluna vulgaris*) but sometimes bell heather (*Erica cinera*) or cross-leaved heather (*Erica tetralix*) (Bunce and Fowler 1989; Rackham 1986, 305–6; Stamp 1950, 145–56). Bilberry and bracken also widely occur, and various coarse grasses including *Nardus stricta*, locally out-com-peting the heather. Areas of poorly draining land can also be found, but these are more a feature of the higher, wetter moors, associ-ated with the main upland masses. These comprise broad, dissected plateaux with extensive areas of flat or gently sloping ground which, given the high levels of precipitation, often suffer from poor drainage (Coppock 1971, 34, 41–4). Here peat often develops: in permanently waterlogged con-ditions plant debris cannot decay in the normal way and accumulates *in situ*. Some-times the peat forms deposits only a few centimetres thick, but often it accumulates as blanket bog', many metres deep. Here, the heather is often out-competed by vigorous grasses, particularly cotton grass (*Eeriophorum ingustifolium*) and purple moor-grass (*Molinia caerulia*) (Rackham 1986, 305–6).

Most English moors were originally forested (Turner and Hodgson 1979). In some, principally those in the far north and extreme west, the hold of the 'wildwood' was always precarious, and the steady accumulation of peat would eventually have rendered the growth of trees more or less impossible. But in most cases the removal of trees by early farmers hastened waterlogging and peat formation on the higher, more level ground, and podzolisation in less elevated terrain. Much of this land was quite intensively settled and farmed in remote prehistory. On Dartmoor, for example, the low tumbled walls of the large-scale organised field systems known as the reaves, and numerous 'hut circles' and other settlement remains, demonstrate that in the Bronze Age settlement and even tillage were once widespread (Fleming 1988). In this case abandonment occurred towards the end of the Bronze Age; elsewhere it came later, during the Iron Age or Roman periods. By the early Middle Ages the higher moors were generally exploited as summer grazing by farms located on lower ground, or by *vaccaries*—specialised grazing establishments owned by great lords or monastic houses.

In medieval times many of the upland moors had, in the technical and legal sense, been forests, mainly in private hands, and most still retained this status at the close of the seventeenth century. In the south-west, both Dartmoor and Exmoor were forests; and there were originally at least 39 named forests in the Pennines and the Lake District, including the Peak Forest in Derbyshire, Bowland in west Yorkshire, and Rossendale in Lancashire (Rackham 1986, 315–16). Here,

even in post-medieval times, notional fines might be levied for 'illicit' grazing, but land use was otherwise much the same as beyond the forest bounds.

Although moors of all kinds were regarded by agricultural writers of the eighteenth century as unproductive 'wastes', they were of course exploited, with varying degrees of intensity, by local communities. The lower moors, at least, would otherwise soon have reverted to woodland. They were mainly used for grazing but other resources were also exploited. Peat was dug for fuel, often creating marked lines or striations bearing a vegetation cover different from the surrounding land: peat digging was especially important where minerals were being smelted. Bracken was extensively cut for cattle bedding, floor covering and sometimes for thatch; heather and furze were gathered as fuel. The treeless character of the moorland terrain ensured that the latter had a much greater economic importance than modern historians might suspect. At Sithney in Cornwall, for example, it was reported as late as 1801 that 'Here are, it is almost literally true, no trees; consequently a considerable part of every estate is under furze, which would frequently, with proper cultivation, produce whatever the cultivated lands now produce' (Turner 1982a, I, 33–4). In areas where coarse grasses, and especially *Molinia*, predominated, moorland hay might be cut. This tussocky grass has the characteristic of shedding its leaves during winter, and making extremely rapid growth between May and early July—too rapid to be grazed effectively but providing a useful store of winter fodder which could be harvested before the hay in the meadows on the lower slopes was ready for cutting (Hanley 1949, 33–4). Molinia hay was particularly palatable to cattle (Hanley 1949, 33) and it was cattle, rather than sheep, that formed the mainstay of moorland economies at the start of the period studied here and constituted the basis of most farmers' wealth (Hey 1984, 69–70; 2000, 196–200). Reared on the poor pastures and tough moorland vegetation, they were sent to the adjoining lowlands—or, as we have seen, to more distant pastures in the Midlands or East Anglia—for fattening. Sheep were also kept—tough, 'rangy' breeds which could pick a living from the highest moors for much of the year.

It was not only regular grazing by livestock and the accumulated deposits of peat which kept the moors free of trees. In addition, many were subject to sporadic burning. Heather makes excellent food for sheep until it becomes woody and unpalatable with age. Fire clears away the old growth, and other less nutritious plants, but the heather itself is fire-resistant and fresh new growth soon appears (Bunce and Fowler 1989; Rackham 1986, 320–1). It is probable that this practice became more systematic and widespread in the course of the eighteenth century but it was a long-established one, to judge from a statute of 1607, which attempted to restrict it to the winter months (Rackham 1986, 321).

Rough, unimproved moorland gave way— sometimes gradually, sometimes sharply—to more tamed and managed land on the lower, sheltered ground, where deeper and more fertile soils could be found. The boundary between the two had fluctuated as demographic pressure rose and fell over the centuries, so that although today it generally lies at around 300 metres OD 'many local anomalies mask past successes and failures in land improvement' (Coppock 1971, 36). Usually this enclosed land formed discrete ribbons of lowland, separated by wide upland tracts—as in the case of the Yorkshire Dales. Sometimes, as on the Lizard Peninsula in Cornwall, moorland and farmland were interdigitated in complex ways.

The upper reaches and higher slopes of dales and valleys were dominated by poor-quality enclosed pastures, often characterised by rather coarse herbage, including bent grass (*Agrostis* sp.), unpalatable to stock and of low nutritional quality. They were often infested in damper places with rushes, sedges, and blue moor grass (*Sesleria calcaria*) (Hanley 1949, 32–3). Other fields were regularly cut for hay, usually those nearest the farmstead, and these often contained such unnutritious herbs as Yorkshire fog (*Holcus lanatus*) and yellow rattle (*Rhinanthus minor*). The settlement pattern in these remote places, close to the moorland edge comprised isolated farmsteads, mainly small cruck-framed buildings, many with only a single hearth (Hey 2000, 198–9). Even at the end of the seventeenth century some 'long houses', in which people and cattle were housed under the same roof, survived in use. Such isolated farms had complex origins. Many had first come into existence in medieval times, as population pressure forced farmers to colonise increasingly marginal land. Others originated as isolated vaccaries or cattle-ranches, or as seasonally occupied 'shielings' or summer grazing stations attached to settlements on lower ground. Some upland farms, however, only began life in the sixteenth or seventeenth century. Indeed, in some moorland districts, especially in parts of Northumberland and Durham, many were still appearing in the landscape at the start of the period studied here, as landowners in the period following the Restoration sought to maximise their incomes by converting customary tenures to leases, and dividing the high grazing grounds from the lowland settlements to which they had traditionally been connected. In the area around Housteads on Hadrian's Wall, for example, research by Robert Woodside and James Crow has suggested that 'Some shielings evolved into permanently settled farmsteads in the seventeenth century, and farms such as Shield-on-the-Wall and Steel Rigg may have begun life in such a way' (Woodside and Crow 1999, 66). But many were on new sites, unrelated to these earlier transhumance stations.

> The exact date for the establishment of these new farmsteads varies between regions and individual settlements. A decree of Charles II dated 1666 concerning tenements in the Manor of Henshaw mentions a Thomas Ridley of 'The Bogg', the original name of East Bog, and the first records for other farms in the region also date from the late seventeenth to early eighteenth century, eg Hotbank in 1698, High Shield in 1700 (Woodside and Crow 1999, 74).

In the lower reaches of the valleys hamlet settlements predominated. Even in the late seventeenth century small areas of open field could sometimes still be found here. And where the valleys were widest, and on the fringes of the uplands, the settlement pattern was characterised by nucleated villages, similar to those of the Midlands, which often contained well-built stone houses, the homes of prosperous yeomen and gentry. Here more extensive areas of arable open field had existed in the Middle Ages, although by the late seventeenth century these were normally in a state of advanced decay.

This book is concerned with agriculture and the rural landscape. But in many northern and western areas it becomes increasingly difficult to maintain such a focus in the course of the eighteenth century because of the impact of large-scale industrialisation. The uplands and their margins were particularly affected by the 'industrial revolution', for two reasons. The steep gradients of valleys provided the necessary conditions for the successful erection of mills and factories which, until well into the nineteenth century, were primarily powered by water; and the most important raw materials required by industry—minerals like iron, copper, lead, and coal—lay within the uplands, or around their margins. The term 'industrial revolution', like 'agricultural revolution', is somewhat contested in modern scholarship, and there has in particular been a tendency to emphasise the gradual nature of the 'revolution' and its early roots in a sixteenth- and seventeenth-century phase of 'proto-industrialisation'—large-scale industry without factories—in which farming was widely combined with cottage-based industrial or craft production (Frost 1981; Hey 1969; Hudson 1992, 111–15; Mendels 1972). Certainly, considerable expansion of output was achieved in many industries before the eighteenth century. National production of coal, for example, seems to have risen from around 21,000 tons in 1560 to nearly three million by 1700 (Nef 1932, 19–32). The descriptions made by contemporary writers show that large areas of the north and west already possessed distinctive industrial landscapes by the early eighteenth century. Approaching Halifax in West Yorkshire in the 1720s, for example, Daniel Defoe noted how houses were spread thickly even on the steeper slopes of the valleys. This was because of the importance of local industry:

> This business is the clothing trade, for the convenience of which the houses are thus scattered and spread upon the sides of the hills . . . even from the bottom to the top; the reason is this; such has been the bounty of nature in this otherwise frightful country, that two things essential to the business, as well as to the ease of the people are found here . . . I mean coals

and running water upon the tops of the highest hills (Defoe 1976 [1724], 492).

Nevertheless, the development of a truly industrial economy really took off from the 1770s, with the massive expansion of the cotton industry and the rapid growth in the production of coal and iron. Although not the subject of this study, the development of industrial landscapes in the north and west in the late eighteenth and nineteenth centuries—the spread of mines and mills, the proliferation of canals and improved turnpike roads, and the emergence of extensive conurbations on the margins of the main upland masses—had innumerable effects, direct and indirect, upon the practice of agriculture.

Draining and Liming

Water was the great enemy of the farmer in the north and west. It affected the yields of arable crops in ways already discussed for the east of England, although here, because of the higher levels of precipitation and lower transpiration rates, the problem was much more acute. But waterlogging also affected pasture land. Poorly drained grass was vulnerable to 'poaching' in the spring, and became infested with rushes, reeds and other rank vegetation. Where drainage was most impeded grass might be overwhelmed by the growth of unpalatable plants (Hanley 1949, 12). The extent of the problem varied greatly, of course, depending on local climatic conditions, topography, and soil type, but even in essentially lowland counties like Staffordshire, Shropshire and Cheshire between 40 per cent and 60 per cent of the land was seriously affected by impeded drainage (Phillips 1989, 36–9).

In some western districts forms of under-drainage seem to have been employed from

an early date. Plott recorded in 1686 how one Mr Astley of Tanhorn in Staffordshire had made drains consisting of trenches lined with pebbles, filled with faggots, and covered with soil (Kettle 1979, 70), although it is unclear whether these were used to relieve limited areas of particularly serious waterlogging, or to drain entire fields. William Marshall reported that in the area around Stotfold in Staffordshire a primitive form of under-draining—using three alder poles arranged to form a simple pipe—had been superseded in the 1750s by the more normal method, which had been learnt from 'soughers' working in the moorland areas of the east of the county (Marshall 1796b, I, 139–41; II, 220–8). 'Soughs' was the usual term in the uplands for underdrains, which were here filled with stones rather than brushwood. They were sometimes quite elaborate affairs, as in parts of Westmoreland, where at the end of the eighteenth century the drains were 'generally walled in the sides, and covered with large stones out of reach of the plough' (Pringle 1805, 322).

So far as the evidence goes, in the 1770s, 1780s and 1790s the amount of land being drained increased both in the lowland vales of the west—especially in Shropshire and Staffordshire—and also on the lower, less marginal moorlands of Staffordshire and Derbyshire, as these were enclosed and reclaimed. A little later the practice seems to have spread further north. Bailey and Culley described in 1805 how the improvement had 'been introduced of late years into the northern counties' (Bailey and Culley 1805, 238). They reported how it had 'lately made its way into Northumberland, and is now mostly practised in the middle and northern parts of the county; the theory is pretty well understood in those districts, and the practice is becoming more prevalent every year' (*ibid.*, 128). Cumberland, they believed, had 'not been behind its neighbours in adopting this beneficial measure' (*ibid.*, 238), while in Westmoreland drainage was 'daily gaining ground' (Pringle 1805, 322). As always, the enthusiasm of agricultural writers needs to be taken with a pinch of salt, but there is little doubt that drainage was indeed making some headway in these regions, at least among the more innovatory and wealthier farmers, in the early decades of the nineteenth century. More importantly, by this time the practice was becoming more common on the lower, more fertile lands of the west, where locally manufactured draining tiles were now sometimes used in preference to the traditional methods. In 1812, draining land on the Branston estate in Burton-upon-Trent was said to have raised its rental value by 10 shillings an acre. Two years later it was said that land there 'which for years would not suffer a hoof to go through it without sinking half a yard deep is now as sound in the most rainy weather as the turnpike road' (Currie 1979, 97). On the Trentham estate in Staffordshire, between 1812 and 1820, 136,000 yards of underground drains were laid (*ibid.*). Surface drains were also extensively used, especially in upland areas, where they were often spaced at intervals of 20 to 30 metres.

Nevertheless, it is important to emphasise that even in the 1830s land drainage had made much less headway in the north and west of England than it had in the arable areas of the south-east. The Tithe Files suggest that activity was concentrated in particular districts—such as south Derbyshire and south-east Staffordshire (Phillips 1999, 59, Figure 18). Of more importance in improving the quality of farmland in the north and west of England were marling and, in particular, liming (Collins 1978; Havinden 1974).

Soil acidity was a serious problem across much of the north and west. High levels of precipitation ensured rapid loss of lime, while poor drainage encouraged the formation of acid peat: most soils in the north and west were base-poor. In a number of places in the western lowlands various types of calcareous subsoil had long been excavated and spread on the fields, such as the black shelly marl which lies some 12 metres below the surface in the area around Radstock in Somerset (Gardner and Garner 1957, 32). But in many lowland areas material of this kind was unavailable, and it was entirely absent from upland districts. However, over extensive tracts of land—particularly in the Pennines and Cheviots—lime was potentially available in the form of limestone. This, unfortunately, could not be applied directly to the fields, as marl or chalk normally were in southern and eastern districts. The latter substances, already broken into manageable pieces by the process of excavation, would then be broken down still further by the action of the elements. Limestone in contrast is much harder and more resistant to weathering: it could not be applied in this way unless first ground to a very fine powder, something impossible on a commercial scale in this period. Instead, it had to be converted into lime, in purpose-built kilns (Gardner and Garner 1957; Williams 1989, 8–11). There was another crucial difference between liming on the one hand, and marling and chalking on the other. Because manufactured lime was much purer it was economical to transport it far from the place of production. Lime could thus become, in time, an almost universal panacea to the problems of soil acidity in northern and western areas.

The benefits of liming had long been appreciated, even if its precise effects were not fully understood. Fitzherbert alludes to agricultural liming as early as 1523; Norden mentions it as an important element in Shropshire agriculture in 1607; while in 1628 the manor of Campsall in Yorkshire was said to contain 'great store of lymestone an excellent compost beinge burned to manure cold grounds' (Havinden 1974, 111, 113; Mingay 1984, 81). In 1664 the farmers of Wharfedale and Airedale were able to describe to the Georgical Committee how they improved their lands with lime (Hey 1984, 68–9). But there is no doubt that liming became more important from the middle decades of the seventeenth century. Samuel Colepeace described it as an established practice in much of Devon in 1667, but it was not yet 'us'd in Cornewall, or westerne parts of Devonshire till of late, and that, by but a few' (Norden 1607, 227; Stanes 1964, 280). Havinden, who examined the Devon evidence in a pioneering study, suggested that the practice spread steadily throughout the south-western peninsula during the late seventeenth and early eighteenth centuries. The parochial enquiries carried out by Dean Milles in 1747–56 suggest that it was by then being practised in around 84 per cent of parishes in Devon (Havinden 1974, 115–17). Not only were local limestones— the Culm measures, and the Plymouth limestone—employed in production. Large quantities of rock were also imported into the county across the Bristol Channel from South Wales. Similarly, on the coastal plain of Northumberland liming was known by the 1670s but it increased steadily in popularity and by the 1720s, according to John Lawrence, it was common practice both there and in county Durham (Brassley 1984, 53).

The improvement of inland waterways allowed lime to be brought into areas where limestone was lacking, and thus provided a major stimulus to production. As David Hey has pointed out, quarrying of the Magnesian limestone in Yorkshire did not develop on a large scale until the rivers were made navigable in the later seventeenth and early eighteenth centuries; while the construction of the Aire and Calder Navigation (after 1699) and the Don Navigation (after 1727) greatly increased the use of the material in that county (Hey 1984, 83). Improvements in transport also allowed coal to be brought cheaply into areas where limestone was available, but not the fuel with which to burn it. In Westmoreland in 1805 it was reported that liming had 'not yet become general', owing to the fact that although limestone was in good supply, the coal necessary to fire the kilns was not, and had to be brought some distance—a situation which the writers hoped would soon be remedied by the construction of a canal to Kendall (Bailey and Culley 1805, 323).

Up until the middle decades of the eighteenth century much lime was produced in temporary sod kilns or clamps. One observer described their operation in 1760: 'They make here a small round pile of wood and place limestone around it, cover it with sods, set the wood on fire and supply fuel until it is sufficiently burnt and this commonly on the spot they want to manure' (Jobey 1966, 2). The lime was burnt for a week or so before being released by dismantling the structure. Yet even in the Middle Ages more robust stone-built lime kilns had existed, and these proliferated during the seventeenth and eighteenth centuries. Some were intermittently fired 'flare kilns', in which the burning fuel and the 'charge' of limestone were kept separate. But from the middle of the eighteenth century many 'draw kilns' were in operation, in which limestone and fuel (now usually coal) were fed into the kiln continuously, and burnt together. Many hundreds of field kilns of eighteenth-century date still survive, in ruined form, in the Yorkshire Dales, the Pennines, and the Cheviot Hills, normally associated with the pits from which the stone was dug. Most

which were largely formed over podzols or acid brown earths and in which waterlogging was mainly caused by the formation of thin iron pan at no considerable depth. On the other hand, there were the higher, more exposed uplands, where the soils were far less inviting (Curtis *et al.* 1976, 70–5). Some were shallow and stony; others were immature *rankers*, consisting of a thin layer of acid organic matter lying directly on base-poor rock. In some places, indeed, there was no soil at all, but only bare rock. The majority of the high plateaux, however, were covered in thick deposits of peat, often forming deep blanket bog.

Much land in the first category—the 'better' moors—had been reclaimed and improved in medieval times, and was subject to both piecemeal enclosure and some large-scale planned enclosure in the seventeenth and early eighteenth centuries. On the Alnwick estate in Northumberland, for example, encroachments on the commons of Rothbury Forest were let at a low rent (between sixpence and a shilling an acre) for 21 years. After this the land was deemed to be improved, and while the rent remained the same the fine charged at the start of successive leases was set at three or four times its original value. In 1702, 37 tenants shared 1,354 acres of such land (Brassley 1984, 48). But moorland enclosure could be effected in many ways. Lords of upland manors sometimes appropriated areas of grazing on the lower slopes in the sixteenth and seventeenth centuries, in the teeth of opposition from their tenants; but the latter also enclosed areas of fell and moor for their own use, intakes which were generally tolerated by manor courts. In addition, 'stinted pastures' or 'cow pastures' were often created on the lower slopes of fells, enclosed areas which provided grazing for small groups of tenants. Their status lay somewhere between enclosed ground and common, but most rapidly moved in the direction of the former: 'once enclosed and separated from the fell, there was a tendency for cow pastures to be divided between those holding stints, leading to the appropriation of separate sections to individual farms' (Winchester 2000, 71). Enclosure and appropriations of the lower moors continued in the early eighteenth century, especially in the White Peak district of the southern Pennines. Defoe described in 1722 riding 'over a large plain called Brassington Moor, which reached full twelve miles in length' (Defoe 1976 [1724], 468): this had disappeared before the period of parliamentary enclosure, like many of the other limestone moors in the district.

Even the higher and more inhospitable moors were sometimes enclosed in the late seventeenth and early eighteenth centuries. As already noted, major landlords in the northern Pennines systematically converted traditional shielings into leasehold farms, enclosing traditional grazing grounds in the process. More common were encroachments on the edges of the main upland plateau. A series of enclosures thus followed the dis-afforestation of Peak Forest and Macclesfield Forest in the seventeenth century. The commons of Hayfield were removed in 1640, those in Hope and adjoining townships in 1675, while Fairfield near Buxton was partially enclosed in 1687. The commons of Castleton were enclosed in 1691 and those in Chapel-en-le-Frith were removed in stages between 1640 and 1714 (Hey 2000, 201–2).

Enclosure of the 'better' moorland, and the margins of the higher moors, continued into the middle and later decades of the eighteenth century—much was effected by parliamentary acts in the 1760s, 1770s and 1780s. But as Figures 26, 27 and 28 indicate, it was only in the period after *c.*1795 that attention really turned to the main blocks of high,

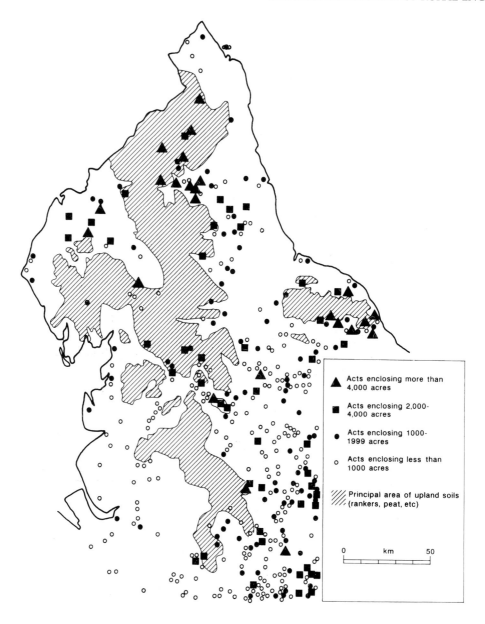

peat-covered plateaux, and the bleak fells. A series of parliamentary acts, some dealing with many thousands of acres of inter-commoned 'waste', were passed during and after the Napoleonic War years. Large areas of common moorland survived, especially in the northern Pennines and the Lake District,

Figure 26   Parliamentary enclosure in the north of England: acts passed before 1795

but by the middle of the nineteenth century the bulk of upland rough grazing had been converted, wholesale, into private property.

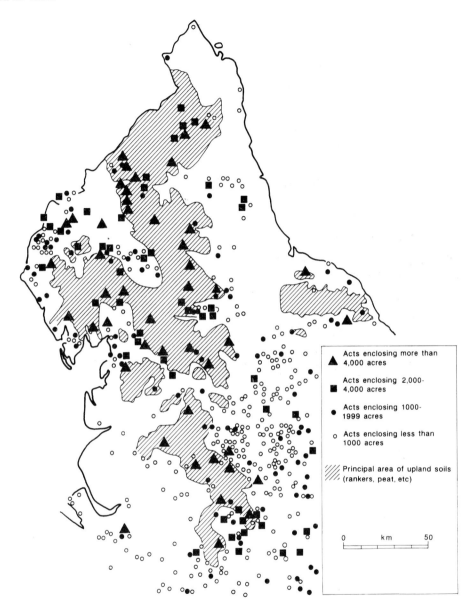

Figure 27   Parliamentary enclosure in the north of England: acts passed between 1795 and 1836

The new allotments had to be walled with great rapidity, usually within twelve months of an award, providing considerable employment—if often in hard conditions—for local or itinerant wallers. The late eighteenth and early nineteenth centuries have justly been described as 'the golden age of the profes-sional waller' (Raistrick 1946, 22). It was a labour-intensive, slow business, if modern experience is anything to go by: a waller

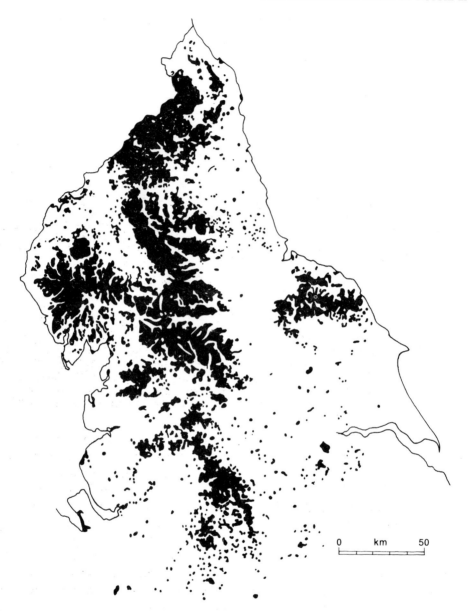

*Figure 28   The distribution of moorland in the
north of England, c.1940*

working on his own will average around 5–5.5 metres per day (Figure 29) (Garner 1995, 6). In many moorland districts the walls created at this time are awe-inspiring, for the abstract grid of private possession was often imposed upon the landscape by enclosure commissioners with little thought to the topography, so that ruler-straight walls climb impossible gradients, or cut obliquely across steep-sided valleys.

Figure 29   Parliamentary enclosure walls on high moorland near Housteads, Hadrian's Wall, Northumberland

In an interesting parallel with hedges, the eighteenth and nineteenth centuries saw the adoption of increasingly standardised methods of constructing field walls. Earlier walls had been of varied but, for the most part, massive or irregular construction. Some were formed of single lines of stones, some in effect were linear piles of stones, some were composed of two distinct faces poorly bound together (Hodges 1991, 26–36). From the eighteenth century, however, most dry-stone walls in England were built with two inclined faces of building stones ('the double') held together by throughstones and cope-stones, and with the space between filled with small stones or 'hearting'. True, in areas of particular hard rock—as in parts of the Lake District—more irregular methods continued to be employed (Garner 1995). It is also true that even when the new norms were adopted some measure of regional variation was dictated by the character of local stone: thus in the Pennines the regular, dark and rather narrow walls built of the millstone grit and coal measures contrast markedly with the broader-based, lighter, and less regular ones constructed from carboniferous limestone. But the overall impression is of a move towards more standardised forms, and indeed, within individual townships or whole groups of townships all the new walls established by a parliamentary enclosure were often built to the same basic specification, laid down in some detail in the award (Raistrick 1946, 10–12).

On the lower, drier moors eighteenth- and nineteenth-century enclosure was often followed by reclamation. Paring and burning, draining, liming and re-seeding were all employed to convert the heather and rough grass into improved pastures. In many places these operations were accompanied by digging or deep ploughing to break up the iron pan which, on podzolised soils, impeded drainage. In some places, especially during the Napoleonic Wars, extensive areas were put to the plough in order to produce oats, potatoes and sometimes wheat. New farm-steads appeared in the midst of the en-closures. In the Pennines these were often 'laithe houses', in which the house and barn were built as a single range; elsewhere symmetrical 'double pile' farmhouses were usually erected (Hey 2000, 204). Sometimes, where the moors were of relatively limited extent, new farms were established only gradually. On the Mendip Hills they only appeared after *c.*1820, although the enclosure of 24,000 acres between 1771 and 1813 had led to extensive reclamation, much of it for arable. The costs were high: on the more attractive soils of the Nordach Series, paring and burning, ploughing and liming cost more than £6 per acre, while on the more podzolised soils of the Priddy Association the need to break up iron pan raised the price to £15 an acre (Williams 1971, 68–70).

Areas of private moorland, enclosed in medieval times or in the sixteenth and seven-teenth centuries, were also reclaimed and ploughed in this period. At Chatsworth in Derbyshire an area called the Old Park lay to the east of the great house and its gardens. It had been private demesne land since at least the sixteenth century, and occupied a gently sloping area above a steep millstone grit escarpment at *c.*225–275 metres OD, some

way below the level of the higher, more exposed moorland immediately to the east. The area had, as its name suggests, originally served as a deer park but it was rendered redundant by the creation, between 1758 and 1765, of a more fashionable landscape park, designed by Capability Brown, on the lower ground beside the River Derwent to the west of the house. In the 1790s, as agricultural prices rose, it was decided that the old park was ripe for improvement. The estate accounts record the various practices involved (Chatsworth House archives, estate accounts, 1798–1806, no catalogue number). Typically, various teams of contractors seem to have specialised in particular tasks. 'John Elliot and Co' were responsible for 'Pairing and burning'—burning off the rough grass and spreading the ashes—and also for spreading lime, most of which was supplied by one John Hallam. There are numerous payments for 'ploughing in the old park', and to teams of women for spreading dung there. James Gibbon and his men were made regular pay-ments from 1798 through to 1806 for 'walling and making soughs [drains] in the Old Park'. Draining was a major item of expenditure and the accounts sometimes distinguish between the costs of the 'main soughs' and of the 'other soughs'. Gibbons and his men were paid for digging the 'soughs'; for 'filling carts and wheeling the refuse from the soughs'; for bringing stones to the site; and for filling the drains with them.

All this activity did not come cheap, although ambiguities in the accounts make the total cost of the project uncertain. Paring, burning and spreading ashes cost 25 shillings per acre, with additional payments for re-moving stones which could, on occasions, exceed this amount. The costs of drainage varied, depending on the dampness of the land and the density of drains required, but main drains cost 2 shillings a rood and minor ones 1 shilling and sixpence. Vast quantities of lime were applied—over 1,700 cartloads in 1798 alone, at a cost of £73. A number of shelter belts were planted around the new fields, and two farmhouses and various outbuildings erected. The work continued from 1798 through to 1806, when 'lime was laid upon the fallows' in the old park. The total costs are hard to estimate, but can hardly have been less than £2,000 for an area of perhaps 300 acres (120 hectares). It is hardly surprising that most serious attempts at moorland reclamation took place, as this one did, during the heady days of the Napoleonic Wars, when agricultural prices reached dizzy heights.

At this time attempts were also being made to reclaim the higher, wetter and more exposed uplands, in some places even to farm them as arable land. John Christian Curwen described in his presidential address to the Workington Agricultural Society for 1812 the recent 'disposition to carry the plough much nearer heaven than what was ever dreamed of a few years ago' (Winchester 1989, 94). Such attempts continued into the early decades of the nineteenth century. Typical was the transformation of Whinfell in Cumberland after its enclosure in 1826, described by Angus Winchester. Here, the gentleman farmer John Nicholson obtained a compact allotment of bleak upland moor, rising to 1,248 feet (385 metres) above sea level. This he surrounded and subdivided with dry-stone walls, and built a new farmstead called Hatteringill. Stones were cleared from the new fields and carted in heaps, the gorse-covered pastures were pared and burnt, then harrowed and sown. Circular stone platforms—'stack bottoms'—were built in the corners of the fields on which stooks of oats could be stood to dry (Winchester 1989, 94–5).

It is sometimes assumed that the enclosure of such upland 'wastes' in the late eighteenth and nineteenth centuries significantly extended the area of productive farmland, including arable land, in England, and was thus a major factor in feeding the growing population. But we need to be a little cautious here. Permanent conversion to arable or improved pasture was largely a feature of the lower, drier moors. The bulk of the uplands were less inviting terrain. True, arable conversion, to judge from the archaeological evidence, was widespread: large areas of moorland are covered by the earthworks known as 'narrow rig', the diminutive form of ridge and furrow (with furrows spaced at c.4 metres or less) principally associated with ploughing of late eighteenth- or early nineteenth-century date. Yet most cultivation of the high moors was short-term and temporary. Indeed, whether many farmers believed that such land would make *permanent* arable is unclear. Ploughing for cereals, as well as being encouraged by the inflated prices of the War years, also provided a quick return which allowed the costs of enclosure to be covered (it took more time to build up a good-quality pasture). Furthermore a phase of arable land use was usually considered an invaluable preparation for the creation of pasture, and after a few years of cropping with oats, wheat and potatoes, the land was seeded and laid down.

Moreover, like many attempts at reclamation in other regions, some of the 'improvement' of the high moors was motivated by more optimism than good sense. Nicholson's ambitious scheme on Whinfell went the way of many: the farm was abandoned by 1850. 'On that windswept hill top Parliamentary enclosure generated a short burst of activity, spanning little more than twenty years at most, and has left a legacy of abandoned features in the landscape today' (Winchester 1989, 95). Reclamation of the lower moors, usually to pasture rather than arable, was generally more successful—Chatsworth Old Park remains, to this day, good-quality grassland. Yet even at relatively low altitudes some of the results were often disappointing. In Cumberland and Westmoreland, where a high proportion of the land enclosed by parliamentary act lay below 250 metres, the Tithe Files of the 1830s frequently contrasted the old enclosed land, on the loamier soils, with the new reclamations. At Frizington, a township situated only slightly above the coastal plain some 10 kilometres to the east of Whitehaven, it was noted that 'the lands which have been inclosed by virtue of a private Act of Parliament are poor wet lands in a high and exposed situation. Many of the fields are entirely covered with rushes' (PRO IR 18 643). The most extensive and successful reclamations of the eighteenth and nineteenth centuries, especially those involving large-scale arable conversion, were in fact restricted not simply to the lower moors, but also to those in more southerly or easterly locations: to the south Pennines, the southern parts of the North York Moors, the Mendips and the west of Cornwall, where the moors and 'downs' today often survive only as names on the map.

In general, moorland reclamation was thus limited and temporary. Where the soils were thin or non-existent, or where the peat lay thick in the form of blanket bog, vast tracts were technically enclosed and bounded with perimeter walls but otherwise remained quite unchanged: devoid of fields and farms, in their native state. Indeed, landowners often had no intention of reclaiming these desolate grounds and enclosure had a very different purpose. Many upland areas were potentially rich in minerals, and this was an age of industrial expansion. Landowners were often keen to enclose in order to ensure the safe enjoyment of mineral rights: this had long been a major motive for enclosure in the

north and west, as David Brown has cogently argued (D. Brown 1992, 72–121). Moreover, enclosure protected landowners' interests in a whole host of ways, especially with regard to industrial and urban development (D. Brown 1992, 122–58). And as we have had cause to observe before, the owners of large estates were seldom motivated solely by economic considerations. As in the grass shires, so too on the high moorlands, enclosure allowed the expansion of recreational hunting on an unprecedented scale.

The shooting of the red grouse had long been a pastime of the rich but its popularity grew in the late eighteenth century, partly, perhaps, because of the growing enthusiasm for wild, upland scenery on the part of the landed classes. Shooting houses—to provide lunchtime shelter for groups of sportsmen—were being erected out on the moors from a relatively early date: that at Rocking Hall on the Bolton Abbey estate for example was built in 1758 (Done 1999, 64). As early as 1773 an act of parliament limited the 'season' for grouse shooting to the period between 12 August and 10 December. By the 1790s grouse were being more strenuously preserved, and landowners both hunted themselves—with their guests—and used access to the moors as a form of patronage, and to gain popularity among potential political supporters. In 1797, for example, advertisements appeared describing how 'His Grace the Duke of Devonshire, from his munificent Disposition, has resolved to devote certain Moors for *Grouse Shooting*, to Gentlemen resident in the Neighbourhood thereof, on applying to Mr Swale of *Settle*, for tickets, and using the same with discretion' (Done 1999, 28).

Improvements in gun technology encouraged more intensive and competitive forms of shooting, and by the start of the nineteenth century systematic 'drives' were taking place in some areas—on the Bishop of Durham's Horsley Moor, for example, in 1803 (Done 1999, 44). Instead of stalking the birds and shooting above the heads of the pointer dogs as they flew away, the grouse were now driven *towards* a line of sportsmen, concealed in shelters called *butts*. Driven birds fly with considerable speed—at up to 90 kilometres an hour—and thus provided a particularly challenging target. The full development of grouse shooting on the moors did not really take place until the middle of the nineteenth century, and was associated with an influx of 'new' money, improvements in access resulting from better roads and the spread of the rail network, and further refinements in firearms technology. But the sport was already of sufficient significance by 1800 to have been a powerful motive for enclosure among landowners keen both to encourage grouse and to protect them from poachers. Indeed, it is possible— as Andrew Done has suggested in his pioneering study of grouse moors—that parliamentary enclosure may have been instrumental in the development of the new mode of shooting, for the proliferation of stone walls on the moors made it more difficult to follow grouse over long distances while, conversely, the walls provided the first rudimentary butts for the sportsmen (Done 1999, 44–5, 70). Certainly, enclosure was often soon followed by the construction of true butts—small enclosures of stone, round, half-round or square in plan—which could be positioned more carefully in relation to the direction of driving, which was usually from the outside of a private moor towards the interior (in order to prevent the grouse from departing onto some neighbour's area of moorland). Shooting houses also proliferated after enclosure, together with shooting lodges—more elaborate structures than shooting houses, providing longer-term

accommodation for hunting parties. Following the enclosure of Grinton Moor in 1816, for example, James Fenton (a coal miner from Doncaster, who had purchased the manor in 1791) erected the elaborate gothic Grinton Lodge, complete with stables, coach house and kennels, to serve as a shooting lodge (Done 1999, 62). The controlled burning of the moors, in order to encourage fresh heather growth on which the grouse could feed, now became a more widespread and systematic practice.

In 1931, to judge from the information collected by the Land Utilisation Survey, the moors of northern and western England still covered an area of some three million acres (Figure 28, p. 130). Around a million acres of this was common land which had somehow escaped enclosure (Hoskins and Stamp 1961, 3); two million acres must therefore have been land technically enclosed yet not reclaimed, most of which had been brought into private ownership in post-medieval times. Of this a high proportion, probably around a million acres, was enclosed by parliamentary act before 1836, and perhaps a further quarter of a million after that date by the same means.

It is true that some of this moorland had been created by the abandonment of re-claimed land during the long depression which began in the late nineteenth century— 'fields formerly enclosed and cultivated which are being allowed to revert to vegetation resembling that of the unenclosed moorland by which they are frequently bordered' (Stamp 1950, 145). But it was only a small proportion. In Cumberland, for example, Stamp compared patterns of land use in the 1870s and in 1931, and concluded that 'the main areas of moorland have remained fixed: changes are restricted to the moorland edge'. It thus follows that upland moor, either never reclaimed or rapidly abandoned, must account for over a quarter of all 'waste' enclosed in England between 1750 and 1830. This is an important fact to remember when we consider how the nation's expanding population was fed in the course of the industrial revolution period.

The Pattern of Farming

There were other changes in patterns of land use in the north and west during the 'long eighteenth century' which we must briefly consider. In some districts, in spite of rapid population growth and escalating grain prices, the area under arable cultivation continued to decline. This was usually where soils were particularly poorly suited to cereal farming, or in the vicinity of major industrial conurbations, where pasture closes, used in particular to produce hay for draught animals and dairy cattle, increased in significance. In the area around Frome Selwood in Somerset in 1801, for example, tillage was said to be in decline because 'of the very great demand for the production of grass land in the populous manufacturing town of Frome' (Turner 1982a, II, 218). At Cromford in Derbyshire a very small proportion was in tilth, 'many cows being kept here for the accommodation of people employed in spinning cotton' (Turner 1982a, I, 111).

Overall, however, most western districts seem to have witnessed some expansion of tillage in the period after 1750, the scale of which in the early nineteenth century can be broadly estimated by comparing the 1801 Crop Returns with the data contained in the 1836 Tithe Files. Once again, there are serious problems with such a comparison. Apart from the fact that rather different parishes are recorded in each source, the Crop Returns make no record of fallow land or rotational grass, while some of the Tithe Files—those of 'pastoral' type—fail to record

the latter information, subsuming the figures for 'seeds' within those for 'pasture'. Allowing for these differences it seems that most districts saw a modest expansion of arable in this period, of between 15 and 30 per cent, but that in Shropshire, Staffordshire, Cheshire and Lancashire there were more dramatic increases, of 33 per cent, 60 per cent, 58 per cent and 90 per cent respectively. In the latter two counties these increases were from a very low level and the landscape remained largely under grass. But the expansion in the first two counties did lead to the development of areas of very extensive arable, largely in the area of deep, well-drained brown earth soils found in south-west Staffordshire, in northern and eastern Shropshire, and in southern and eastern Herefordshire. All were areas with, for the west of England, comparatively low rainfall, in which tillage had long been relatively important. Here the area under cultivation could reach levels comparable to those in the arable south and east, in excess of 50 per cent in many parishes by the mid-1830s, and the landscape underwent changes similar to—although generally less dramatic than—those seen in eastern districts. In particular, there was much thinning and removal of hedges, and felling of hedgerow timber and pollards. Such developments were most marked on large estate farms. The Groundlow Fields Farm in Tittensor, on the Trentham estate, had 56 irregular fields in 1830, most—to judge by their sinuous boundaries—created through the piecemeal enclosure of open fields. By 1843 these had been replaced by fifteen large closes, bounded by ruler-straight hedges (Currie 1979, 99–101). The government enquiry of 1791 gives the impression that, while hedge removal was most marked in the eastern counties, it was also widespread in some western arable districts. In Staffordshire the grubbing out of hedges was aid to be common, while in Shropshire 'the opening of Fields together has prevailed much' (Lambert 1977, 748–9). Other aspects of 'improved farming' were also widely adopted in these districts. In particular, the area sown with turnips seems to have increased during the later eighteenth century and, in particular, the early nineteenth century. In both Staffordshire and Shropshire, for example, they made up 6.8 per cent of the cropped acreage, excluding fallows and grass, recorded in the 1801 Crop Returns. By c.1836, according to the Tithe Files, they constituted 19 per cent and 15 per cent respectively.

We might expect that the adoption of 'improved' rotations, coupled with an increased incidence of liming and draining and removal of hedges and hedgerow timber, would have raised cereal yields significantly in western districts. In fact, comparison of estimates made around 1800, with those contained in the Tithe Files of c.1836, suggest that in most western districts yields per acre actually *fell* in this period, whereas in southern and eastern counties they generally increased or at least remained stable (Table 1, p. 156). We should not make too much of this observation, for there are good reasons for suspecting that the Tithe Files tend to underestimate cereal yields (Turner *et al.* 2001, 125). But certainly, no very great improvements are indicated.

In spite of the localised expansion of arable farming, even in the 1830s most western counties remained largely devoted to livestock farming, the practice of which underwent a number of local and regional adjustments in the course of the eighteenth and nineteenth centuries. Dairying increased in importance in many districts (as in parts of Staffordshire) within easy reach of major industrial centres, while sheep replaced cattle as the main animal grazed on the upland moors. This latter change was in part the consequence of improvements in sheep breeds: the development of Blackfaces and Cheviots, which survived better than traditional breeds on high moorland. This expansion of upland sheep farming was part of a wider phenomenon which was associated, most notoriously, with the Highland Clearances in Scotland between the 1780s and 1850s (Rackham 1986, 318–19).

Improvements in livestock breeds have long held the attention of historians of the agricultural revolution (Clutton-Brock 1982; Russell 1986; Trow Smith 1959). Recent research—especially in the field of zoo-archaeology—has tended to emphasise the *gradual* nature of developments in sheep and cattle during the post-medieval centuries (Davis and Beckett 1999). Evidence from a number of excavated sites examined by Davis and Beckett, mainly in the north and west of England, suggests that 'improvement in England was already under way in the fifteenth and sixteenth centuries, and that improvements in livestock should be viewed more as a long-term and gradual development originating in the fifteenth century, rather than as a *revolutionary* one which commenced sometime after 1760'. This change was, essentially, between the medieval situation in which 'animals were slaughtered relatively old and relatively small', to the nineteenth-century one in which slaughtered livestock were 'relatively young but larger animals' (Davis and Beckett 1999, 14). The speed with which animals matured was as important as their size, the latter anyway a poor guide to the amount and quality of the meat each beast contained, and in this, selective breeding, by innumerable farmers over a long period of time, was of crucial importance. But new breeds were 'only made possible by general improvements in livestock nutrition'. Davis and Beckett noted the significance of the new fodder crops and floated water meadows in improving feed, but in the period after *c.*1700 perhaps of equal importance were the improvements in grazing which occurred not only in the Midlands but, more particularly, in the north and west, where the majority of England's sheep and cattle continued to be both reared and fattened. Indeed, improvements in grazing would have raised the amount of meat produced even without significant changes in breeds, simply because better grass could carry more animals.

Unfortunately, we have little *direct* evidence concerning the effects of the various improvements noted in this chapter: the liming, re-seeding, more intensive dunging and draining which were employed both to raise the quality of existing pasture fields and to convert areas of drier, low-altitude moorland to improved pasture. But some indication of their consequences can be gained from more recent figures for the productivity of different grades of grassland, produced at the start of the post-Second World War period of agricultural intensification (Hanley 1949, 13). Rough grass moors, dominated by purple moor grass and fescue, can have meat yields as low as 8 kilograms per annum. Through drainage and liming these could be converted to bent grass pasture, which might be expected to produce something in the region of 30–40 kilograms of meat (or 400–500 litres of milk) per annum. Pastures of this latter type could also be improved. By draining, liming, and re-seeding the proportion of bent grass could be lowered, and that of rye grass and clover increased: the resulting low-grade ryegrass pasture or superior bent grass pasture might produce between 50 and 80 kilograms of meat (or around 900 litres of milk) per annum (Hanley 1949, 13). In other words, the kinds of techniques widely employed to improve northern and western pastures in the eighteenth and nineteenth centuries had the potential to increase productivity very substantially. In reality the scale of improvement will have been much less than these figures suggest, for many lowland pastures were probably already of reasonable quality at the start of the period studied here. Nevertheless, changes to enclosed upland pastures, and to the lower and drier moors, must have been significant. The improvement of grazing land was certainly the key development in the agricultural revolution of the north and west of England.

CHAPTER 6

High Farming

The Nature of High Farming

The term 'high farming' is generally used by historians to describe the system of agriculture which existed in England during the early and mid-Victorian period—roughly, from the 1830s to the start of the great agricultural depression of the late 1870s (F.M.L. Thompson 1968). Originally the phrase simply meant particularly exemplary, modern farming, but by the 1840s agricultural writers like Phillip Pusey were using the term very much in its modern sense. The agricultural improvements of the 'long eighteenth century' had essentially involved the processing or recycling of materials produced on the farm itself, using high inputs of labour—this was true of marling, bush drainage, and the production and diligent application of animal manure. There were important exceptions to this, especially in the north and west, where lime was manufactured on an industrial scale and transported over long distances. Nevertheless, the essentially self-sufficient character of eighteenth-century 'improved' farming is one of its most striking features. High farming was very different. It was a high-input, high-output system which, crucially, relied on materials, often manufactured, imported from *outside* the farm. In addition, more durable fixtures (in particular, permanent forms of drainage), and machines, were now substituted for recurrent inputs of labour. It was primarily a system of arable farming—most fully developed on large farms and on

the lighter lands—which nevertheless placed more emphasis on livestock production than the earlier 'revolution'. Self-consciously scientific, it was the rural counterpart to the later phases of the industrial revolution; indeed, as we shall see, the two were linked in innumerable ways. The new scientific and experimental approach to agriculture was reflected in the establishment, in 1838, of the English Agricultural Society, soon renamed the Royal Agricultural Society; in the foundation in 1845 of the Cirencester Agricultural College; and in the establishment in 1843 of the Rothampstead Experimental Station in Hertfordshire by Sir John Lawes (Wade Martins 1995, 101–2; Chambers and Mingay 1966, 170; Goddard 1988).

Contemporary writers like Pusey were quite specific about the particular practices which distinguished the new husbandry (Pusey 1843). Firstly, there was the use, on a large scale, of 'artificial' fertilisers, a term which contemporaries employed to encompass not only manufactured substances which aided crop growth, but also organic materials imported from beyond the farm, often indeed from beyond the boundaries of the kingdom. Secondly, there was the increased use of oil cake, a by-product of the rape and linseed oil extraction industries, as animal fodder. Thirdly, there was the adoption of new forms of drainage, and new types of farm building. Lastly, there was the more widespread use of seed drills and steam-powered threshing machines.

Some of these new features were paid for

by the tenant, some were the responsibility of the landlord. The tenant's main investment was in oil cake and artificial manures. Oil cake had been used on English farms since the middle of the eighteenth century. It had first been employed as a manure, ground up and applied directly to the fields (3,300 rape cakes were purchased for the home farm at Holkham in Norfolk as early as 1732 (Holkham Hall archives, MS 1067, bundle 23)). By the 1760s, however, it was being fed to bullocks (Wade Martins and Williamson 1999a, 124). Its use increased through the 1830s, and more rapidly in the 1840s, when falling transport costs and the expansion of the rail network made it cheaper and more easily available. While roots (now not only turnips, but also mangold wurzels and swedes) continued to be the principal livestock fodder, the use of cake increased inexorably. National consumption rose from around 24,000 tons in 1825 to 160,000 in 1870, by which time few farms in the main arable areas of England were more than 10 miles from a dealer (F.M.L. Thompson 1968, 73–4). Oil cake increased the quantity of meat which could be produced on arable farms, both by allowing more livestock to be kept and by permitting them to be fattened more quickly. With improved communications and growing urban affluence, the market for meat was increasingly buoyant, and farmers in the south and east of England were very keen to expand this aspect of their businesses. But in addition, higher stocking levels increased the amounts of manure produced and thereby further boosted cereal yields.

Yields were also raised in this period by the widespread adoption of artificial fertilisers. Imports of guano from South America were already taking place by the 1830s; by the 1850s its use was widespread in many arable areas. By the 1830s the improving effects of bone dust (especially when applied to the turnip course) were already widely appreciated. The value of imports of this material rose from £78,000 in 1832 to £254,000 in 1837 (Brigden 1986, 188). Bone dust was ineffective on alkaline soils, however; only in acidic conditions was the active ingredient, calcium phosphate, released. Hence the importance of the experiments carried out by John Bennett Lawes, involving the treatment of bone with sulphuric acid, in order to produce superphosphates. He later substituted mineral phosphates for bone, patented the method in 1842, and thus initiated the fertiliser industry. The value of superphosphates used by farmers rose from nil in 1840 to £1,440,000 in the period 1864–7 and to £4,080,000 in the period 1877–81 (F.M.L. Thompson 1968, 74–5). Some of the raw material for the manufacture of superphosphate came from coprolites—that is, phosphatic nodules of clay, sponges and other fossils, which are found in a number of places in south-east England but in particular on top of the Gault clay in a narrow band running through Cambridgeshire and Hertfordshire, from Ashwell northeastwards as far as Burwell (Hodge et al. 1984, 158–60; Grove 1976; Taylor 1973, 242–3). The industry flourished between c.1850 and the start of the agricultural depression in the 1880s. To extract the coprolites the land was dug in trenches to a depth of up to 7 metres; once the nodules had been removed the trench was backfilled with material dug from an adjacent, parallel trench. The land was eventually returned to agricultural use, but the former workings are still clearly apparent from the air, and in some places the latest workings were never backfilled, because the industry collapsed so rapidly. As a result, elongated ponds and associated linear mounds often remain, a prominent feature of the landscape, most notably in the area around Stow-cum-Quy Fen in Cambridge-shire (Taylor 1973, 243).

The advantages and disadvantages of the various new fertilisers were debated in the *Journal of the Royal Agricultural Society*. Between 1855 and 1860 over a fifth of articles were devoted to this subject (Goddard 1991, 170). Many others were concerned with farm machinery, the production and use of which escalated rapidly in the course of the nineteenth century. Both seed drills and threshing machines—powered now by steam engines, rather than horse power, and mobile rather than fixed—were widely adopted in arable areas during the 1830s, 1840s and 1850s. In the 1850s they were joined by a new invention, the reaping machine. Two American machines, the McCormick and the Hussey, were shown at the Great Exhibition in 1851 and were rapidly adopted by English farmers in the eastern counties (Read 1858, 280). By the 1860s some of the larger farms, generally on the heavier land, were beginning to use steam traction engines for ploughing.

These various new innovations were not adopted to the same extent, or with the same alacrity, in all areas of England. They tended to appear first on the largest farms, and most were adopted with the greatest enthusiasm on the light soils. It was, in particular, on these hungry lands that the use of artificial fertilisers was most intense by the middle of the century. In west Norfolk, according to C.S. Read, the use of fertilisers was particularly important: there was, he wrote, no other district 'in which such an amount of the necessities of life are raised by artificial manure', so much so that 'the manure agent's little bill is more than the landlord's rent' (Read 1858, 269, 276). Small farms on heavier or more fertile soils, in contrast, seem to have made less use of fertilisers, although all, by the 1850s, appear to have used substantial quantities of oil cake (Wade Martins and Williamson 1999a, 134–6).

New Drains and Buildings

It was now more important than ever for landowners to attract tenants with working capital, farmers of substance, and estates in all areas seem to have poured money into the erection of farm buildings (Wade Martins 1995, 103–12). The new methods of husbandry, moreover, required new *types* of building. The costs were high but landowners were now able to take advantage of new government loan schemes, primarily intended to fund land drainage but also used to finance other improvements.

Interest in the design of improved farmsteads is manifested in the Royal Agricultural Society's farm building competition, and in a number of publications of which John Bailey Denton's *Farm Homesteads of England* (1863) is the most famous. Rebuilding now occurred on a large scale, no longer mainly on the light arable soils of the east, and on the heartlands of the great estates (in the form of elaborate and flamboyant 'model farms'), but also in the more pastoral landscapes of the north and west, and to some extent on the heavy clays of the south and east.

In the north and west, most efforts were directed towards the provision of housing for milking cattle, and dairying facilities: the expanding market provided by nearby industrial conurbations, and the improved transportation offered by the railways, encouraged the expansion of dairying in many districts (Brigden 1986). Sometimes farms were demolished and completely rebuilt to some convenient, 'rational' layout. More usually, older arrangements were augmented, or partially rebuilt. As well as improved dairying provision, extensive piggeries were often supplied, the pigs being fed on the waste products from butter- and cheese-making. Contemporary accounts suggest that existing farm buildings were generally inadequate for the new intensive modes of farming, and often in a poor state of repair. Andrew Thompson, who prepared reports for the Enclosure Commissioners on the requests for loans made by estates in Staffordshire and the surrounding counties in the 1850s and 1860s, typically reported on the state of the buildings at Marl Pit Farm in Bagots Bromley: 'The present buildings are the very worst I have seen on Lord Bagot's estate and consist of very old and inconvenient boarded and thatched erections, all in a very ruinous state, and I am surprised that the occupier should have been able to carry on so long with them' (Phillips 1996, 108).

In the clayland areas of the south and east, and in East Anglia, the provision of cattle housing was also the main concern of land-lords, agents and tenants; but here cow houses and dairies were less important than cattle sheds for fattening bullocks (Wade Martins and Williamson 1999a, 142–9). Here, too, reports frequently suggest that buildings were old, dilapidated, and unsuited to the new modes of farming, especially in clayland districts. Evidently, in the buoyant years around 1800 it had been easy to attract suitable tenants to poorly equipped holdings, but times had changed, and, if tenants with the capital required for the new modes of farming were to be attracted, action was required. In the 1860s and 1870s surveys of the Duke of Norfolk's estates and the Earsham estate in south Norfolk, and of the Flixton estate in north Suffolk, all suggest that many farm buildings were inadequate, dilapidated or both (NRO Smiths Gore 20.10.78, no. 225, 1520; ESRO HA 12 D4/26; NRO MEA 3/539). The report on the Duke of Norfolk's estates thus describe buildings 'not adapted to the present mode of farming' (NRO Smiths Gore 20.10.78, no. 225, 1520); the surveyor, William Keary, warned that only poor tenants, with low levels of capital,

would be prepared to farm there. Never-theless, we should not exaggerate the extent of investment on clayland farms in East Anglia and the south-east. Many were owned by relatively small proprietors, others formed outlying and seldom-visited portions of large estates, and had no real function in advert-ising the improving zeal of the owner. Such inactivity is fortunate for us, for it is in these areas that large numbers of timber-framed barns, dating from the period before 1700, still survive.

Both on the southern and eastern clays, and in other arable areas, entirely new 'model' farms were occasionally provided. But more usual was piecemeal addition, especially of new cattle sheds, within or around already existing yards. The key development of the late eighteenth and early nineteenth centuries had been the replace-ment of rudimentary yards and shelters with permanent yards and properly constructed shelter sheds. The high farming period saw the construction, on many farms, of more sophisticated cattle housing—ranges of loose boxes, often with central feeding passage and a turnip- or cake-house at one end. This allowed farmers to give their livestock individual attention (Wade Martins and Williamson 1999a, 120–4).

The scientific, rational approaches to farming propagated by the Royal Agricultural Society of England were particularly apparent in the design of buildings, and there was a growing awareness that, exposed to the elements, much of the nitrogen and other chemicals was lost from manure. The main writers on farm buildings, such as John Bailey Denton, thus argued that the open yard should be completely roofed over, so as to provide protection for both the livestock and their manure (Denton 1863, 68). Many farmers were wary, however, concerned about the problems lack of ventilation could cause to cattle. Roofed yards were only really adopted on the model 'home farms' of large estates, or by leading agricultural improvers. More widely shared was a concern for labour efficiency, and thus an interest in the careful planning of yards and buildings to ensure the most efficient movement of feed, straw and manure. In most districts there was a clear tendency for farmstead layout to become more regular, with buildings clustered tightly around one or more yards rather than being more haphazardly arranged (Wade Martins and Williamson 1999a, 96–7). On some model farms, by the 1860s, tramways were provided to facilitate the movement of materials; these were true industrial farms, and indeed, the impact of technology and industrialisation were everywhere apparent. Improvements in transport ensured that sheds and barns were no longer built, of necessity, of local materials: slate was now widely used for roofing, and cast iron for windows and fittings (Wade Martins 1995, 60–71). More importantly, with the widespread adoption of steam threshing, barns gradually declined in importance, and by the 1860s were seldom erected.

The widespread construction of new farm buildings in the middle decades of the nineteenth century has left an enduring mark upon the rural landscape. But more important in the expansion of agricultural production was the spread of land drainage. Its importance was stressed again and again by agricultural writers, Phillip Pusey for example arguing that 'Thorough draining is to the land as foundations are to a house' (Pusey 1843). The simple underdrains which had spread steadily in arable areas of eastern England in the course of the eighteenth century—and to some extent, in the north and west—had usually been installed by tenants. Most were temporary structures which in many cases lasted little longer than

the duration of a lease. The early nineteenth century, however, saw an increasing interest in more permanent forms of land drain which, by definition, became the landlord's responsibility. The efficiency of drainage was improved and the practice now spread into new districts (Phillips 1989 and 1999; Harvey 1980, 81–2).

Ceramic land drains had been sporadically used in the late eighteenth and early nineteenth centuries, either in the form of semicircular or horseshoe tiles laid on flat 'soles', or as hand-made pipes (Figure 30). But they were expensive, and their spread was slow. The high farming period, however, seems to have witnessed a marked increase in interest in the technique. The advantages accruing from the improvement were relentlessly championed by agricultural writers like J. Smith, whose influential volume *Remarks on Thorough Draining and Deep Ploughing* was published in 1831. Between 1840 and 1855 over 10 per cent of the articles in the *Journal of the Royal Agricultural Society of England* dealt with the topic (Goddard 1991, 165–90). More importantly, there were important technical developments. In 1835 Robert Beart of Godmanchester (Huntingdonshire) invented machines for the mass production of tiles and soles, and a number of similar inventions soon followed (Phillips 1999, 64). At the same time, experiments were being made into methods of cheaply producing cylindrical drainage pipes, endeavours which culminated in the pipe-making machine designed by Thomas Scraggs, which was patented in 1842. Whereas it cost over £4 to drain an acre of land using hand-made tiles and soles, with cylindrical pipes the costs fell significantly, to less than £3 (Phillips 1999, 64).

Of equal significance in encouraging the wider adoption of the improvement were legislative changes. A tax levied on all

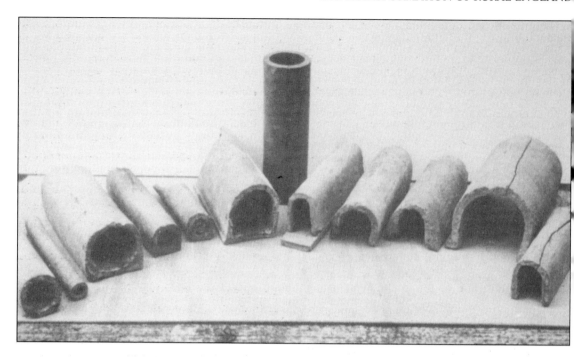

Figure 30   Various forms of nineteenth-century drainage pipes. The horseshoe pipes, which rested on flat soles, declined in popularity in the 1840s as mass-produced cylindrical pipes became available

bricks and tiles between 1784 and 1850 was amended in 1826 to exempt those produced 'for the sole purpose of draining marshy land', provided that they were marked with the word 'DRAIN' 'in so plain and distinct a manner that the same may be easily and distinctly legible to any officer of the excise' (thereby providing a useful dating method for later archaeologists: all pipes and tiles so labelled must date from between 1826 and 1850) (Harvey 1980, 81). Moreover, in 1840 and 1845 acts were passed which established the principle that the owners of entailed estates (the majority of large landowners) could borrow money to finance land improvements; this was followed by acts of 1846 and 1850, by which the government provided £2 million for drainage and other improvements. Between 1847 and 1860 five Land Improvement Companies were established by parliamentary act, to provide landowners with the capital necessary for drainage, new farm buildings, and other improvements.

Between 1847 and 1899 just under £5.5 million was advanced by these organisations, a very substantial sum.

Many landowners were reluctant to borrow, preferring to finance drainage from estate revenue, as for example at Holkham in Norfolk where more than £2,000 per annum was spent on underdrainage without recourse to the loan companies, the tenants being charged a percentage interest, added to the rent of the drained land. In other words, the sums advanced by the drainage companies significantly under-represent the scale of drainage investment in the middle decades of the nineteenth century (Phillips 1999, 66). It has, nevertheless, been cogently argued that an examination of the records of the loan

and 32 bushels of wheat an acre (Craigie 1883, 40–1). Yields from western arable areas, in contrast, still lagged noticeably behind, at 22–25 bushels per acre. The equivalent figures for barley would be 34–43 bushels and 28–32 bushels respectively (Craigie 1883, 40–1).

The improvements in yields which occurred before c.1830 were often accompanied, to varying extents, by the adoption of a less intensive course of cropping—by a decrease in the area under cereals and an expansion of that under fodder crops. Those achieved during the high farming period, in contrast, were sometimes accompanied by the adoption of *more* intensive rotations. On some estates, by the 1860s, landowners were bowing to the demands of their tenants and allowing them to break the sacrosanct principle of the Norfolk four-course and follow whatever course of cropping they chose until the final few years of the lease (Wade Martins and Williamson 1998, 140).

Of equal significance during this period, however, was the increase in the volume of meat produced by English farmers. In part this was a consequence of further improvements to pasture land consequent upon the wider adoption of underdrains; in part it resulted from the widespread use of oil cake as feed, which increased in particular the numbers of livestock kept in primarily arable areas. Between 1854 and c.1870, according to Michael Turner's calculations, the number of sheep in England increased by around 2.5 million, the number of cattle by perhaps 600,000 (Turner 1998, 158). Indeed, it is probable—as John Walton has recently suggested—that much of the additional grain produced during the high farming period actually went to feed livestock rather than humans. High doses of fertilisers increased the proportion of stalk to grain in both wheat and barley (the straw was cut and used as fodder) while at the same time increasing the volume of the grain at the expense of its density, thus making it more suitable for consumption by livestock. Both of these effects were, according to Walton, compounded by the particular varieties of wheat and barley increasingly adopted in the course of the nineteenth century (Walton 1999, 40–3).

These high levels of production were only maintained through high levels of investment in forms of farming which were, to varying extents, environmentally unfriendly. Unsustainable schemes of reclamation were carried out in areas of marginal land, wreaking additional havoc on the ecology of the heathlands, chalk downs, and some moorland areas. Even contemporaries worried about some of the effects of the new farming: they knew, for example, that the increasing use and efficiency of underdrains led to faster, and more complete, run-off from the land, leading to increased pressure on rivers and other arterial drainage channels (Phillips 1999, 67; Denton 1863). But the benefits of high farming may not have been entirely clear-cut even in conventional economic terms. Whether many farmers made substantial profits from the system—once the costs of machinery, manure and oil cake were taken into account—is uncertain. In 1861 Charles Wrattislaw calculated that a successful mixed farm enterprise demanded an annual investment of £9 an acre (Wrattislaw 1861, 182); although farm accounts, where they survive, seldom suggest anything quite as high as this, they do suggest that profits were often relatively low, compared with levels of investment. Accounts for the home farm on the Merton estate in Norfolk between 1850 and 1869, for example, show dramatic swings, from a profit of £814 in 1868 to a loss of £250 in 1860: outgoings included over £1,000 per annum in artificial fertilisers, roughly equivalent to the cost of labour in many years (NRO WLS XVIII/17 411X).

Much of the investment demanded of tenants was of medium- or long-term benefit to the productivity of the land, and it is not surprising that this period saw increasing agitation over rights to compensation for unexhausted improvements (Wade Martins and Williamson 1998, 139–40). High levels of investment ensured that, in the view of most contemporaries, the new mode of farming was best suited to large farms. C.S. Read, for example, believed that high farming was only to be found on farms of over 300 acres, and asserted that 'The small farmer is rarely a high farmer' (Read 1887, 27). In reality, the connection was perhaps less to do with levels of investment than with the fact that the greatest gains could be made on the more marginal soils, where small farms had long been uneconomic. In this sense, and in these locations, high farming in its purest form was a precarious enterprise, in which high investment brought profits only for so long as agricultural prices remained high.

CHAPTER 7

The Agricultural Revolution and the Landscape

Feeding the Nation

We can now return to the question posed at the start of this enquiry. How, in the eighteenth and nineteenth centuries, was it possible to feed the rapidly increasing population of the world's first industrial nation? As we have seen, an important contribution was made by a steady improvement in cereal yields, in particular those for wheat, the main bread grain. On a national basis, changes in wheat yields can be reconstructed in a number of ways. The set of figures presented in Table 1, showing trends in the late eighteenth and nineteenth centuries, is based on contemporary estimates, made for whole counties, by individuals or government officials. As actual statements of productivity these figures are unquestionably misleading: some at least of these sources systematically overestimated or underestimated yield figures. Those from the 1836 Tithe Files are, in particular, serious underestimates, to judge from comparisons with other contemporary data (Turner *et al.* 2001, 125). This is probably because—at a time of rapidly rising yields— tithe commissioners were attempting to ascertain *average* figures of production, and of necessity based these on the experience of local farmers over the previous decade or so, when yields had been lower. Nevertheless, while inaccurate in absolute terms, these figures do allow us to see some broad *relative* differences between the performance of

different geographical regions, and suggest in particular a distinction between western counties, in which yields at best remained stable during the late eighteenth and early nineteenth centuries, and the southern and eastern counties, in which they generally displayed some upward movement. These figures also indicate—even allowing for some pessimism on the part of tithe commissioners—that yields increased much faster in the period of 'high farming' between *c.*1830 and 1870 than they did in the previous forty years or so.

Much more sophisticated national figures have recently been produced as the result of a painstaking research project carried out by Michael Turner, John Beckett and Bethanie Afton (Turner *et al.* 2001) (Table 2). These are based on actual yields recorded from specific farms, rather than on contemporary estimates made for general areas, and cover the whole of the eighteenth and nineteenth centuries. They are unquestionably the best figures so far produced for crop yields during the agricultural revolution and 'high farming' periods. Yet they too have their problems. Comparatively little data of this kind survives, so that even for the early nineteenth century the figures are usually based on only seven or eight observations for each year, spread across the entire country. Moreover, we need to interpret them with some care. In particular, as I noted in the opening chapter, we must remember that natural as well as human agency could influence the scale and direction of changes in productivity. Never-theless, the story these data tell seems relatively straightforward, if rather surprising.

Table 1: Wheat Yield Estimates for Selected English Counties (bushels per acre)

	A c.1770	B 1795	C 1800	D 1801	E Late C18th	F c.1836	G 1870s
Bedfordshire	19.0	21.0	20.0	17.0	19.3	22.7	30.5
Berkshire	28.0	-	20.0	-	24.0	24.2	32.0
Buckinghamshire	25.0	24.0	20.0	24.0	23.3	21.0	30.0
Cambridgeshire	-	-	23.0	22.0	22.5	22.4	33.0
Cheshire	25.0	21.5	22.0	-	22.8	20.6	28.0
Cornwall	-	-	24.0	24.0	24.0	17.9	29.7
Derbyshire	-	19.0	-	26.0	22.5	22.3	28.0
Devon	-	18.0	24.0	19.0	20.3	15.6	24.6
Dorset	20.0	17.5	16.0	-	17.8	20.4	30.7
Durham	25.0	-	21.5	20.0	22.2	17.1	28.0
Essex	24.0	18.5	24.0	24.5	22.2	24.6	33.6
Hampshire	20.0	17.5	24.0	21.0	20.6	21.5	28.5
Hertfordshire	24.0	20.0	22.0	25.0	22.8	21.6	26.3
Huntingdonshire	18.0	-	20.0	23.0	20.3	22.0	30.5
Kent	-	20.5	22.0	26.5	23.0	25.6	34.0
Lancashire	26.0	38.5	21.0	33.5	29.8	22.9	29.2
Lincolnshire	21.0	-	24.0	21.0	22.0	22.9	31.6
Norfolk	24.0	-	26.0	-	25.0	23.3	31.6
Northumberland	18.0	-	24.0	24.5	22.2	19.5	28.6
Oxfordshire	26.0	15.0	24.0	-	21.7	22.9	36.0
Shropshire	-	15.0	20.0	16.0	17.0	19.5	21.0
Somerset	-	-	20.0	21.0	20.5	21.0	31.6
Staffordshire	23.0	18.0	22.0	28.5	22.9	21.3	29.9
Suffolk	24.0	24.0	19.0	-	22.3	22.2	30.4
Surrey	-	12.0	20.0	25.0	19.0	20.9	28.0
Sussex	22.0	20.0	22.0	24.0	22.0	25.6	31.0
Warwickshire	28.0	20.0	20.5	23.0	22.9	23.1	31.7
Wiltshire	20.0	22.5	20.0	24.5	21.8	22.0	28.0
Yorkshire, East Riding	25.0	-	22.5	26.0	24.5	18.6	29.0
Yorkshire, North Riding	21.0	-	22.5	22.5	22.0	19.4	28.0
Yorkshire, West Riding	20.0	21.0	22.5	21.5	21.3	21.0	25.0

SOURCES:
A, estimates from Arthur Young, from Craigie 1883.
B, estimate of an 'average' yield, from a government enquiry of 1795, HO42, from Turner 1982b.
C, estimates of the harvest of 1800, from House of Lords Enquiry, in Turner 1982b.
D, estimated yields from the 1801 Crop Returns, in Turner 1982b.
E = average of A + B + C + D.
F, county averages from the Tithe Files, as calculated by Kain 1986.
G, average from Royal Commission on Agriculture reports, from Craigie 1883.

Table 2: Mean Wheat Yields, 1720–1900
(from Turner, Beckett and Afton 2001)

Period	Number of observations	Mean (bushels per acre)
1720s	32	19.99
1730s	25	21.14
1740s	40	21.75
1750s	28	22.42
1760s	47	21.82
1770s	57	19.68
1780s	41	18.88
1790s	83	18.97
1800s	91	20.98
1810s	76	21.17
1820s	86	23.60
1830s	110	26.67
1840s	113	30.60
1850s	134	27.47
1860s	112	28.57
1870s	90	28.92
1880s	54	26.47
1890s	32	27.05

In the half-century between *c.*1730 and 1780 yields remained fairly stable at around 21.5 bushels per acre. The period between 1780 and 1820, in contrast, witnessed some decline. Although the point was not emphasised by Turner and his co-workers, this was largely because these forty years saw a significant deterioration in the climate, with a higher than average number of very wet summers: in the late Jim Holderness's words, the period was characterised by 'the comparatively high frequency of poor harvests' (Holderness 1989, 99). This, we must assume, was enough to counteract the effects of all the many changes—the adoption of the four-course rotation, liming, draining and the like—which I have described in earlier chapters, and average yields hovered around 20 bushels an acre.

The run of poor harvests came to an end in 1821, and with the return of more normal conditions the various improvements adopted over the previous half-century now began to have an immediate effect on average yields, which for the decade 1820–29 rose suddenly to 23.6 bushels per acre. The 1820s also saw a significant, if localised, increase in the use of oil cake and bone fertiliser, which may have contributed something to the clear leap in the figures. But it was the following decade which saw their more widespread adoption and, from *c.*1840, substantial imports of guano; while through the 1840s and 1850s increasing use was made of superphosphates. The impact of the new techniques of 'high farming' is obvious in the figures. Yields increased dramatically: to 26.7 bushels an acre in the 1830s; and thereafter to a plateau, oscillating within a bushel or two of 28.5 bushels, which was maintained from the 1840s until the onset of the next period of poor weather in the 1880s. Artificial inputs, the more widespread adoption of land drainage, and other innovations thus raised average yields by around 20 per cent within a decade or two, and then maintained them at a new, high level.

However we interpret these sets of figures, the most important point is really this: improvements in yields alone would never have been enough to feed the growing population. Between 1830 and 1870 the population of England and Wales increased by 9 million (from around 14 to around 23 million), or 64 per cent, while wheat prices—which fell steeply after the end of the Napoleonic Wars—registered no markedly upward trend. Yet wheat yields, having risen through the 1830s and 1840s by around 20 per cent, stubbornly refused to climb further. In part the resultant gap in supply was filled by imports, which rose significantly following the repeal of the Corn Laws in 1846: in the

1840s they accounted for around 8 per cent of home consumption; by the 1860s they accounted for some 40 per cent. Nevertheless, given that during this period little extra land appears to have been brought into cultivation in England, some significant shortfall in the supply of wheat is indicated.

But developments in the period *before* *c.*1830 are much more perplexing. The population of England and Wales rose from perhaps 6 million in 1750 to around 14 million in 1830. Yet average wheat yields can have increased by only around 10–15 per cent. Moreover, the actual increases in *production* were sometimes more limited still, because improvements in yields were, as I have emphasised, often accompanied by a shift to less intensive modes of cropping, as the adoption of rotations featuring two or more fodder courses decreased the frequency of cereal courses. It is true that to some extent the yawning gap in requirements was filled by the conversion of a small wheat export surplus of around one million hundredweight in the 1740s (Ormrod 1985) to a small import deficit of 6.8 million by 1840 (Mitchell and Deane 1962, 98). But this must have been more than offset by the steady rise in the consumption of wheat, as opposed to other bread grains, which occurred in this same period, as an increasingly urban population rejected more traditional forms of bread made of oats, rye or barley (Collins 1975). In 1800 66 per cent of the population of England and Wales consumed wheat grain; by 1850 this had risen to 88 per cent (Collins 1975, 114).

To some historians, the answer to this apparent conundrum lies in the fact that the period from 1750 to 1830 saw a significant expansion of the cultivated acreage, through the enclosure and ploughing of 'waste'. It could thus be argued that while yields did not rise significantly, much more grain was produced simply because more land was put to the plough. Yet, as we have seen, although much common land was enclosed in this period, probably approaching 4 million acres, a high proportion of this was of such poor quality that it could never be reclaimed (the bulk of the high moorland in the north and west of England), while much that was reclaimed, especially on the poorer heathlands of the south, soon reverted to rough grazing. At the very most, the area of ploughland in England can have been increased through enclosure by only around 22 per cent in the period *c.*1750–1830.[1] In short, however we juggle the figures, enclosure and reclamation of marginal land and improvements in yields per acre can at the very best have increased wheat production by around 40 per cent between *c.*1750 and 1830: a period in which the demand for wheat more than doubled.

Transforming England

A landscape history perspective, looking at the 'agricultural revolution' within its spatial and environmental context, thus throws some doubt on certain established interpretations. But such a perspective can also suggest new lines of enquiry. Perhaps the most important argument contained in this book is a simple one: there was not one agricultural revolution in the eighteenth and early nineteenth centuries, but many. The classic revolution of the light soils, involving the cultivation of new

[1] This figure assumes that around 24 per cent of England was enclosed, by both parliamentary and non-parliamentary means, between *c.*1750 and 1830; that around 60 per cent, or *c.*3.3 million acres, of this was common land; that two-thirds of this was converted to arable; and that the arable area in 1750 already amounted to *c.*10 million acres: very optimistic estimates.

fodder crops, the enclosure of open fields and the reclamation of sheepwalks, was only one pattern of change. In the Midlands, vast areas of arable land were put down to grass, while on the claylands of the east the key developments were the spread of under-drainage and, in some districts, the simplification of ancient woodpasture landscapes. In the East Anglian Fenland improvements to drainage, the enclosure and reclamation of areas of common fen, and the claying of peat soils were fundamental developments, while in the north and west the widespread improvement of moorlands and pastures by liming and 'soughing' was perhaps the most important change. But as I have emphasised, this is a very general account, and there were many local variations, with particular regions and districts following their own distinct paths of development.

And yet, viewed from the perspective of landscape history, it is evident that underlying this diversity there were some more general themes. In particular, when James Caird came, in 1852, to draw a map of English farming he did not produce one anything like as complicated as those of early modern farming regions, created by scholars like Joan Thirsk or Eric Kerridge. He did not illustrate a complex mosaic of arable and pastoral areas intermingled throughout the country. Instead he posited a much simpler arrangement, a dichotomy between an essentially arable south and east, and an essentially pastoral north and west (Figure 32: Caird 1852, i). The Tithe Files—compiled a decade and a half earlier—naturally reveal a more complex picture (Figure 33). A number of districts deviated markedly from Caird's broad pattern. The Norfolk Broads and the 'hay belt' around London, for example, remained largely under grass, while Caird arguably exaggerated the importance of arable in the Weald of Kent and Sussex, and certainly

underplayed its extent in certain western districts, especially parts of Shropshire, Herefordshire and Staffordshire. Nevertheless, this more analytical source does confirm, in general terms, the broad thrust of Caird's bald generalisation. It reveals, in the words of Roger Kain, 'a marked distinction in amounts of arable and grass between the east and west of the country' (Kain 1986, 458). This pattern was already in place by the start of the century, to judge from the 1801 Crop Returns (Turner 1981, 297) but it became much sharper through the 1820s and 1830s with, in particular, the expansion of arable in the Fens.

The area of arable expanded significantly in the period c.1750–1830, not merely through the reclamation of 'waste' but through the ploughing up of pasture land long held in severalty. But more significant than any *general* increase in the extent of arable land was this new concentration in the east of England. Traditionally, historians have focused on two ways in which the production of arable crops could be achieved: by raising yields per acre, and by expanding the area under cultivation at the expense of under-utilised 'waste'. There is, however, a third way: by changing the geography of agricultural production, so that less of a particular crop is grown in places unsuitable for its cultivation, and more in the places best suited.

A number of variables effect crop yields and these have been studied in some detail by plant biologists, and modelled in a variety of ways. One model, the CERES model for predicting wheat growth, takes into account aspects of soil, together with variations in rainfall and temperature, and has been employed successfully in most regions of the world (Ritchie 1984). It has also been used to examine the production of wheat in an eighteenth-century context, in an important

OUTLINE MAP OF ENGLAND,

Showing the distinction between the Corn and Grazing counties; and the line of division between high and low Wages.

All to the East of the black line, running from North to South, may be regarded as the chief Corn Districts of England; the average rental per acre of the cultivated land of which is 30 per cent. less than that of the counties to the West of the same line, which are the principal Grazing, Green Crop, and Dairy districts.

The dotted line, running from East to West, shows the line of Wages; the average of the counties to the North of that line being 37 per cent. higher than those to the South of it.

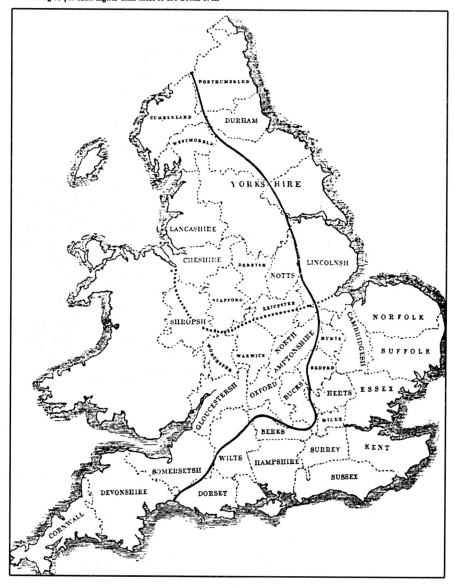

Figure 32   English farming regions, as depicted by James Caird in 1852

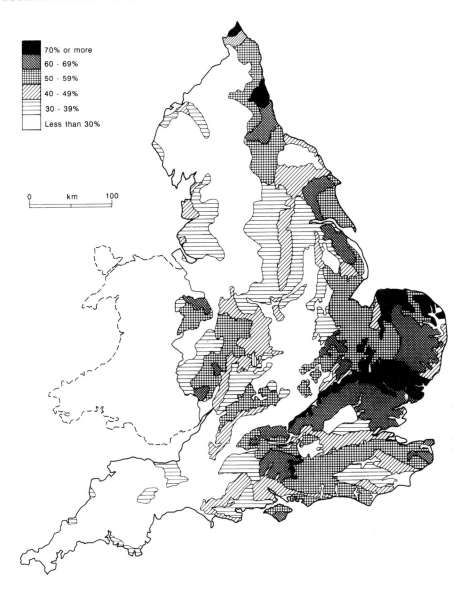

Legend:
- 70% or more
- 60 - 69%
- 50 - 59%
- 40 - 49%
- 30 - 39%
- Less than 30%

0   km   100

Figure 33   The distribution of arable land in England, c.1836, compiled from the Tithe Files

paper by the economic historian Liam Brunt (Brunt 1997). As Brunt observed, temperature is a significant determinant of wheat yields:

> For most of the lifecycle of the wheat plant there is no relationship between temperature and the future grain yield of the plant—temperature only affects the date at which the wheat plant reaches maturity . . . But once the wheat plant has matured and started to produce grain then the temperature becomes important (Brunt 1997, 9).

Essentially, lower July temperatures help to increase the grain size, by lengthening the period of 'filling', while high August temp-eratures help to dry out the grain and prevent sprouting. But rainfall 'is by far the most important climatic factor determining the wheat yield in Western Europe'. This is because 'the grain yield is susceptible to rainfall fluctuations *throughout* the growth cycle': when the wheat plant is developing; in early summer when the grains are 'filling'; and in late summer, when the grains are harvested (Brunt 1997, 7). In short, wheat produces the heaviest yields in areas of modest rainfall.

Brunt examined a number of variables in eighteenth- and early nineteenth-century agriculture, including the use of particular rotations, in an attempt to ascertain whether it was environmental factors or peculiarities of farming practice which ensured that eighteenth-century English farmers generally produced significantly higher yields than their Continental neighbours. He concluded that climatic factors were most important, giving English farmers an advantage 'of up to 3 bushels per acre'. In addition, factors of soil quality 'may also have given English farmers an advantage of up to 2 bushels'. Nature, not nurture, was the prime determinant of differences in national crop yields (Brunt 1997, 9).

Brunt was interested in comparing English with (in particular) French agriculture. The evidence presented in the foregoing chapters, however, allows us to use some of these findings to throw light on changes occurring *within* England, in the course of the long eighteenth century. Looked at in this way, it is immediately apparent that one of the most important developments of the period was that the arable area increased to the greatest extent in those parts of the country best suited by climate for the production of cereal crops, the dry south and east of England. It is true that tillage also expanded in certain districts in the west of England—especially in Herefordshire, Shropshire and Staffordshire. All, significantly, were areas of comparatively low rainfall within the generally wetter west. But the contribution made by these to the nation's grain requirements was limited. In spite of the widespread adoption of many of the key improvements here, cereal yields seem to have stubbornly refused to rise. In the mid-1830s, to judge from the Tithe Files, 'all grain yields were highest in eastern and south eastern counties'. By this time a third of all English grain was produced by just six eastern counties (Lincolnshire, Essex, Cambridgeshire, Norfolk, Suffolk and Huntingdon) (Kain 1986, 461). And it was in the expansion of cultivation in the east of England, as we have seen, that the new fodder crops made their greatest contribution to agricultural productivity, by allowing a dramatic reduction in the area of grassland while still maintaining livestock numbers, and thus the quantities of manure required to keep the land in heart.

The relative contribution made to England's grain supplies by these various southern and eastern districts probably varied considerably. Precise figures are hard to obtain because, as we have seen, the output of grain was a function of three interrelated variables, and we seldom have reliable information about all of them: the amount of land under cultivation, the yields per acre, and the type of rotation employed. We might guess, however, that while the 'light land revolution' did play a significant role, it was the ploughing of the eastern clays and the Fens which provided the bulk of the additional wheat required to feed England's expanding population. Not only did these soils make particularly good wheat land. It was on soils of this type, and particularly those formed over clayey drift, that the climatic differences between east and west were, and are, most marked:

Most of eastern England from Yorkshire south to Essex suffers from a net water deficit in the summer months. The drift soils are particularly valuable at this stage because the lower subsoil layers, often being relatively impervious, retain water received from the upper layers during winter. In western Britain, with higher rainfall, this facility is of little advantage and the frequent poorly-drained characteristics of the drift soils only serve to make them more difficult to cultivate (Curtis *et al.* 1996, 70–5).

The arable acreage probably increased by around 70 per cent on the boulder clays of East Anglia, Essex and Hertfordshire; even greater increases took place on the coastal plains of the north-east. But it was the ploughing of the East Anglian and Lincolnshire Fens which must have made the greatest contribution to wheat supplies. Comparatively little land had been under cultivation, on either silt-clay or peat soils, in c.1700: probably around 10 per cent of their combined land area. By the 1830s around 55 per cent of both districts was in tilth. At this time, the installation of underdrains and the practice of 'claying' were still making progress, and the arable acreage was still expanding. The Tithe Files nevertheless suggest that around 30 per cent of the cultivated acreage was devoted to wheat and that this yielded, on average, some 27 bushels per acre. On this basis, between the late seventeenth century and c.1836 the wheat output of the fen soils may have increased from around half a million bushels per annum to around 3.5 million. Further expansion of arable here during the high farming period, coupled with further enhancement of yields, makes it probable that around 8 million bushels of wheat per annum were being produced in the Fenlands by the 1870s, perhaps

sixteen times the quantity in c.1700. The arablisation of the Fens arguably made the single greatest contribution to England's escalating demand for wheat in the eighteenth and nineteenth centuries, and it is curious that the history of Fenland farming has formed such a minor part of conventional histories of the 'agricultural revolution'.

'Not by bread alone'

I have tended to concentrate in this book on the production of wheat. This is partly because this is what most obsessed contemporaries, worried by the inability of the nation to feed its teaming poor, and about the possible social unrest which food shortages might engender. But it is also because, in the final analysis, wheat remained—and remains—the single most important source of nutrition in the country (Turner *et al.* 2001, 116). Indeed, in the period under discussion here it became steadily *more* important as the principal bread grain, as the consumption of oats and rye declined (Collins 1975). Yet the changes outlined in the preceding chapters—in the practice of farming, and in patterns of land use—also affected the production of other crops and commodities.

Changes in the output of barley have been touched on several times in the course of this book. On average, across England as a whole, yields rose from around 25 to 49 bushels an acre between the 1720s and the 1830s (Turner *et al.* 2001, 153). But this average conceals the fact that increases on the poorest light land—the heaths of East Anglia, for example—were even more dramatic, yields virtually tripling in some districts in this period, from around 14 to around 40 bushels (Wade Martins and Williamson 1999a, 164–5). The yields of barley thus improved more than those of wheat during the agricultural revolution period, and this almost certainly reflects the importance of liming, marling and under-drainage in the enhancement of cereal yields: barley is more susceptible than wheat to both excess soil acidity and waterlogging. But the volume of this crop produced in England was also increased in other ways. Firstly, barley only produces good yields in areas of moderate rainfall (D.H. Robinson 1949, 195). It is even more sensitive to excess precipita-tion than wheat, especially in late summer, and the increasing concentration of arable in the drier east of England will, of necessity, have served to raise average national yields. Secondly, on the more fertile soils of south-ern and eastern England—on the better clays and fertile loams of East Anglia and the Home Counties in particular—the 'improved' rotation most commonly adopted in the second half of the eighteenth century was not the famous 'Norfolk four-course' but a variant featuring an additional course of barley after the wheat: that is, wheat > barley > turnips > barley > clover. Not only did more fertile soils permit such intensive courses of cropping. Unless intensively cropped, some of these soils were *too* fertile for the pro-duction of good-quality barley, which was prone to 'lodge'. There is an important contrast here, in other words, with the effect of the new rotations on the production of wheat. While their adoption frequently led to a decrease in the amount of wheat under cultivation, it often led to an *increase* in the barley acreage. Most of the barley was turned into malt and used in the brewing industry. But much was used as animal feed, and some was destined for consumption as bread, for in parts of the north especially barley bread continued to be consumed on some scale well into the nineteenth century.

Oats continued to be a significant crop, especially in the north of England, and once again yields increased throughout the nine-teenth century. This too was used both for livestock feed, especially for horses, and also for human consumption. But the quantity grown declined steadily, and whereas in 1801 over a quarter of the national cropped acre-age had been occupied by oats, by c.1836 this figure had fallen to just over an eighth (12.8 per cent) (Turner 1981, 296; Kain 1986, 460). The acreage devoted to rye declined more dramatically, however. This crop had been widely cultivated on acid soils, even in the south-east, at the start of the eighteenth century but had virtually disappeared from most districts by the early nineteenth century, remaining significant only in very limited areas of the north and west (Overton 1996a, 103). In large measure this reflects the fact that, with the spread of marling and liming, and improved drainage, it was possible to grow more profitable and nutritious cereal crops in such contexts. Bailey and Culley in 1805 thus noted how in Northumberland 'The soils which formerly were occupied in growing rye are now so much improved by the use of lime, that they produce abundant crops of excellent wheat' (Bailey and Culley 1805, 79). Rye was one of several crops which, important in the early eighteenth century, fell from favour in the agricultural revolution period, including buckwheat and vetches. But one crop, in particular, increased in popularity, and is of particular relevance to the central theme of this book.

Although the subject of a pioneering study by Salaman in 1949, the potato has received little attention from historians. The crop had been grown in gardens since the sixteenth century, and by the eighteenth century was widely cultivated by farmers and labourers. It is a major source of carbohydrates, and also of vitamin C. Indeed, a crop of potatoes yields nearly twice as much nutritional value per acre as cereals (de Rougemont 1989, 280). The Crop Returns of 1801 indicate that their cultivation on a small scale was widespread, but as a major field crop they were mainly a feature of marginal, often rather acid lands in the north and west of England—especially in Cumberland, Cheshire and Lancashire. The latter county boasted the most extensive area of the crop, 8 per cent of the cropped acreage. Across England as a whole potatoes accounted for around 2 per cent of the cultivated area (Turner 1981, 296).

There are signs, however, that they were being planted on an increasing scale at this time, and by the 1820s William Cobbett could refer to the 'modern custom of using potatoes to supply the place of bread' (Cobbett 1822, 48). Unfortunately the Tithe Files are somewhat cavalier in their treatment of the crop (Kain 1986, 56). In many districts potatoes were not tithable, or subject to only small tithes and subsumed within the general category of 'fodder crops' (Kain 1986, 243). But they do appear to have been more widely grown, especially on reclaimed wetlands in eastern England, where they often replaced turnips as a fallow crop. Potatoes thrive on acid, peat soils, especially those with a high summer water table and a temperate climate. Fenland reclamation must have been an important factor in their increased cultivation. The steady improvement in communications in the course of the nineteenth century was a further encouragement. Although acre for acre potatoes yield twice as much nutrition as cereals, 'they are less concentrated as a food source . . . because of their high water content, their storage life is shorter, and the cost of transport much greater' (de Rougemont 1989, 280). The establishment of the railway network, in particular, made it possible for the crop to be cultivated on a large scale at some distance from its principal markets, London and the conurbations of the north

and west. I would not want to overemphasise the contribution made by the increased cultivation of this rather neglected crop, but that contribution was, nevertheless, a significant one. Between 1801 and 1880 the area under potatoes may have increased by some 70 per cent, from c.2 per cent to some 3.4 per cent of the cropped arable acreage— some 325,000 acres, figures which exclude the unrecorded but doubtless large quantities grown in gardens and allotments (Turner 1981, 296; BPP LXXVI, 674). Potatoes may well have played a major part in filling any gap in the nation's requirements for carbohydrates left by a shortfall in cereal production.

There were thus important changes in the production of crops other than wheat in the course of the eighteenth and nineteenth centuries. But equally important, although more difficult to quantify, were improvements in livestock production. Historians have long concentrated on the changes made in arable farming in this period. But as we have seen, over large areas of England the key development of the eighteenth century was in fact the expansion of pasture. The average quality of grassland was, moreover, improved not merely by the kinds of interventions described in Chapters 2 and 5—better drainage, liming, the use of potash, etc—but also by virtue of the fact that, with the changes in agrarian geography which took place during the eighteenth century, the bulk of grazing land was now concentrated towards the west of the country, where high levels of rainfall allowed good grass growth both early and late in the summer.

But even the classic improvements in arable farming—the adoption of turnips and clover—were as much about increasing livestock production as they were about enhancing the cultivation of cereals. After all, the adoption of the 'Norfolk four-course' or its variants generally served to increase the acreage of fodder crops at the expense of cereals: it is perverse logic, indeed, that views this development solely in terms of grain production. While in most of the main arable areas the adoption of the new crops was accompanied by a marked reduction in the area under pasture, livestock numbers were at least maintained. And while historians have often viewed sheep and bullocks in arable districts as, in effect, machines for producing manure, adjuncts to the real business of arable husbandry, in reality livestock were crucial to farm incomes, even in periods of high corn prices. Farming journals and similar sources show that farmers paid as much attention to the buying and selling of stores, and to other matters of livestock husbandry, as they did to their grain crops. Even in arable Norfolk, William Marshall in 1787 argued that the 'affluent fortunes' made by farmers came not from growing cereals, but through dealing in stock (Marshall 1787, 345; Wade Martins and Williamson 1995). Indeed, with the adoption of the new, larger and faster-maturing breeds, the income from meat and wool was probably more important than it had been before the 'improvements', especially on the more marginal heathland soils. In the course of the nineteenth century—with the advent of the new techniques of high farming, the large-scale use of oil cake as supplementary feed, and substantial improvements in cattle housing—it is clear that the importance of livestock in ostensibly 'arable' areas increased still further, and much of the additional grain produced in this period was probably, as Walton has suggested, used as fodder (Walton 1999).

Insofar as historians have paid much attention to the development of livestock husbandry in this period they have tended to concentrate on the improvements made to sheep and cattle breeds by men like the Collings brothers or Robert Bakewell (Trow Smith 1959). Recent archaeological research has emphasised the gradual nature of such changes in the course of the post-medieval period (Davis and Beckett 1999). But changes there were during the period studied here and these were closely related to the wider developments in landscape, land management and land use which have been the main concern of this book. As Pitt noted in Northamptonshire in 1813:

> The common-field sheep . . . are much inferior to the ancient-pasture sheep, longer in the leg, and smaller and less compact in the carcass, and, in some instances, horned; these sheep were meant for the fold, and if they would endure that, and the necessary length of walk daily, to and from pasture in the fallow, or elsewhere, little attention was paid to other circumstances (Pitt 1813b, 203).

The new, faster-maturing breeds would never have been developed if the old forms of arable farming—fallows, folds, and the rest—had persisted. Improvements in fodder were of crucial importance, as contemporaries were well aware (Ryder 1964, 7). By 1830 most maturing livestock enjoyed a more sedentary lifestyle, and were fattened on clover and turnips, or on pastures better drained, and more intensively limed and fertilised, than a century earlier. Not surprisingly, the available figures suggest phenomenal improvements in meat production in the course of the eighteenth and nineteenth centuries. Michael Turner has examined the surviving returns of censuses of live and dead stock carried out by the government in 1798 and 1803, in preparation for an expected French invasion; and, extrapolating from these, he has suggested that there may have been around 2.4 million cattle and 12.2 million sheep in the country in *c.*1800 (Turner 1998, 156). By the late 1860s, these figures had grown to 3.6 million and 18.9 million respectively. Using rather different, indirect methods of calculation, Mark Overton has suggested that across the period 1700–1850 there may have been an increase in annual meat production of around 150 per cent, and in dairy production of around 220 per cent (Overton 1996a, 75).

True, increases in meat production did not keep pace with population growth, and inequalities of consumption were a significant aspect of the widening gulf between rich and poor in the period. And indeed, in general, although the achievements of the agricultural revolution allowed the English population to double in the period *c.*1750–1830, a large proportion of the rural workforce, in particular, were appallingly fed, especially in the period of bad harvests between 1780 and 1820.

Explaining Agrarian Change

This is a book about the development of farming and the rural landscape. But these topics cannot be understood in isolation from broader patterns of economic and institutional change. These are matters which have been discussed at length by more competent authorities than myself (Overton 1996a), but it might be useful, nevertheless, to highlight those factors and influences which, in the light of the arguments presented here, may have had the greatest impact upon the development of agriculture during the eighteenth and nineteenth centuries.

We began our story in the late seventeenth century, with England as a complex mosaic of farming regions. The pattern and distribution of these was closely related to soil types: in particular, in the lowland areas of the south and east, light land districts were primarily

devoted to cereal production, while heavy and damp soils were used for fattening livestock, and for dairying. But patterns of regional specialization were also determined in part by antecedent structures, tenurial and social, inherited from the medieval past. In particular, the Midland clays, potentially good grazing country, remained for the most part an arable region in the early modern period because of the complex intermixture of properties in, and consequent resistance to enclosure of, the 'regular' and extensive open fields generally found there. In the course of the agricultural revolution period this pattern was radically changed, and the simpler one that emerged was primarily related not to soils, but to *climate*. Arable land became concentrated in the south and east of England, where grassland and other forms of grazing declined markedly, with the reclamation of sheepwalks, the ploughing of clay pastures, and the draining of fens.

This transformation of agricultural geography was not, of course, alone responsible for increases in production. The overall area under arable cultivation expanded between 1750 and 1830 and the productivity of both existing grassland and existing arable increased. These improvements were, as I hope I have shown, achieved in diverse ways in different areas, but more assiduous drainage and increased levels of liming and marling were perhaps the most significant developments. So much is tolerably clear.

But what lay behind these changes? Why did England's agricultural geography change fundamentally in the agricultural revolution period; and why were simple and often long-familiar techniques like underdraining and marling now adopted on such a large scale? We can identify a number of key factors, some relatively straightforward, others more complex, which underpinned this 'revolution' in agriculture.

Firstly, changes in patterns of landholding (the increasing size and consolidation of large estates) coupled with legal and institutional changes (the development of parliamentary enclosure) finally permitted the enclosure of those areas of England in which properties were intermixed, or use-rights were shared, in the most complex ways. It is important to emphasise, once again, that enclosure did not simply or directly lead to a massive expansion of tillage at the expense of 'waste'. Across very large areas of England it actually led to the laying down of arable to grass, while a very high proportion of the common grazing enclosed either remained in its virgin state or else was reclaimed for only a very short period of time. But enclosure did pave the way for the more efficient draining of the Fens, and allowed the ploughing up of great tracts of sheepwalk on the light lands of the south and east, and in general assisted the emergence of England's new agricultural geography.

Yet this development required something else: the widespread adoption of the new crops and rotations. Turnips, clover and the 'Norfolk four-course' may have served to increase cereal yields in some places but their main contribution was to allow an expansion of ploughland at the expense of grazing in sheep-corn districts, especially in eastern England and, to a lesser extent, in eastern clayland districts which had formerly been devoted to pasture farming. They allowed stocking levels to be maintained even as permanent grazing dwindled, in some places, to almost nothing (Figure 14, p. 73). While it is true that the new fodder crops now occupied much of the land which had formerly been used to produce grain, this loss was more than offset by the sheer scale to which tillage was expanded. But the expansion of cultivation in these areas required something more. As we have seen, in many districts other things had to happen in order to make the soils more suitable for cereal farming in general, and turnip cultivation in particular. In some places drainage needed to be improved; in others soil acidity had to be neutralised; in yet others surplus trees and hedges needed to be removed. All these changes required substantial amounts of labour. Moreover, large inputs of labour were essential for the efficient working of the new rotations. Manure produced by stall-fed cattle had to be brought into the fields; the turnip crop had to be diligently hoed in the summer.

> If, as is sometimes the case . . . weeds are allowed to grow, turnips can become anything but a cleaning and restorative crop. There is no particular virtue in a turnip as a 'cleaning' agent; the crop merely offers a chance of cleaning the land and building up fertility, and it is the management rather than the crop itself which is important (Hanley 1949, 139).

A large, 'flexible' workforce was thus required, both to expand the area under cultivation and to adopt the various practices required to raise yields on existing arable land, and a substantial body of under-employed landless workers did indeed exist in most of the prime arable areas of England, as a result of increases in average farm size and massive expansion in the rural population. Moreover, in most of these areas—parts of the north-east excepted—the creation of such a workforce was greatly aided by the effects of the industrial revolution.

The links between the industrial and agricultural revolutions were many and various. The expanding industrial centres in the north and west provided a massive market for agricultural goods. At the same time, a more sophisticated transport infrastructure—turnpike roads, river navigations, and canals

—developed to service the new economy. By 1830 there were 1,100 turnpike trusts administering 22,000 miles of road, and 4,250 miles of navigable inland waterway in England (Cossons 1987, 254). This allowed easier movement of grain and other agricultural products (Chartres 1995, 130–2), and thus encouraged specialisation in production in places distant from the expanding urban and industrial markets: not only in the south and east, but also in those areas in the west which were, compared with neighbouring districts, better suited to cereal growing. This in turn gave further *discouragement* to small-scale grain production in unsuitable locations in the north and west, farmers shifting in many cases into forms of agriculture better suited to the needs of expanding industrial conurbations—dairying and hay production in particular. Coupled with the expansion of coalfields, improved transport also lowered the price of lime and increased both the extent and intensity of its use, bringing advantages to both arable and pasture farmers in the north and west.

But industrialisation had other effects. The development of large-scale, water-powered forms of production in the north and west of England, the steady expansion of coalfields, and changes in the character of iron production, all led in the second half of the eighteenth century to the progressive *de*-industrialisation of many other regions, in which various forms of proto-industrial production had formerly constituted a major part of the economy. The most dramatic decline was in textile production which had, since medieval times, been important in East Anglia and Essex (Coleman 1962). But other industries in the south and east also dwindled in importance in the course of the eighteenth century, such as the iron industry of the Weald, its single main competitive advantage—the availability of large quantities of charcoal—progressively undermined by the development of smelting with coke. Many southern and eastern districts had long been densely populated and, while in relative terms demographic growth was fastest in the north and west, there was no reduction in the numbers of people in these increasingly rural districts. Indeed, labour mobility was restricted by institutional structures—by the operation of the Poor Law, which limited relief to those who could claim a settlement, through birth or marriage, in a particular community.

All this had important effects on wages. In Hunt's words,

> Between 1760 and 1800 the wages geography of Britain changed to the advantage of the industrialising areas. London remained a high-wage centre and wages were still high in some counties nearby. But southern counties more distant from London suffered a substantial fall in real wages (Hunt 1986, 960).

It was not only that real wages fell across much of the south and east. More important was the fact that employment became increasingly short-term and casualised—'flexible', in the words of right-wing economists. Labourers were increasingly employed for the day, on piecework, or to undertake a specific task for an amount agreed beforehand (Raynbird 1846; Forby 1796; Wade Martins and Williamson 1997; Collins 1987). The available work was often spread thinly among the poor, moreover, in order to keep them from claiming on the poor rates—a perennial concern among landowners and farmers.

By the early nineteenth century living conditions among rural labourers in many arable districts—the majority of whom now possessed neither land of their own nor access to commons—were appalling. But a workforce now existed which was ideally suited to the farming practices of the 'new husbandry'. Indeed, it is likely that increases in yields in some areas in this period may have owed much to the simple fact that ground was now being prepared, and crops nurtured, with greater care—mirroring the similar improvements effected during the population explosion of the high Middle Ages (Campbell 1991). But in addition a 'flexible' workforce was ideally suited for the tasks required when clayland pastures, or the heaths and wolds of sheep-corn districts, were being put to the plough. Economic historians often discuss the levels of investment required in the agricultural improvements of the eighteenth and nineteenth centuries. But the most important tasks in the main arable areas—installing underdrains, marling, removing or realigning hedgerows or felling pollards—primarily involved high (if sporadic) inputs of labour. Indeed, as we have seen, the distinguishing feature of the agricultural revolution was that it relied on the recycling of materials produced on the farm, rather than imported from beyond its boundaries. The farm was a closed circuit: labour was the principal external input.

In a variety of ways, therefore, the agricultural and industrial revolutions were intimately connected, and the new geography of farming reflected, as much as anything, the improvements in transport and the relentless integration of the national economy which took place in the course of the eighteenth and nineteenth centuries. Defoe and other eighteenth-century writers on political economy repeatedly emphasised the growing interdependence of the regional economies of England. But it was William Cobbett, early in the following century, who most succinctly expressed the way in which industrialisation in one region might encourage agricultural expansion elsewhere.

Commenting on how all the harvested wheat he had seen on his recent travels through the north 'would not make the one-half of what I have many times seen in one single rickyard of the vales of Wiltshire', he continued: 'But this is all very proper: these coal-diggers, and iron-smelters, and knife-makers, compel us to send the food to them, which, indeed, we do very cheerfully, in exchange for the produce of their rocks, and the wondrous works of their hands' (Cobbett 1830, 495).

As the industrial revolution progressed, of course, all this changed. Improvements in technology and transport, and in urban living standards, in the period after c.1830, and a growth in alternative forms of employment in the southern and eastern counties, together transformed the character of agriculture. Farms began to rely increasingly on manufactured products, and on materials brought to them not only from beyond their boundaries but from beyond the shores of the nation: drainage pipes, guano, oil cake, superphosphates. Machines—threshing machines, reaper-binders—were increasingly substituted for human labour, and farm buildings were designed to maximise labour efficiency. As urban living standards rose, livestock became ever more important within primarily arable districts, while in grassland farming areas dairying frequently increased in importance. Both developments, like the expansion of the potato acreage, were ultimately dependent on the ease of communication now afforded by the national rail network. High farming was born, and the application of science boosted productivity to unprecedented heights.

The Making of the Modern Landscape

The high levels of investment necessary to sustain 'high farming' could only continue for as long as the market for agricultural produce remained buoyant. But from the late 1870s prices began to fall, and farming started to slide into a long period of depression (Perry 1974, 21–33). The principal cause was the expansion of the American railway network into the prairies of the mid-west, which meant that European markets were flooded with large quantities of cheap grain. Prices, rents and land values all fell steeply in the course of the 1880s. After a brief period of stabilisation, a further intense depression occurred in the 1890s, this time affecting not only arable farmers but also livestock producers, as cheap meat and dairy produce were imported, on refrigerated ships, from the New World and Australia. The technological improvements, particularly in transport, which had encouraged the development of high farming now led to a crisis in English agriculture. The depression continued, with varying degrees of intensity, up until the time of the First World War. Agricultural fortunes then revived for a short time, but the peace brought a renewed slump which continued, on and off, until the start of the next World War in 1939 (Perry 1974, 32–3).

The effects of agricultural depression on the landscape were complex and have not been sufficiently researched. The main development was the emergence of new patterns of land use as England's agrarian geography underwent a further series of changes. Firstly, the area of arable contracted, reversing the trend of the previous century and a half. In 1869 15.3 million acres were under the plough in England and Wales. By 1900 this had fallen to 12.2 million acres, and by 1939 to 8.9 million (Stamp 1950, 480–1). Grass replaced ploughland because livestock prices held up better than those for cereals, and dairying in particular remained a profitable enterprise, for large urban conurbations continued to provide a good market for fresh milk. Secondly, and catering for this same market, there was a steady expansion in market gardening and fruit-growing, especially in the Fens, providing a welcome alternative to wheat production. Thirdly, there was a widespread 'retreat from the margins'—from the edges of the upland moors, from the thinner, hungrier soils of heath and down, even from the less fertile clays of lowland England, especially in the Weald and on the London clays of south Essex. The journalist George Millin described Essex in 1891 as a 'civilised waste', and provided a graphic account of the county's abandoned and weed-choked fields (Millin 1999 [1891], 51). Hunter Pringle, in the Royal Commission report for 1894, described areas in the south of the county where 'whole farms and tracts of country have been given up to nature' and produced maps showing an abundance of derelict land (BPP XVI, 1, 704, 801). Here, as in the Weald, abandonment was soon reversed as hard-pressed wheat growers turned land over to pasture, or farmed their holdings less intensively. More serious, and of longer-term significance, was the situation in the northern uplands, and on the poor light lands of the south and east.

In heathland districts land was abandoned wholesale and many landed estates became little more than vast game farms. Agriculturalists now regarded the earlier expansion of tillage here with less enthusiasm than had Young or his contemporaries. In 1888 James Caird roundly declared that 'there is no doubt that vast areas of poor down and heath land, in the south of England, were converted to arable at the beginning of this century—land that cannot be tilled profitably now, and that cannot be restored to its former condition within any reasonable limit of time, if ever' (Caird 1888, 124–5). The East Anglian Breckland was particularly badly hit. On the 5,000-acre Downham Hall estate in

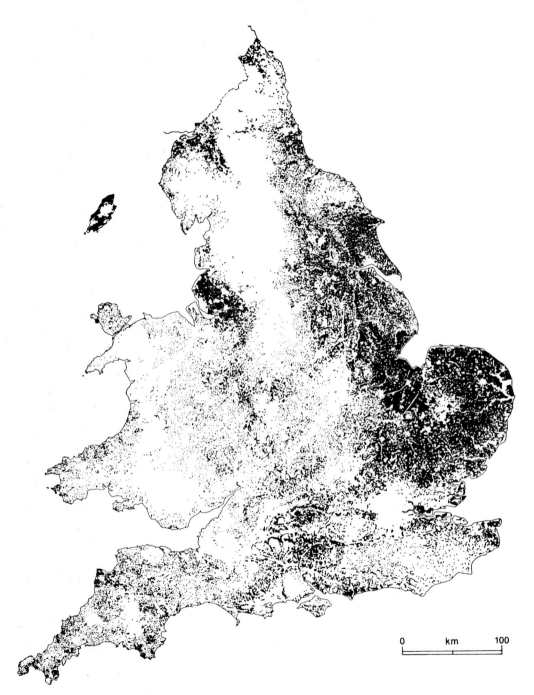

Figure 34   The distribution of arable land in England, c.1940, as mapped by the Land Utilisation Survey (after Stamp 1950)

Suffolk in 1923, for example, not a single farm was let and most of the land was derelict (Skipper and Williamson 1997, 22). Like many other Breckland estates in the 1920s, Downham was purchased by the Forestry Commission and almost entirely planted with conifers. The Commission had been established by the government at the end of the First World War in an effort to maintain the nation's strategic timber supplies, and also to revitalise the depressed economies of the more agriculturally marginal regions of Britain (Ryle 1969). Many areas of both acid heath and upland moor were bought and planted up by the Commission through the 1920s and 1930s, bringing dramatic changes to these landscapes which are with us still.

The agricultural geography of England was mapped, with a detail never accomplished before or matched since, by the Land Utilisation Survey in the 1930s, towards the end of the depression years (Stamp 1950, 85) (Figure 34). The most striking changes since the nineteenth century were the virtual disappearance of arable land from the Weald and other areas of difficult clay soils in the south-east of England, and the sharp decline of arable farming throughout the west. With the notable exception of the Lancashire Plain, where there had been a significant expansion of ploughland, the darkest areas on the map all lie in the east of the country, in a band stretching from London northwards to Northumberland. In Stamp's words, 'the cultivation of wheat . . . became more and more restricted to good arable soils . . . in the drier eastern counties, where a harvest of good grain was assured' (Stamp 1950, 389). The great divide between arable east and pastoral west which had emerged in the agricultural revolution period was thus sharpened still further in this era of relative decline.

The environmental effects of the long depression years were evidently mixed. On the one hand, large-scale afforestation took place not only over abandoned arable fields but also at the expense of virgin heathland and moor, land which had escaped the agricultural intensification and mania for 'improvement' of the early nineteenth century. In addition, many important semi-natural habitats, including much surviving common land in the south and east of England, suffered from neglect and poor management, and tumbled down to secondary woodland of marginal botanical interest. On the other hand, farming at lower levels of intensity, together with the general expansion of grassland at the expense of tillage, undoubtedly favoured wildlife and the environment. The neat, manicured and well-managed landscape of high farming was replaced by something rougher and wilder: hedges grew high and wide, drainage works were neglected, damp areas returned to once drained fields. All in all, farming might have been in decline, but wildlife flourished. Low farm incomes had other effects. The removal of hedges came to a virtual standstill, and little was done to farm buildings: something which explains, of course, why so many of the barns, cattle houses, granaries and the rest erected during the agricultural revolution and high farming periods survived into the second half of the twentieth century—in the intervening years farmers had no money to invest in anything more modern.

All this was dramatically changed, as is now well known, by the Second World War, by post-War government policies, and latterly by Britain's entry into the European Economic Community. With the recovery of farming fortunes, an onslaught on the environment was begun by farmers now armed with all the new technologies which had developed during the previous fifty years—tractors, herbicides, JCBs, improved drainage systems (Shoard 1980; Mabey 1980). The arable acreage expanded dramatically, not only in areas which had been in tillage before the depression but also in quite new districts: the remaining areas of ancient chalk downland in southern England thus came under renewed attack and the Midland pastures began to revert once more to plough-land as the arable frontier moved steadily eastwards. In both new and old arable areas, hedges began to disappear at a rapid rate: they were redundant in a landscape of arable monoculture, and got in the way of combine harvesters and other large machinery. Ponds were filled in, trees felled and copses grubbed out, and many areas of wetland drained and ploughed. These developments were most dramatic in the arable east, but the west and north were not immune to hedge removal, and to the general decline of landscape features rendered redundant by technological change as, for example, barbed wire replaced stone walls as the most efficient method of providing a stock-proof barrier. Moreover, whereas in the lowlands the expansion of conifer plantations now occurred only on a limited scale—albeit often at the expense of existing ancient, semi-natural woodland—in the upland districts it continued at a dramatic rate, swamping many thousands of hectares of moorland. At the time of writing the high tide of arable intensification seems to have passed, and a host of other threats to the rural landscape has emerged, arising not so much from farming as from such things as road schemes and sprawling suburbanisation. These matters, however, take us far from the themes of this book, and cannot be discussed here.

Conclusion

It might appear that the 'transformation of rural England' discussed in this volume is an arcane matter, of interest only to students of agricultural history. But the changes I have outlined have a much wider relevance: to archaeologists, landscape historians, and to all those interested in the history of the countryside and in the infinitely complex relationship between man and the natural world.

Many landscape historians probably carry around in their heads Rackham's useful map of 'planned' and 'ancient' countryside. I would invite them also to internalise the other, admittedly over-simple, maps in Figure 35, and the nature of the differences between them. The successive 'transformations' of England they indicate together help explain many aspects of the rural landscape, from variations in settlement patterns and field size to the distribution of landscape parks. Social historians, too, might derive some benefit from their perusal. They have often embraced early modern farming regions as an aid to understanding past local and regional communities. But the impact of the disintegration of this pattern in the course of the eighteenth and nineteenth centuries has, perhaps, received less attention.

Archaeologists might also learn something. They are increasingly aware that the distributions of sites and earthworks which form an important aspect of their study are structured and patterned, to a significant degree, by later processes. In particular, the plough is the enemy of the past, levelling upstanding earthworks and pulverising the more fragile artefacts, especially certain kinds of pottery, in the ploughsoil. Patterns of land use in the historic period are thus of some importance in understanding the nature of archaeological data, and two relevant observations arise from this study. Firstly, it is clear that the expansion of tillage into marginal areas during the agricultural revolution period

(a)

(b)

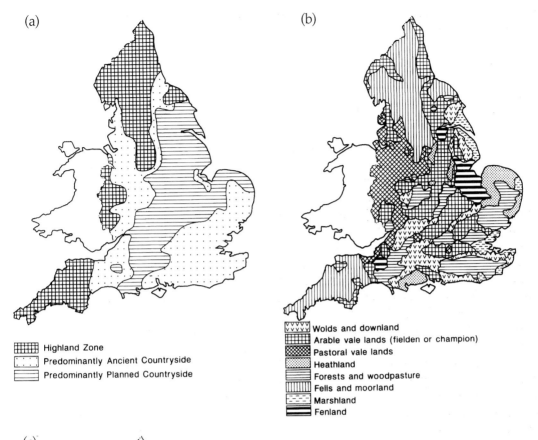

Wolds and downland
Arable vale lands (fielden or champion)
Pastoral vale lands
Heathland
Forests and woodpasture
Fells and moorland
Marshland
Fenland

Highland Zone
Predominantly Ancient Countryside
Predominantly Planned Countryside

(c)

Figure 35   Transformations of England. The distinction between champion areas, and districts of more dispersed settlement and irregular field systems and enclosed fields, is still echoed in the modern landscape in the distinction between Rackham's planned and ancient countryside (a). Over this broad dichotomy, however, was imposed the farming regions of the early modern period, mapped here by Joan Thirsk (b). This in turn was overlain by the simpler pattern of farming which emerged in the agricultural revolution period, as mapped by Caird in 1852 (c). The three maps together provide a simple but useful conceptual framework for understanding the development of the English landscape

must have levelled many upstanding earth-works from the prehistoric past. Much of this land was subsequently abandoned, reverting to its original state of moorland or heath; when interpreting apparent gaps in archae-ological distributions in such areas we should never forget, or underestimate, the extent of 'improvement', even in the most unlikely of contexts, during the eighteenth and nine-teenth centuries. Secondly, it is possible that the dichotomy which emerged in this period—between the arable east, and pastoral west—has helped structure a number of familiar distributions. The paucity of ridge and furrow in many eastern counties—especially East Anglia—in spite of the presence here of both heavy clay soils and open field agriculture, compared with its abundance in the grass 'shires' of the Midlands, may reflect post-medieval land use patterns as much as variations in medieval ploughing practice (Liddiard 1999). The distribution of other forms of medieval and post-medieval earthwork display a similar bias towards the Midlands and the west. Pillow mounds—the low, cigar-shaped mounds constructed as artificial rabbit warrens—are almost unknown in eastern England although documentary evidence suggests that they were once common here (Loveday and Williamson 1988; Williamson 1998a).

Indeed, patterned distruction may have helped frame our more general perceptions of English archaeology. The traditional pre-eminence of Wessex in studies of the Neolithic and Bronze Age is only partly a consequence of the existence in this region of the largest and most sophisticated ceremonial monuments, such as Stonehenge, Silbury Hill or Avebury. It also reflects the fact that large areas of ancient chalk grassland and associated prehistoric monu-ments—round barrows, field systems—

survived here into the nineteenth century in a way that they did not on the chalk wolds of Lincolnshire and Yorkshire, which were much more intensively ploughed in the eighteenth and nineteenth centuries. Recent aerial surveys have to some extent rectified this imbalance but the 'Wessex perspective' still dominates. In a similar way, much of the landscape history of medieval England has been written from a Midlands perspective, and this is partly because it was here that, until the post-war decades, extensive traces of the medieval landscape existed in archae-ological form, fossilised by the long drift of the 'shires' into pasture. Elsewhere the medieval landscape was either obliterated by enclosure and continued arable land use, or else survived in less obviously 'archaeo-logical' form, as upstanding lanes and boundaries. Again, modern scholarship has increasingly turned its attention to other regions of medieval England, but many of the main issues in landscape history, especially the origins of villages and of open-field agri-culture, are still addressed very much from a Midlands perspective.

In reality, of course, much of the 'medieval' landscape preserved under grass here was, strictly speaking, of *post*-medieval date. The majority of ridge and furrow dates to the period after *c*.1500, in the sense that the land in question was last ploughed in the neces-sary fashion after this date. And we are, perhaps, sometimes too quick to label earth-works of settlement desertion as 'medieval'. In some cases, such remains represent con-traction of post-medieval date and they are, indeed, no less important or interesting for that. This is, arguably, one part of a wider problem. In general landscape archaeologists and landscape historians have tended to emphasise the medieval (or earlier) origins of the English rural landscape, in part perhaps to counter claims that boundaries, hedges and footpaths are of relatively recent origin and that their removal or alteration, in the name of farming efficiency or development, is therefore a matter of small importance. Much of the fabric of the countryside, especially in areas of 'ancient countryside', is indeed very old. Yet, as I hope I have shown, the changes of the eighteenth and nineteenth centuries have everywhere left a profound mark. At a conservative estimate around 30 per cent of the hedged and walled landscape of England was created in the period after 1700 and even in areas of 'ancient countryside', already largely enclosed before this date, substantial if often subtle alterations to the field pattern occurred. Many of our 'traditional' landscapes are almost entirely the creation of this period: much of the East Anglian Fenland, for example, or the grass 'shires' of the Midlands. It is worth remembering this, perhaps, in an age increasingly concerned with 'curation', and in which the Countryside Agency laboriously maps and categorises 'traditional' landscapes in a laudable attempt to guide future planning policy. Landscapes are not timeless: they were created and endlessly modified by specific sets of economic and social circumstances, often in the relatively recent past, and their preservation is only an issue now because new forms of production or exploitation have often rendered their existing fabric redundant. Preservation is a complex issue, often more to do with patterns of middle-class residency and tourism than with anything else. In practice, landscape conservation often shades off into pastiche, as new forms of building or land-division are clothed self-consciously in the garbs of the old and, in many cases, the not-so-old. There is nothing intrinsically wrong in this, perhaps, but it is as well to recognise precisely what it is that we are doing.

The agricultural revolution certainly created new landscapes. But it also destroyed, or damaged beyond recognition, vast areas of ancient, semi-natural habitat. Conservationists sometimes talk as if the twentieth and twenty-first centuries had a monopoly on environmental vandalism. What the eighteenth and nineteenth centuries managed to achieve, with much less impressive instruments of destruction, was easily as awesome. The ancient chalk grasslands of the wolds, vast areas of heathland, great tracts of wet fenland were obliterated in an orgy of improvement. These were habitats which had remained stable for millennia. While the pockets that remain provide some indication of what we have lost, these, too, were often modified by the high tide of improving zeal. Many of the surviving areas of heathland in eastern England, for example, were under the plough in the early nineteenth century. In some 'alternative' circles the closed-circuit system of farming which characterised the agricultural revolution, typified by the Norfolk four-course, is lauded as a model of environmentally sensitive husbandry (Seymour 1975, 10–11), and so indeed it was compared with the chemical-based systems which developed in the nineteenth century, and which are with us still. But in one important respect the 'new husbandry' was intrinsically damaging. Implicit in its adoption was the collapse of the ancient distinction between permanent pasture and permanent arable. As a result, complex habitats, millennia in the making, fell to the plough.

The agricultural revolution succeeded in feeding England's expanding population, and allowed the industrial revolution to take place, but not without significant costs. In essence, rampant demographic growth and escalating production of material goods were achieved at the expense of environmental destruction, increasing social inequality, and a severance of the intimate ties between people and the land. Yet this is a world with which we should be familiar, for it is the one in which we live. The scale of the game is global now, but the essential rules remain the same.

References

Allen, R.C. 1988. 'Inferring Yields from Probate Inventories', *Journal of Economic History* 48, 117–25.

Allen, R.C. 1991. 'The Two English Agricultural Revolutions, 1450–1850'. In B. Campbell and M. Overton (eds) *Land, Labour and Livestock*, Cambridge, 236–54.

Allen, R.C. 1992. *Enclosure and the Yeoman: The Agricultural Development of the South Midlands 1450–1850*, Oxford.

Allen, R.C. 1994. 'Agriculture during the Agricultural Revolution'. In R. Floud and D. McCloskey (eds) *The Economic History of Britain since 1700*, Vol. I, Cambridge, 96–122.

Allison, K.J. 1957. 'The Sheep-Corn Husbandry of Norfolk in the Sixteenth and Seventeenth Centuries', *Agricultural History Review* 5, 12–30.

Anon. ('N') 1752. 'The Management of Three Farms in the County of Norfolk', *Gentleman's Magazine* 22, 502.

Avery, B.W., Findlay, D.C. and Mackney, D. 1974. *Soil Map of England and Wales*, Soil Survey, Harpenden.

Babbington, C.C. 1860. *Flora of Cambridgeshire*, Cambridge.

Bacon, R.N. 1844. *The Report on the Agriculture of Norfolk*, Norwich.

Bailey, J. and Culley, G. 1805. *General View of the Agriculture of Northumberland and Westmoreland*, London.

Bailey, M. 1989. *A Marginal Economy? East Anglian Breckland in the Later Middle Ages*, Cambridge.

Bailey, M. 1990. 'Sand into Gold: The Evolution of the Foldcourse System in West Suffolk, 1200–1600', *Agricultural History Review* 38, 40–57.

Baker, A.H.R. 1973. 'Field Systems of Southeast England'. In A.H.R. Baker and R.A. Butlin (eds) *Studies of Field Systems in the British Isles*, Cambridge, 377–429.

Banks, S.J. 1988. 'Nineteenth-Century Scandal or Twentieth-Century Model? A New Look at Open and Close Parishes', *Economic History Review* 41, 51–73.

Bateman, J. 1876. *The Great Landowners of England and Wales*, London.

Beastall, T.W. 1978. *The Agricultural Revolution in Lincolnshire*, Lincoln.

Beckett, J.V. 1977. 'English Landownership in the Later Seventeenth and Early Eighteenth Centuries: The Debate and the Problems', *Economic History Review* 30, 567–81.

Beckett, J.V. 1983. 'The Debate Over Farm Size in Eighteenth-Century England', *Agricultural History Review* 68, 1, 308–25.

Beckett, J.V. 1984. 'The Pattern of Landownership in England and Wales 1660–1880', *Economic History Review* 38, 1–22.

Beckett, J.V. 1986. *The Aristocracy in England 1660–1914*, Oxford.

Beckett, J.V. 1990. *The Agricultural Revolution*, London.

Beresford, M.W. 1948. 'Ridge and Furrow and the Open Fields', *Economic History Review* 2nd series, 2, 34–45.

Bettey, J.H. 1977. 'The Development of Water Meadows in Dorset during the Seventeenth Century', *Agricultural History Review* 25, 37–43.

Bettey, J.H. 1999. 'The Development of Water Meadows in the Southern Counties'. In H. Cook and T. Williamson (eds) *Water Management in the English Landscape: Field, Marsh and Meadow*, Edinburgh, 175–95.

Bettey, J.H. 2000. 'Downlands'. In J. Thirsk (ed.) *The English Rural Landscape*, Oxford, 27–49.

Birtles, S. 1999. 'Common Land, Poor Relief, and Enclosure: the Use of Manorial Resources in Fulfilling Parish Obligations, 1601–1834', *Past and Present* 165, 74–106.

Boswell, G. 1779. *A Treatise on Watering Meadows,* London.

Bowden, P.J. 1985. 'Agricultural Prices, Wages, Farm Profits and Rents'. In J. Thirsk (ed.) *The Agrarian History of England and Wales*, Vol. V.2, Cambridge, 1–118.

Bowie, G. 1987a 'New Sheep For Old: Changes in Sheep Farming in Hampshire, 1792–1879', *Agricultural History Review* 35, 15–24.

Bowie, G. 1987b. 'Water Meadows in Wessex: A Re-evaluation for the Period 1640–1850', *Agricultural History Review* 35, 151–8.

Bowie, G. 1990. 'Northern Wolds and Wessex Downlands: Contrasts in Sheep Husbandry and Farming Practices, 1770–1850', *Agricultural History Review* 38, 117–26.

Boys, J. 1813. *General View of the Agriculture of the County of Kent*, London.

Bradley, R. 1727. *A General Treatise of Husbandry and Gardening*, London.

Brandon, P. 1974. *The Sussex Landscape*, London.

Brassley, P. 1984. 'Northumberland and Durham'. In J. Thirsk (ed.) *The Agrarian History of England and Wales*, Vol. V.1, Cambridge, 39–58.

Briault, E.E. 1942. *The Land of Britain: Sussex (Land Utilisation Survey Pts 13 and 14)*, London.

Brigden, R. 1986. *Victorian Farms*, London.

Broad, J. 1980. 'Alternate Husbandry and Permanent Pasture in the Midlands, 1650–1800', *Agricultural History Review* 28, 77–89.

Broad, J. 1997. 'Landscape, Farming and Employment in Bernwood 1660–1880'. In J. Broad and R. Hoyle (eds) *Bernwood: the Life and Afterlife of a Forest*, Preston, 73–89.

Brown, A.F.J. 1996. *Prosperity and Poverty: Rural Essex, 1700–1815*, Chelmsford.

Brown, D. 1992. 'Enclosure and Improvement: an investigation into the Motives for Parliamentary Enclosure'. Unpublished Ph.D. thesis, Wolverhampton Polytechnic.

Brown, R. 1799. *General View of the Agriculture of the West Riding of Yorkshire*, London.

Brown, T. and Foard, G. 1998. 'The Saxon Landscape: a Regional Perspective'. In P. Everson and T. Williamson (eds) *The Archaeology of Landscape: Studies Presented to Christopher Taylor*, Manchester, 67–94.

Brunt, L. 1997. *Nature or Nurture? Explaining English Wheat Yields in the Agricultural Revolution*, University of Oxford Discussion Papers in Economic and Social History no. 19, Oxford.

Brunt, L. 2000. *Where There's Muck, There's Brass: The Market for Manure in the Industrial Revolution*, University of Oxford Discussion Papers in Economic and Social History no. 35, Oxford.

Bunce, R.G.E. and Fowler, D. 1989. *Heather in England and Wales*, London.

Burrell, E.D.R. 1960. ' Historical Geography of the Sandlings of Suffolk, 1600 to 1850'. Unpublished M.Sc. thesis, University of London.

Butlin, R.A. 1973. 'Field Systems of Northumberland and Durham'. In A.H.R. Baker and R.A. Butlin (eds) *Studies of Field Systems in the British Isles*, Cambridge, 377–429.

Caird, J. 1852. *English Agriculture 1851-2*, London.

Caird, J. 1878. 'General View of British Agriculture', *Journal of the Royal Agricultural Society of England* 2nd series 14, 273–332.

Campbell, B.M.S. 1983. 'Agricultural Progress in Medieval England: Some Evidence from East Norfolk', *Economic History Review* 2nd series 36, 26–46.

Campbell, B.M.S. 1991. 'Land, Labour, Livestock and Productivity Trends in English Seigniorial Agriculture, 1208–1450'. In B.M.S. Campbell and M. Overton (eds) *Land, Labour and Livestock*, Manchester, 144–82.

Campbell, B.M.S. 2000. *English Seigniorial Agriculture, 1250–1450*, Cambridge.

Campbell, B.M.S. and Overton, M. 1993. 'A New Perspective in Medieval and Early Modern Agriculture: Six Centuries of Norfolk Farming c.1250–1850', *Past and Present* 141, 38–105.

Carr, R. 1976. *English Fox Hunting: A History*, London.

Castle, D.A., McCunnall, J. and Tring, I.M. 1984. *Field Drainage: Principles and Practices*, London.

Chambers, J.D. and Mingay, G.E. 1966. *The Agricultural Revolution 1750–1880*, London.

Chapman, J. 1987. 'The Extent and Nature of Parliamentary Enclosure', *Agricultural History Review* 35, 25–35.

Chapman, J. and Seeliger, S. 1995. 'Formal Agreements and the Enclosure Process: The Evidence from Hampshire', *Agricultural History Review* 43, 35–46.

Chartres, J. 1995. 'Market Integration and Agricultural Output in the Seventeenth, Eighteenth, and Early Nineteenth Centuries', *Agricultural History Review* 43, 117–36.

Chorley, G.P.H. 1981. 'The Agricultural Revolution in Northern Europe, 1750–1880: Nitrogen, Legumes and Crop Production', *Economic History Review* 34, 71–93.

Clark, G. 1988. 'Agriculture and the Industrial Revolution'. In J. Mokyr (ed.) *The British Industrial Revolution: An Economic Perspective*, London, 227–66.

Clarke, J.A. 1848. 'On the Great Level of the Fens', *Journal of the Royal Agricultural Society of England* 8, 80–133.

Clay, C. 1985. 'Landlords and Estate Management in England'. In J. Thirsk (ed.) *The Agrarian History of England and Wales*, Vol. V.2, Cambridge, 119–251.

Clemenson, H. 1982. *English Country Houses and Landed Estates*, London.

Clutton-Brock, J. 1982. 'British Cattle in the Eighteenth Century', *Ark* 9, 55–9.

Cobbelt, W. 1822. *Cottage Economy*, London.

Cobbelt, W. 1830. *Rural Rides in the Southern, Western and Eastern Counties*, London.

Coleman, D.C. 1962. 'Growth and Decay During the Industrial Revolution: The Case of East Anglia', *Scandinavian Economic History Review* 10, 115–27.

Collins, E.J.T. 1975. 'Dietary Changes and Cereal Consumption in Britain in the Nineteenth Century', *Agricultural History Review* 23, 97–115.

Collins, E.J.T. 1978. 'The Economy of Upland Britain 1750–1950'. In R.B. Tranter (ed.) *The Future of Upland Britain*, Reading, Vol. II, 586–651.

Collins, E.J.T. 1987. 'The Rationality of "Surplus"Agricultural Labour: Mechanisation in English Agriculture in the Nineteenth Century', *Agricultural History Review* 35, 36–46.

Colyer, R. J. 1973. 'Some Aspects of Cattle Production in Northamptonshire and Leicestershire in the Nineteenth Century, *Northamptonshire Past and Present* 5, 45–54.

Cook, H. 1999. 'Soil Water Management: Principles and Purposes'. In H. Cook and T. Williamson (eds) *Water Management in the English landscape: Field, Marsh and Meadow*, Edinburgh, 15–27.

Copland, S. 1866. *Agriculture Ancient and Modern*, London.

Coppock, J.T. 1971. *An Agricultural Geography of Great Britain*, London.

Cossons, N. 1987. *The BP Book of Industrial Archaeology*, London.

Craigie, P.G. 1883. 'Statistics of Agricultural Production', *Journal of the Royal Statistical Society* 46, 1, 1–45.

Crutchley, J. 1794. *General View of the Agriculture of Rutland*, London.

Currie, C.R.J. 1979. 'Agriculture 1793 to 1875'. In M.W. Greenslade and D.A. Johnson (eds) *Victoria County History of Staffordshire*, Vol. VI, London, 91–121.

Curtis, L.F., Courtney, F.M. and Trudgill, S.T. 1976. *Soils in the British Isles*, London.

Curwen, J.C. 1809. *General Hints on Agricultural Subjects*, London.

Cutting, R. and Cummings, I. 1999. 'Water Meadows: their Form, Operation, and Plant Ecology'. In H. Cook and T. Williamson (eds) *Water Management in the English Landscape: Field, Marsh and Meadow*, Edinburgh, 157–78.

Daniels, S. 1988. 'The Political Iconography of Woodland in Later Eighteenth-Century England'. In D. Cosgrove and S. Daniels (eds) *The Iconography of Landscape*, Cambridge, 51–72.

Darby H.C. 1940. *The Medieval Fenland*, Cambridge.

Darby, H.C. 1966. *The Draining of the Fens*, 2nd edn, Cambridge.

Darby, H.C. 1983. *The Changing Fenland*, Cambridge.

Darley, G. 1978. *Villages of Vision*, London.

Davis, S.J.M. and Beckett, J.V. 1999. 'Animal Husbandry and Agricultural Improvement: The Archaeological Evidence from Animal Bones and Teeth', *Rural History: Economy, Society, Culture* 10, 1, 1–18.

Davis, T. 1794. *General View of the Agriculture of the County of Wilts: With Observations on the Means of its Improvement*, London.

Deetz, J. 1977. *In Small Things Forgotten*, New York.

Defoe, D. 1976 [1724]. *The Tour through the Whole Island of Great Britain*, Penguin edn, Harmondsworth.

Denison, J. 1840. 'On the Duke of Portland's Water Meadows at Clipstone Park', *Journal of the Royal Agricultural Society of England* 1, 359–70.

Denton, J. Bailey 1863. *The Farm Homesteads of England*, London.

De Rougemont, G.M. 1989. *Collins Field Guide to the Crops of Britain and Europe*, London.

Done, A. 1999. 'The Impact of Grouse Shooting on the Development of the Cultural Landscape of the Yorkshire Dales'. Unpublished M.A. Dissertation, University of Leeds College of Ripon and York.

Druce, C. 1886. *The Flora of Oxfordshire*, London.

Duffey, E. 1974. *Grassland Ecology and Wildlife Management*, London.

Dugdale, W. 1662. *The History of Inbanking and Drayning of Diverse Fens and Marshes . . .*, London.

Dyer, C. 2000. 'Woodlands and Wood-Pasture in the West of England'. In J. Thirsk (ed.) *The English Rural Landscape*, Oxford, 97–121.

Elliott, G. 1973. 'Field Systems of Northwest England'. In A.H.R. Baker and R.A. Butlin (eds) *Studies of Field Systems in the British Isles*, Cambridge, 42–92.

Ellis, W. 1750. *The Modern Husbandman*, 8 vols, London.

Emery, F. 1974. *The Oxfordshire Landscape*, London.

Ernle, Lord (R.E. Prothero) 1912. *English Farming, Past and Present*, London.

Evans, H. 1845. 'Norfolk Draining', *Journal of the Royal Agricultural Society of England*, 4, 43–4.

Everitt, A. 1976. 'The Making of the Agrarian Landscape of Kent', *Archaeologia Cantiana* 112, 1–32.

Eyre, S.R. 1955. 'The Curving Ploughland Strip and its Historical Implications', *Agricultural History Review* 3, 80–94.

Fleming, A. 1988. *The Dartmoor Reaves*, London.

Folkingham, W. 1610. *Feudographica*, London.

Forby, the Rev. 1796. 'Reply to the Editor's Circular Letter', *Annals of Agriculture* 26, 137–41.

Fox, H.S.A. 1981. 'Approaches to the Adoption of the Midland System'. In T. Rowley (ed.) *The Origins of Open-Field Agriculture*, London, 64–111.

Fox, H.S.A. 1989. 'The People of the Wolds'. In M. Aston, D. Austin, and C. Dyer (eds) *The Rural Settlements of Medieval England: Studies Presented to Maurice Beresford and John Hurst*, Oxford, 44–69.

Frost, P. 1981. 'Yeomen and Metalsmiths: Livestock in the Dual Economy in South Staffordshire 1560–1720', *Agricultural History Review* 29, 29–41.

Fussell, G.E. (ed.) 1936. *Robert Loder's Farm Accounts, 1610–1620*, Camden Society 3rd series, 53.

Gardner, H.W. and Garner, H.V. 1957. *The Use of Lime in British Agriculture*, London.

Garner, L. 1995. *Dry Stone Walls*, Aylesbury.

Ginter, D.E. 1991. 'Measuring the Decline of the Small Landowner'. In B.A. Holderness and M. Turner (eds) *Land, Labour and Agriculture*, London, 27–48.

Glennie, P. 1988. 'Continuity and Change in Hertfordshire Agriculture, 1550–1700: Trends in Crop Yields and their Determinants', *Agricultural History Review* 36, 145–61.

Glennie, P. 1991. 'Measuring Crop Yields in Early Modern England'. In B. Campbell and M. Overton (eds) *Land, Labour and Livestock*, Manchester, 255–83.

Glyde, J. 1856. *Suffolk in the Nineteenth Century*, London.

Goddard, N. (1988). *Harvests of Change: The Royal Agricultural Society of England 1838–1988*, London.

Goddard, N. 1991. 'Information and Innovation in Early-Victorian Farming Systems'. In B.A. Holderness and M. Turner (eds) *Land, Labour and Agriculture 1700–1920*, London, 165–90.

Grey, J. 1840. 'A View of the Past and Present State of Agriculture in Northumberland', *Journal of the Royal Agricultural Society of England* 2, 51–92.

Grigg, D. 1987. 'Farm Size in England and Wales, from Early Victorian Times to the Present', *Agricultural History Review* 35, 2, 179–90.

Grove, R. 1976. 'Coprolite Mining in Cambridgeshire', *Agricultural History Review* 24, 36–43.

Habbakuk, H.J. 1953. 'Economic Functions of English Landowners in the Seventeenth and Eighteenth Centuries', *Explorations in Entrepreneurial History* December, 92–121.

Haggard, R. 1899. *A Farmer's Year*, London.

Hall, A.D. and Russell, E.J. 1911. *A Report on the Agriculture and Soils of Kent, Surrey and Sussex*, London.

Hall, D. 1982. *Medieval Fields*, Aylesbury.

Hall, D. 1995. *The Open Fields of Northamptonshire*, Northamptonshire Record Society Vol. 38, Northampton.

Hall, D. 1998. 'Enclosure in Northamptonshire', *Northamptonshire Past and Present* 9, 4, 351–68.

Hall, D. 1999. 'The Drainage of Arable Land in Medieval England'. In H. Cook and T. Williamson (eds) *Water Management in the English Landscape: Field, Marsh and Meadow*, Edinburgh, 28–40.

Hall, D., Wells, C.E. and Huckerby, E. 1995. *The Wetlands of Greater Manchester*, Lancaster.

Hammond, B. and Hammond, J.L. 1911. *The Village Labourer 1760–1832*, London.

Hanley, J.A. 1949. *Progressive Farming*, 4 volumes, London.

Harris, A. 1958. 'The Lost Villages and the Landscape of the Yorkshire Wolds', *Agricultural History Review* 6, 97–100.

Harris, A. 1961. *The Rural Landscape of the East Riding of Yorkshire, 1700–1850*, London.

Harris, H. 1971. *The Industrial Archaeology of the Peak District*, Newton Abbot.

Harrison, M.J., Mead, W.R. and Pannett, D.J. 1965. 'A Midland Ridge and Furrow Map', *Geographical Journal* 131, 366–9.

Darby H.C. 1940. *The Medieval Fenland*, Cambridge.

Harvey, N. 1980. *The Industrial Archaeology of Farming in England and Wales*, London.

Havinden, M. 1961. 'Agricultural Progress in Open-Field Oxfordshire', *Agricultural History Review* 9, 73–83.

Havinden, M. 1974. 'Lime as a Means of Agricultural Improvement: The Devon Example'. In C.W. Chalklin and M.A. Havinden (eds) *Rural Change and Urban Growth*, London, 104–34.

Havinden, M. 1981. *The Somerset Landscape*, London.

Hellen, J.A. 1972. 'Agricultural Innovation and Detectable Landscape Margins: The Case of Wheelhouses in Northumberland', *Agricultural History Review* 20, 140–50.

Hey, D. 1969. 'A Dual Economy in South Yorkshire', *Agricultural History Review* 17, 108–19.

Hey, D. 1984. 'Yorkshire and Lancashire'. In J. Thirsk (ed.) *The Agrarian History of England and Wales*, Vol. V.2, Cambridge, 59–88.

Hey, D. 2000. 'Moorlands'. In J. Thirsk (ed.) *The English Rural Landscape*, Oxford, 188–209.

Hills, R.L. 1967. *Machines, Mills and Uncountable Costly Necessities*, Norwich.

Hodge, C., Burton, R., Corbett, W., Evans, R. and Scale, R. 1984. *Soils and their Uses in Eastern England,* Harpenden.

Hodges, R. 1991. *Wall-to-Wall History: The Story of Roystone Grange,* London.

Holderness, B.A. 1972. '"Open" and "Close" Parishes in England in the Eighteenth and Nineteenth Centuries', *Agricultural History Review* 20, 126–39.

Holderness, B.A. 1981. 'The Victorian Farmer'. In G.E. Mingay (ed.) *The Victorian Countryside,* Vol. I, London, 227–4.

Holderness, B.A. 1984. 'East Anglia and the Fens'. In J. Thirsk (ed.) *The Agrarian History of England and Wales* Vol. V, 2, Cambridge, 119–245.

Holderness, B.A. 1989. 'Prices, Productivity and Output'. In G.E. Mingay (ed.) *The Agrarian History of England and Wales,* Vol. VI, Cambridge, 84–189.

Hoskins, W.G. 1949. 'The Leicestershire Crop Returns of 1801'. In W.G. Hoskins (ed.) *Studies in Leicestershire Agricultural History,* Leicester, 1–22.

Hoskins, W.G. 1955 *The Making of the English Landscape,* London.

Hoskins, W.G. and Stamp, L. Dudley. 1961. *The Common Lands of England and Wales,* London.

Howkins, A. 1994. 'Peasants, Servants and Labourers: The Marginal Workforce in British Agriculture c.1870–1914', *Agricultural History Review* 42, 49–62.

Hudson, P. 1992. *The Industrial Revolution,* London.

Hunt, E.H. 1986. 'Industrialisation and Regional Inequality: Wages in Britain 1760–1914', *Journal of Economic History* 46, 4, 935–66.

Hutton, K. 1976. 'The Distribution of Wheelhouses in the British Isles', *Agricultural History Review* 24, 30–36.

Jennings, B. 2000. 'A Longer View of the Wolds'. In J. Thirsk (ed.) *The English Rural Landscape,* Oxford, 62–77.

Jesse, R.H.B. 1960. *A Survey of the Agriculture of Sussex,* London.

Jessop, A. 1887. *Arcady: For Better, For Worse,* London.

Jobey, G. 1966. 'A Note on Sow Kilns', *Journal of the University of Newcastle-upon-Tyne Agricultural Society* 29, 2–3.

Johnson, W. 1978. 'Hedges: A Review of Some Early Literature', *Local Historian,* 195– 204.

Jones, E.L. 1960. 'Eighteenth-Century Changes in Hampshire Chalkland Farming', *Agricultural History Review* 8, 5–19.

Jones, E.L. 1967. 'Agriculture and Economic Growth in England, 1660–1750: Agricultural Change'. In E.L. Jones (ed.) *Agriculture and Economic Growth in England 1650–1815,* London, 152–71.

Kain, R.J.P. 1986. *An Atlas and Index of the Tithe-Files of Mid Nineteenth Century England and Wales,* Cambridge.

Kain, R.J.P. 1995. *The 1836 National Tithe-Files Database on CD Rom: A Socio-economic Survey of Land Use and the Economy,* Marlborough.

Kent, N. 1793. *Hints to Gentlemen of Landed Property,* London.

Kerridge, E. 1953. 'The Sheep Fold in Wiltshire and the Floating of the Watermeadows', *Economic History Review* VI, 282–9.

Kerridge, E. 1956. 'Turnip Husbandry in High Suffolk', *Economic History Review* 2nd series, 8, 390–2.

Kerridge, E. 1967. *The Agricultural Revolution,* London.

Kerridge, E. 1969. 'The Agricultural Revolution Reconsidered', *Agricultural History* 43, 463–76.

Kettle, A.J. 1979. 'Agriculture 1500–1793'. In M.W. Greenslade and D.A. Johnson (eds) *Victoria County History of Staffordshire,* Vol. VI, London, 49–90.

Lambert, S. (ed.) 1977. *House of Commons Sessional Papers of the Eighteenth Century: George III; Reports of the Commissioners of Land Revenue, 8–11, 1792,* Delaware.

Lane, C. 1980. 'The Development of Pastures and Meadows in the Sixteenth and Seventeenth Centuries', *Agricultural History Review* 27, 18–30.

Le Gear, R.F. 1983. 'The Agricultural Chalk Mines in North West Kent', *Archaeologia Cantiana* 99, 67–72.

Lewis, C., Mitchell-Fox, P. and Dyer, C. 1997. *Village, Hamlet and Field: Changing Medieval Settlements in Midland England*, Manchester.

Liddiard, R. 1999. 'The Distribution of Ridge and Furrow in Norfolk: Ploughing Practice and Subsequent Land Use', *Agricultural History Review* 47, 1–6.

Lloyd-Pritchard, M.F. 1953. 'The Vicar of Mattishall and his Tithes', *Agricultural History* 27, 141–7.

Longman, G. 1977. *A Corner of England's Garden: An Agrarian History of South West Hertfordshire, 1600–1850*, 2 volumes, London.

Loveday, R. and Williamson, T. 1988. 'Rabbits or Ritual? Artificial Warrens and the Neolithic Long Mound Tradition', *Archaeological Journal* 145, 290–313.

Low, D. 1838. *Practical Agriculture*, London.

Mabey, R. 1980. *The Common Ground*, London.

Macdonald, S. 1975. 'The Progress of the Early Threshing Machine', *Agricultural History Review* 23, 63–77.

Markham, C.A. 1906. 'Early Foxhounds'. In R. Serjeantson (ed.) *Victoria County History of Northamptonshire*, Vol. II, London, 355–73.

Marshall, G., Palmer, M. and Neaveson, P. 1992. 'The History and Archaeology of the Calke Abbey Limeyards', *Industrial Archaeology Review* 14, 2, 145–76.

Marshall, W. 1787. *The Rural Economy of Norfolk*, 2 volumes, London.

Marshall, W. 1788. *The Rural Economy of Yorkshire*, 2 volumes, London.

Marshall, W. 1796a. *Planting and Rural Ornament*, London.

Marshall, W. 1796b. *The Rural Economy of the Midland Counties*, 2 volumes, London.

Marshall, W., 1798. *The Rural Economy of the Southern Counties*, 2 volumes, London.

Marshall, W. 1808. *A Review of the Reports of the Board of Agriculture from the Northern Departments of England*, York.

Martin, J.M. 1979. 'The Smallholder and Parliamentary Enclosure in Warwickshire', *Economic History Review* 32, 328–43.

Mate, M. 1985. 'Medieval Agricultural Practice: The Determining Factors', *Agricultural History Review* 33, 22–31.

Mathew, W. 1993. 'Marling in British Agriculture: A Case of Partial Identity', *Agricultural History Review* 41, 97–110.

Mendels, F.F. 1972. 'Proto-Industrialisation: The First Phase of the Industrialisation Process', *Journal of Economic History* 32, 241–61.

Millin, G. 1999 [1891]. *Life in the Victorian Village: The Daily News Survey of 1891*, 2 volumes, London.

Mingay, G.E. 1961–2. 'The Size of Farms in the Eighteenth Century', *Economic History Review* 2nd series, 14, 469–88.

Mingay, G.E. 1984. 'The East Midlands'. In J. Thirsk (ed.) *The Agrarian History of England and Wales*, Vol. V.1, Cambridge, 89–128.

Mingay, G.E. (ed.) 1989a. *The Agrarian History of England and Wales Volume VI, 1750–1850*, Cambridge.

Mingay, G.E. 1989b. 'Agricultural Productivity and Agricultural Society in Eighteenth-Century England', *Research in Economic History*, Supplement 5, 31–47.

Mingay, G.E. 1997. *Parliamentary Enclosure in England: An Introduction to its Causes, Incidence and Impact*, London.

Mitchell, B.R. and Deane, P. 1962. *Abstract of British Historical Statistics*, Cambridge.

Moon, H.P. and Green, F.H.W. 1940. *The Land of Britain: Hampshire (Land Utilisation Survey, Pt 78)*, London.

Mosby, J.E.G. 1938. *The Land of Britain: Norfolk (Land Utilisation Survey, Pt 70)*, London.

Neave, S. 1993. 'Rural Settlement Contraction in the East Riding of Yorkshire between the Mid Seventeenth and Mid Eighteenth Centuries', *Agricultural History Review* 49, 124–36.

Neeson, J.M. 1993. *Commoners: Common Right, Enclosure and Social Change in England 1700–1820*, Cambridge.

Nef, J. 1932. *The Rise of the British Coal Industry*, London.

Newbold, C. 1999. 'Historical Changes in the Nature Conservation Interest of the Fenlands of Cambridgeshire'. In H. Cook and T. Williamson (eds) *Water Management in the English Landscape: Field, Marsh and Meadow*, Edinburgh, 210–26.

Newton, R. 1972. *The Northumberland Landscape*, London.

Nisbet, J. 1906. 'Forestry'. In R. Serjeantson (ed.) *Victorian County History of Northamptonshire*, Vol. 2, 341–52.

Norden, J. 1607. *The Surveyor's Dialogue*, London.

O'Brien, P.K. 1985. 'Agriculture and the Home Market for English Industry, 1660–1820', *English Historical Review* 100, 773–800.

Ormrod, D. 1985. *English Grain Exports and the Structure of Agrarian Capitalism, 1700–1760*, Hull.

Orwin, C.S. and Sellick, R.J. 1970. *The Reclamation of Exmoor Forest*, revised edn, Newton Abbot.

Oschinsky, D. 1971. *Walter of Henley and Other Treatises on Estate Management and Accounting*, Oxford.

Overton, M. 1979. 'Estimating Crop Yields from Probate Inventories: An Example from East Anglia 1585–1735', *Journal of Economic History* 39, 363–78.

Overton, M. 1990. 'The Critical Century? The *Agrarian History of England and Wales 1750–1850*'. Review in *Agricultural History Review* 38, 185–9.

Overton, M. 1991. 'The Determinants of Crop Yields in Early Modern England'. In B. Campbell and M. Overton (eds) *Land, Labour and Livestock*, Manchester, 284–322.

Overton, M. 1996a. *Agricultural Revolution in England: The Transformation of the Agrarian Economy 1500–1850*, Cambridge.

Overton, M. 1996b. 'Re-establishing the Agricultural Revolution', *Agricultural History Review* 44, 1–20.

Paine, C. (ed.) 1993. *The Culford Estate 1780–1935*, Bury St Edmunds.

Patten, J. 1971. 'Fox Coverts for the Squirearchy', *Country Life*, 23 September, 726–40.

Perry, P.J. 1974. *British Farming in the Great Depression*, London.

Pettit, P.A. 1968. *The Royal Forests of Northamptonshire: A Study of their Economy 1558–1714*, Northamptonshire Record Society Vol. 23, Northampton.

Phillips, A.D.M. 1989. *The Underdraining of Farmland in England During the Nineteenth Century*, Cambridge.

Phillips, A.D.M. 1996. *The Staffordshire Reports of Andrew Thompson to the Inclosure Commissioners, 1858–68: Landlord Investment in Staffordshire Agriculture in the Mid Nineteenth Century*, Stafford.

Phillips, A.D.M. 1999. 'Arable Land Drainage in the Nineteenth Century'. In H. Cook and T. Williamson (eds) *Water Management in the English Landscape: Field, Marsh and Meadow*, Edinburgh, 53–72.

Pitt, W. 1796. *General View of the Agriculture of Staffordshire*, London.

Pitt, W. 1813a. *General View of the Agriculture of the County of Leicestershire*, London.

Pitt, W. 1813b. *General View of the Agriculture of the County of Northampton*, London.

Plumb, J.H. 1952. 'Sir Robert Walpole and Norfolk Husbandry', *Economic History Review* 2nd series, 5, 86–9.

Postgate, M.R. 1962. 'The Field Systems of Breckland', *Agricultural History Review* 10, 80–101.

Postgate, M.R. 1973. 'Field Systems of East Anglia'. In A.H.R. Baker and R.A. Butlin (eds) *Studies of Field Systems in the British Isles*, Cambridge, 281–324.

Prince, H. 1964. 'The Origins of Pits and Depressions in Norfolk', *Geography* 49, 15–32.

Pringle, A. 1805. *General View of the Agriculture of Westmoreland*, London.

Pusey, P. 1841. 'Some Account of the Practice of English Farmers in the Improvement of Peaty Grounds', *Journal of the Royal Agricultural Society of England* 2, 400–14.

Pusey, P. 1843. 'On the Progress of Agricultural Knowledge Over the Past Four Years', *Journal of the Royal Agricultural Society of England* 3, 169–216.

Pusey, P. 1845. 'Remarks on the Foregoing Evidence' [i.e. re. Evans 1845], *Journal of the Royal Agricultural Society of England* 4, 44.

Pusey, P. 1846. Editor's footnote to Roal, 1846.

Pusey, P. 1849. 'On the Theory and Practice of Water Meadows', *Journal of the Royal Agricultural Society of England* 10, 462–79.

Rackham, O. 1976. *Trees and Woodlands in the British Landscape*, London.

Rackham, O. 1986 *The History of the Countryside*, London.

Ragg, J.M., Beard, G.R., George, H., Heaven, F.W. and Jones, R.J.A. 1984. *Soils and their Use in Midland and Western England*, London.

Raistrick, A. 1946. *Pennine Walls*, York.

Raynbird, H. 1846. 'On Measure Work', *Journal of the Royal Agricultural Society of England* 7, 119–40.

Raynbird, W. and Raynbird, H. 1849. *On the Farming of Suffolk*, London.

Read, C.S. 1858. 'Recent Improvements in Norfolk Farming', *Journal of the Royal Agricultural Society of England* 19, 265–310.

Read, C.S. 1987. 'Large and Small Holdings', *Journal of the Royal Agricultural Society of England* 23, 1–28.

Reed, M. 1979. *The Buckinghamshire Landscape*, London.

Reed, M. 1981. 'Pre-Parliamentary Enclosure in the East Midlands, 1550 to 1750, and its Impact on the Landscape', *Landscape History* 3, 60–8.

Reed, M. 1983. 'Enclosure in North Buckinghamshire, 1500–1750', *Agricultural History Review* 31, 104–42.

Richardson, R.C. 1984. 'Metropolitan Counties: Bedfordshire, Hertfordshire, and Middlesex'. In J. Thirsk (ed.) *The Agrarian History of England and Wales*, Vol. V.1, Cambridge, 239–69.

Riches, N. 1937. *The Agricultural Revolution in Norfolk*, Chapel Hill, North Carolina.

Ritchie, J.T. 1984. 'Validation of the CERES Wheat Model in Diverse Environments'. In W. Day and R.H. Atkin (eds) *Wheat Growth and Modelling*, Bristol, 280–96.

Roal, J. 1846. 'On the Converting of Mossy Hillside to Catch Meadows', *Journal of the Royal Agricultural Society of England* 6, 518–22.

Roberts, B.K. 1973. 'Field Systems of the West Midlands'. In A.H.R. Baker and R.A. Butlin (eds) *Studies of Field Systems in the British Isles*, Cambridge, 195–205.

Roberts. B.K. and Wrathmell, S. 1998. 'Dispersed Settlement in England: A National View'. In P. Everson and T. Williamson (eds) *The Archaeology of Landscape: Studies Presented to Christopher Taylor*, Manchester, 95–116.

Robinson, J.M. 1980. *Georgian Model Farms*, London.

Robinson, D.H. 1949. *Fream's Elements of Agriculture*, 13th edn, London.

Robinson, E. and Powell, D. 1984. *The Oxford Authors: John Clare*, Oxford.

Roden, D. 1973. 'Field Systems of the Chiltern Hills and their Environs'. In A.H.R. Baker and R.A. Butlin (eds) *Studies of Field Systems in the British Isles*, Cambridge, 325–74.

Rosenheim, J.M. 1989. *The Townshends of Raynham*, Middletown, Connecticut.

Royal Commission on Historical Monuments, England. 1979. *An Inventory of the Historical Monuments in the County of Northamptonshire, Vol. 2: Archaeological Sites in Central Northamptonshire*, London.

Royal Commission on Historical Monuments, England. 1981. *An Inventory of the Historical Monuments in the County of Northamptonshire, Vol. 3: Archaeological Sites in North-West Northamptonshire*, London.

Royal Commission on Historical Monuments, England. 1982. *An Inventory of the Historical Monuments in the County of Northamptonshire, Vol. 4: Archaeological Sites in South-West Northamptonshire*, London.

Ruggles, T. 1786. 'Picturesque Farming', *Annals of Agriculture* 6, 175–84.

Russell, E. and Russell, R. 1985. *Old and New Landscapes in the Horncastle Area*, Lincoln.

Russell, N. 1986. *Like Engend'ring Like: Heredity and Animal Breeding in Early Modern England*, Cambridge.

Ryder, M.L. 1964. 'The History of Sheep Breeds in Britain', *Agricultural History Review* 12, 1–12.

Ryle, G. 1969. *Forest Service: The First Forty-five Years of the Forestry Commission in Great Britain*, Newton Abbot.

Salaman, R.N. 1949. *The History and Social Influence of the Potato*, Cambridge.

Salmon, N. 1728. *The History of Hertfordshire*, London.

Saunders, H.W. 1916. 'Estate Management at Raynham 1661–86 and 1706', *Norfolk Archaeology* 19, 39–67.

Seymour, J. 1975. *The Complete Book of Self-Sufficiency*, London.

Shaw Taylor, L. 2000. Abstract of thesis, in *Journal of Economic History* 60, 508–11.

Sheil, R.S. 1991. 'Soil Fertility in the Pre-Fertiliser Era'. In B. Campbell and M. Overton (eds) *Land, Labour and Livestock*, Manchester, 51–77.

Sheppard, J.A. 1973. Field systems of Yorkshire. In A.H.R. Baker and R.A. Butlin (eds) *Studies of Field Systems in the British Isles*, Cambridge, 145–87.

Sheppard, J.A. 1992. 'Small Farms in a Sussex Weald Parish 1800–1860', *Agricultural History Review* 40, 127–41.

Shoard, M. 1980. *The Theft of the Countryside*, London.

Short, B. 1992. 'The Evolution of Contrasting Communities within Rural England'. In B. Short (ed.) *The English Rural Community: Image and Analysis*, Cambridge, 19–43.

Silvester, R. 1988.*The Fenland Project, No. 3: Norfolk Survey, Marshland and the Nar Valley*, published as *East Anglian Archaeology*, 45.

Silvester, R. 1999. 'Medieval Reclamation of Marsh and Fen'. In H. Cook and T. Williamson (eds) *Water Management in the English Landscape: Field, Marsh and Meadow*, Edinburgh, 122–140.

Skipper, K. 1989. ' Wood-pasture: the Landscape of the Norfolk Claylands in the Early Modern Period'. Unpublished M.A. thesis, Centre of East Anglian Studies, University of East Anglia.

Skipper, K. and Williamson, T. 1997. *Thetford Forest: Making a Landscape, 1922–1997*, Norwich.

Smith, J. 1831. *Remarks on Thorough Draining and Deep Ploughing*, Stirling.

Smith, R. 1851. 'Some Account of the Formation of Hillside Catchworks on Exmoor', *Journal of the Royal Agricultural Society* 12, 139–48.

Smith, W. 1806. *Observations on the Utility, Form and Management of Water Meadows*, Norwich.

Snell, K.D.M. 1985. *Annals of the Labouring Poor: Social Change and Agrarian England 1660–1900*, Cambridge.

Stamp, L. Dudley 1950. *The Land of Britain: Its Use and Misuse*, London.

Stanes, R.G.F. 1964. 'A Georgical Account of Devonshire and Cornewalle: Samuel Colepresse 1667', *Transactions of the Devon Association* 96, 279–81.

Steane, J. 1974. *The Northamptonshire Landscape*, London.

Stevenson, H. 1870. *The Birds of Norfolk*, London.

Stevenson, W. 1815. *General View of the Agriculture of the County of Dorset*, London.

Strickland, H.E. 1812. *A General View of the Agriculture of the East Riding of Yorkshire*, York.

Sturgess, R.W. 1966. 'The Agricultural Revolution on the English Claylands', *Agricultural History Review* 14, 104–21.

Surtees, R.S. 1929. *Town and Country Papers*, London.

Tate, W.E. 1978. *A Domesday of English Enclosure Acts and Awards*, Reading.

Taylor, C. 1973. *The Cambridgeshire Landscape*, London.

Taylor, C. 1975. *Fields in the English Landscape*, London.

Taylor, C. 1983. *Village and Farmstead: a History of Rural Settlement in England*, London.

Taylor, C. 1999. 'Post-medieval Drainage of Marsh and Fen'. In H. Cook and T. Williamson (eds) *Water Management in the English Landscape: Field, Marsh and Meadow*, Edinburgh, 141–56.

Taylor, C. 2000 'Fenlands'. In J. Thirsk (ed.) *The English Rural Landscape*, Oxford, 167–87.

Theobald, J. 2000. 'Changing Landscapes, Changing Economies: Holdings in Woodland High Suffolk 1600–1850. Unpublished PhD thesis, Centre of East Anglian Studies, University of East Anglia.

Thirsk, J. 1964. 'The Common Fields', *Past and Present* 29, 3–25.

Thirsk, J. 1970. 'Seventeenth-century Agriculture and Social Change'. In *Land, Church and People* supplement to *Agricultural History Review* 18, 148–77.

Thirsk, J. 1985. 'Agricultural Innovations and their Diffusion'. In J. Thirsk (ed.) *The Agrarian History of England and Wales* Vol. V.2, Cambridge, 533–89.

Thirsk, J. 1984. 'The South-West Midlands: Warwickshire, Worcestershire, Gloucestershire and Herefordshire'. In J. Thirsk (ed.) *The Agrarian History of England and Wales* Vol. V.1, 159–96.

Thirsk, J. 1987. *England's Agricultural Regions and Agrarian History 1500–1750*, London.

Thompson, F.M.L. 1968. 'The Second Agricultural Revolution', *Economic History Review* 21, 62–77.

Thompson, L.S. 1957. *Soils and Fertility*, London.

Trimmer, C.P. 1969. 'The Turnip, the New Husbandry and the English Agricultural Revolution', *Quarterly Journal of Economics* 83, 375–95.

Trow Smith, R. 1959. *A History of British Livestock Husbandry 1700–1900*, London.

Turner, J. and Hodgson, J. 1979. 'Studies in the Vegetational History of the North Pennines', *Journal of Ecology* 67, 629–46.

Turner, M.E. 1975. 'Parliamentary Enclosure and Landownership Change in Buckinghamshire', *Economic History Review* 28, 565–81.

Turner, M.E. 1980. *English Parliamentary Enclosure*, Folkestone.

Turner, M.E. 1981. 'Arable in England and Wales: Estimates from the 1801 Crop Return', *Journal of Historical Geography* 7, 291–302.

Turner, M.E. 1982a. *Volume 190: Home Office Acreage Returns HO67. List and Analysis*, 3 parts, London.

Turner, M.E. 1982b. 'Agricultural Productivity in England in the Eighteenth Century: Evidence from Crop Yields', *Economic History Review* 35, 489–510.

Turner, M.E. 1984a. *Enclosures in Britain 1750–1830*, Basingstoke.

Turner, M.E. 1984b 'The Landscape of Parliamentary Enclosure'. In M. Reed (ed.) *Discovering Past Landscapes*, London, 132–66.

Turner, M.E. 1986 'English Open Fields and Enclosures: Retardation or Productivity Improvements?', *Journal of Economic History* 41, 669–92.

Turner, M.E. 1998. 'Counting Sheep: Waking Up to New estimates of Livestock Numbers in England c.1800', *Agricultural History Review* 46, 142–61.

Turner, M.E., J.V.Beckett, J.V. and Afton, B. 2001. *Farm Production in England 1700–1914*, Oxford.

Tusser, T. 1812. *Five Hundred Points of Good Husbandry* (ed. W. Mavor), London.

Underdown, D. 1985. *Revel, Riot and Rebellion: Popular Politics and Culture in England 1603–1660*, Oxford.

Vancouver, C. 1813a. *General View of the Agriculture of Hampshire*, London.

Vancouver, C. 1813b. *General View of the Agriculture of Essex*, London.

Wade Martins, S. 1995. *Farms and Fields*, London.

Wade Martin, S. and Williamson, T. 1994. 'Floated Water-Meadows in Norfolk: A Misplaced Innovation', *Agricultural History Review* 42, 20–37.

Wade Martins, S. and Williamson, T. 1995. *The Farming Journal of Randall Burroughes 1794–1799*, Norfolk Record Society, Norwich.

Wade Martins, S. and Williamson, T. 1997. 'Labour and Improvement: Agricultural Change in East Anglia c.1750–1870', *Labour History Review*, 62, 3, 275–95.

Wade Martins, S. and Williamson, T. 1998. 'The Lease and East Anglian Agriculture, 1660–1870', *Agricultural History Review* 46, 2, 127–41.

Wade Martins, S. and Williamson, T. 1999a. *Roots of Change: Farming and the Landscape in East Anglia 1700–1870*, Exeter.

Wade Martins, S. and Williamson, T. 1999b. 'Inappropriate Technology? The History of Floating in the North and East of England'. In H. Cook and T. Williamson (eds) *Water Management in the English Landscape: Field, Marsh and Meadow*, Edinburgh, 196–209.

Walker, D. 1795. *General View of the Agriculture of Hertfordshire*, London.

Walton, J. 1990. 'On Estimating the Extent of Parliamentary Enclosure', *Agricultural History Review* 38, 79–82.

Walton, J. 1991. 'Parliamentary Enclosure, the Bootstrap, and a Red Herring or Two', *Agricultural History Review* 39, 52–4.

Walton, J. 1999. 'Varietal Innovation and the Competitiveness of the British Cereals Sector, 1760–1930', *Agricultural History Review* 46, 29–57.

Wedge, J. 1794. *General View of the Agriculture of Warwickshire*, London.

Wells, S. 1830. *The History of the Drainage of the Great Level of the Fens*, London.

Wheeler, W.H. 1896. *The History of the Fens of South Lincolnshire*, Boston.

Williams, M. 1970. *The Draining of the Somerset Levels*, Cambridge.

Williams, M. 1971. 'The Enclosure and Reclamation of the Mendip Hills, 1770–1830', *Agricultural History Review* 19, 65–81.

Williams, R. 1989. *Limekilns and Limeburning*, Aylesbury.

Williamson, T. 1995. *Polite Landscapes: Gardens and Society in Eighteenth-Century England*, London.

Williamson, T. 1997. *The Norfolk Broads: A Landscape History*, Manchester.

Williamson, T. 1998a. 'Questions of Preservation and Destruction'. In P. Everson and T. Williamson (eds) *The Archaeology of Landscape*, Manchester, 1–24.

Williamson, T. 1998b. *The Archaeology of the Landscape Park: Garden Design in Norfolk, England, c.1680–1840*, Oxford.

Williamson, T. 1999. 'Post-medieval Field Drainage'. In H. Cook and T. Williamson (eds) *Water Management in the English Landscape: Field, Marsh and Meadow*, Edinburgh, 41–52.

Williamson, T. 2000. 'Understanding Enclosure', *Landscapes* 1, 56–79.

Williamson, T. 2002. *Field Boundaries,* London.

Winchester, A. 1989. 'The Farming Landscape'. In W. Rollinson (ed.) *The Lake District: Landscape History*, Newton Abbot, 76–101.

Winchester, A. 2000 *Harvest of the Hills: Rural Life in Northern England and the Scottish Borders, 1400–1700*, Edinburgh.

Woodside, R. and Crow, J. 1999. *Hadrian's Wall: An Historic Landscape*, London.

Wordie, J.R. 1983. 'The Chronology of English Enclosure, 1500–1914', *Economic History Review* 36, 483–505.

Wordie, J.R. 1984. 'The South: Oxfordshire, Buckinghamshire, Berkshire, Wiltshire, and Hampshire'. In J. Thirsk (ed.) *The Agrarian History of England and Wales*, Vol. V.1, Cambridge, 51–77.

Wratislaw, C. 1861. 'The Amount of Capital Required for the Profitable Occupation of a Mixed Arable and Pasture Farm in a Midland County', *Journal of the Royal Agricultural Society of England* 22, 167–88.

Wright, T. 1792. *An Account of the Advantages of Watering Meadows by Art, as Practised in the County of Gloucestershire*, London.

Yarranton, A. 1663. *The Improvement Improved: by a second edition of the Improvement of Land by Clover*, London.

Yelling, J.A. 1977. *Common Field and Enclosure in England 1450–1850*, London.

Young, A. 1771. *The Farmer's Tour Through the East of England*, 4 volumes, London.

Young, A. 1773. *Observations on the Present State of the Waste Lands of Great Britain*, London.

Young, A. 1795. *General View of the Agriculture of the County of Suffolk,* London.
Young, A. 1804a. *General View of the Agriculture of Norfolk,* London.
Young, A. 1804b. *General View of the Agriculture of the County of Hertfordshire,* London.
Young, A. 1813a. *General View of the Agriculture of the County of Hertfordshire,* London.
Young, A. 1813b. *General View of the Agriculture of the County of Lincolnshire,* London.

Index